The ONS Productivity Handbook

A Statistical Overview and Guide

Edited by Dawn Camus

Office for National Statistics

palgrave
macmillan

First published 2007 by
PALGRAVE MACMILLAN
Houndmills, Basingstoke, Hampshire RG21 6XS and 175 Fifth Avenue, New York, NY 10010, USA
Companies and representatives throughout the world.

PALGRAVE MACMILLAN is the global academic imprint of the Palgrave Macmillan division of St. Martin's Press, LLC and of Palgrave Macmillan Ltd. Macmillan® is a registered trademark in the United States, United Kingdom and other countries. Palgrave is a registered trademark in the European Union and other countries.

ISBN 978-0-230-57301-7

This book is printed on paper suitable for recycling and made from fully managed and sustained forest sources. Logging, pulping and manufacturing processes are expected to conform to the environmental regulations of the country of origin.

A catalogue record for this book is available from the British Library.

10	9	8	7	6	5	4	3	2	1
16	15	14	13	12	11	10	09	08	07

Printed and bound in Great Britain by Hobbs the Printers Ltd, Totton, Hampshire.

A National Statistics publication

National Statistics are produced to high professional standards set out in the National Statistics Code of Practice. They are produced free from political influence.

About the Office for National Statistics

The Office for National Statistics (ONS) is the government agency responsible for compiling, analysing and disseminating economic, social and demographic statistics about the United Kingdom. It also administers the statutory registration of births, marriages and deaths in England and Wales.

The Director of ONS is also the National Statistician and the Registrar General for England and Wales.

Contact points

For enquiries about this publication and general enquires, contact the National Statistics Customer Contact Centre.

Tel: 0845 601 3034 (minicom: 01633 812399)
E-mail: info@statistics.gsi.gov.uk
Fax: 01633 652747
Post: Room 1015, Government Buildings, Cardiff Road, Newport NP10 8XG

You can also find National Statistics on the Internet at:
www.statistics.gov.uk

Front cover illustration: Corbis

Contents

Acknowledgements and Contributors

Editor:
Dawn Camus

Authors:

Fathimath Ali

Stephen Almond

Keith Brook
Department of Trade & Industry

Dawn Camus

Tony Clayton

Sumit Dey-Chowdhury

Peter Goodridge

Jonathan Haskel
Queen Mary, University of London

Isabell Kohten
Department of Trade & Industry, formerly ONS

Andrew Machin

Sanjiv Mahajan

Fenella Maitland-Smith

Catherine Marks

Joe Robjohns

Paul Schreyer
Organisation for Economic Co-operation and Development

Claire Swadkin

Geoff Tily

Dev Virdee

Gavin Wallis
HM Treasury, formerly ONS

James Watson
Department of Trade & Industry

With thanks:

Jon Beadle

Ivan Bishop
Department of Trade & Industry

Steve Drew

Andrew Evans

David Knight

Benjamin Marriott
Department of Trade & Industry

Colin Mowl

Tuu-Van Nguyen

Nicholas Oulton
Bank of England

Geoff Reed
Department of Trade & Industry

Diana Shaw

Sally Srinivasan
Bank of England

All authors and contributors are from the Office for National Statistics unless otherwise stated.

ONS is grateful for contributions to this book by staff from several UK government departments, the OECD and independent academics. All responsibility for any errors or omissions is, of course, our own.

List of Tables and Figures

Tables

Figures

Foreword

I am delighted to welcome you to *The ONS Productivity Handbook*. This is the first time that information on how all ONS productivity measures and theories are sourced and formulated has been brought together in one volume. As such, it forms a wonderful resource for anyone working on or studying how productivity is measured and influenced. The content reflects consultation with users of ONS statistics to ensure that it addresses all important areas and issues within productivity analysis.

Statistics relating to productivity are vital to understanding the economy and how it changes. This, and the impressive range of ONS productivity statistics and analysis, leads to widespread interest in measures published at international, national and regional levels and also for different sections of the economy. This handbook meets and reflects these interests.

As with all ONS statistics, it is crucial that both experts and the general public can depend on the accuracy and relevance of ONS productivity measures. I believe that the clarity, completeness and accessibility of this volume will enhance this confidence. Additionally, by laying out our plans for further work in this area, this publication encourages future input from all users.

Together with the online version, *The ONS Productivity Handbook* should be the ideal reference source for everyone who uses ONS productivity measures to gain insight into the UK economy and its place in the world in the 21st century. I hope you will enjoy reading it.

Karen Dunnell
National Statistician

Overview

The Office for National Statistics, in response to the needs of UK policy makers and others who use our data, has produced an expanding range of productivity statistics and analyses in recent years. As government policy has focused more explicitly on measures to increase productivity and output, so the demand for better statistics has grown. Two important reviews of economic statistics – on structural change and regional issues by Christopher Allsopp, and on measurement of government output and productivity by Tony Atkinson – have helped to provide direction.

This investment is raising the quality of UK productivity statistics compared to those produced by other countries. In some areas, such as analysis of the effect of ICT investment and measurement of public services productivity, ONS can claim to be among a small group of the world's leading statistics agencies.

The improvements achieved, and those still in the pipeline, cover a wide range of inputs to productivity measurement. Up to now they have been available in a fragmented form. *The ONS Productivity Handbook* sets out to present the current position so that users have a clear appreciation of the changes that have taken place and the challenges being addressed.

This Handbook is not intended as a competitor to the *OECD Productivity Manual*, which is the authoritative international source on methodology for productivity analysis.

Taking the international standards as given, this is the first comprehensive guide to implementation and practice, showing how UK statistics have developed, and are developing, to help a wide range of users in government and beyond.

Productivity is a complex field, and by setting out the sources and uses of productivity statistics in a single publication, the Handbook makes ONS productivity material more readily accessible and coherent. It also serves to make more users aware of the data resources available and to encourage external input to further improvement.

ONS is responsible for a relatively small proportion of productivity analysis in the UK, but it provides most of the basic data on which the work of others depends. Productivity estimates usually rely on multiple sources, making it difficult to achieve consistency between the numerator (output) and denominator (input), between countries and regions, and over time. There is also the difficulty of measuring quality change, which affects both output and input. All of these issues are explored in the Handbook.

The ONS Productivity Handbook has been created in collaboration with statisticians and economists in several UK government departments, OECD staff and leading academics. We would like to thank all contributors to this first edition and welcome readers to our shared project.

Chapter 1

Introduction

What is productivity, how is it measured and why is it important? These questions are a useful starting point from which we can define and explain the range of productivity measures ONS produces.

Productivity represents the relationships between inputs and outputs in the production process. As a practical concept, productivity helps define both the scope for raising living standards and the competitiveness of an economy. Productivity has, therefore, an increasing role in formulating and assessing government policy.

This introductory chapter provides a definition of productivity along with an explanation of how and why it is used. It also covers the importance of productivity as an economic measure.

Giving broad definitions of output and input and the challenges in measuring productivity, the chapter goes on to explain the difference between levels and growth rates of productivity. Finally, it outlines different measures of productivity, their uses and the links between them.

Defining productivity

Productivity matters because it is the main determinant of national living standards.

The definition of productivity in the Oxford English Dictionary is deceptively simple:

1. the quality or fact of being productive; capacity to produce

2. econ. The rate of output per unit of input, used esp. in assessing the effective use of labour, materials, etc

The first definition of productivity can be thought of as being about the ability to produce outputs, such as goods or services, taking into consideration the amount of inputs, such as raw materials, capital and labour, used to produce them. High productivity means producing as much output as possible using as little input as possible.

The second, economic, definition is a formal quantification of the first:

$$\text{Productivity} = \frac{\text{Output}}{\text{Input}}$$

Productivity is defined as the ratio between output and input. Therefore increasing productivity means greater efficiency in producing output of goods and services from labour, capital, materials and any other necessary inputs.

In practice, however, measuring productivity is one of the more difficult challenges in economic statistics. Users wanting a detailed discussion of the theoretical background and how best to approach the measurement of productivity should use the Organisation for Economic Co-operation and Development (OECD) *Productivity Manual*. This ONS handbook instead provides a practical approach for users so that readers can gain an understanding of how UK productivity is currently approached and measured.

1.1   Why does productivity matter?

Productivity isn't everything, but in the long run it is almost everything. A country's ability to improve its standard of living over time depends almost entirely on its ability to raise output per worker (Paul Krugman, OECD, 2006).

Defining productivity may be the start, but the key question is: why does productivity matter? How, as an economic concept, does it relate to people living their day-to-day lives?

In everyday life, people care about their living standards and would like to see them improved as much as possible for themselves and for others. The main economic indicator for living standards has traditionally been national income, although it is widely acknowledged as being imperfect. Consequently various alternatives have been considered over time and ONS attaches growing importance to measuring welfare within the National Accounts framework.

Economic theory, economic behaviour and actual consumer spending patterns suggest that the majority of people want an increase in the quantity and quality of goods and services available. At the same time, they would like it at as small a cost as possible.

Improving productivity results in improved living standards. This is because an increase in productivity translates into an increase in output (amount and quality) without any increase in input (labour and materials). In this context, labour can be seen as the amount of effort required to produce something.

The term 'living standards' also covers the way the output of these goods and services is distributed within a population. It is not just overall productivity of an economy that is important but also how it varies across the economy and across the people living in it. Therefore the productivity of different geographical areas is important, as is the productivity of different industries or types of firms. Issues of regional productivity and productivity by industry are discussed in **Chapter 11** and **Chapter 8**.

The link between living standards and productivity is generally recognised and organisations aimed at improving living standards, such as the Centre for the Study of Living Standards in Canada, regard productivity as the key to increasing living standards.

1.2   Constructing productivity statistics

To find out how productivity changes over time, or how productive one economy is compared to another, a set of statistical measures is needed. Unlike some economic statistics, productivity cannot be directly observed or measured. As a derived statistic, estimates of both output and input are required. There are different measures of output, such as total output and value added, and different types of input, including capital, labour and raw materials. In practice, measuring productivity means measuring the outputs and inputs of an economic unit, for instance a sector, industry or firm.

Changes in output can be achieved by adding more inputs, or by changing the relationships between inputs and outputs (in economic terms this means a shift in the production function). Productivity growth occurs through improved efficiency, such as using fewer inputs to produce the same outputs, or through inputs being used more effectively to produce outputs of greater value.

Productivity analysis is not confined to the economy as a whole (macroeconomics). The practice also takes place in firms and other organisations (microeconomics) that conduct sophisticated analysis of their own operations.

For productivity statistics to show dependable trends over time, they need to be produced from consistent measures of outputs and inputs. This means that the output estimates used must be consistent with the whole economy measures available from the National Accounts. Input estimates should be consistent with UK population and employment figures. Additionally input and output measures should be consistent with each other. Obtaining consistent measures of output and input is one of the main challenges in estimating productivity, which has both conceptual and measurement aspects. This is discussed in detail in **Chapter 5**. However, before considering consistency, there is the question of what outputs and inputs actually are.

1.2.1 Output

Productivity estimates tend to use one of three different measures of output:

1. total output
2. gross value added (GVA)
3. gross domestic product (GDP)

One potential source of confusion is the term 'gross'. GVA and GDP are net of inputs used, meaning that they equal the value of production less the value of inputs. Put another way, they measure the value added to inputs during the course of production. GVA and GDP are, therefore, both value-added measures. The difference between them relates to the price valuation used, as explained later. GVA and GDP are 'gross' in the sense that they are gross of the depreciation of capital assets. A fuller explanation of these concepts is given below.

The choice between which output measure to use is mainly determined by what types of input are included in the productivity calculation, as will be explained later.

1.2.1.1 Total output

Total output, or output, is the value of the goods and services produced. It is broadly equal to the value of the sales plus any increase (and less any decrease) in the value of the inventory of finished goods not sold and work in progress.

1.2.1.2 Gross value added

GVA is the difference between total output and intermediate consumption for any given sector or industry. That is the difference between the value of goods and services produced and the cost of raw materials and other inputs that are used up in production. Therefore, GVA can be simply related to total output:

GVA = total output - intermediate consumption

> **Intermediate consumption** is the cost of raw materials and other inputs that are used up in the production process.

1.2.1.3 Gross domestic product

GDP measures the total economic activity and, like GVA, is 'gross' in that capital consumption (loosely defined as depreciation of fixed assets) is not offset from production.

> **The National Accounts** are a set of current values, volume measures and volume indices which, together, summarise all the economic activity of a nation. This can be defined as a central framework for the presentation and measurement of the stocks and flows within the economy. In the UK this framework provides many key economic statistics including gross domestic product (GDP) and gross national income (GNI) as well as information on, for example, saving, disposable income and investment.
>
> **A volume measure** is a quantity describing the number of units produced. For instance, if you spend £100 on items that cost £10 each, expenditure is £100 and the volume measure is 10 (£100/£10 = 10).

GDP can be measured in three ways:

1. production (GDP(P)) – as the sum of all the gross value added by all producers in the economy

2. income (GDP(I)) – as the total of the income generated through this productive activity

3. expenditure (GDP(E)) – as the expenditure on goods and services produced

In principle, these three estimates must yield the same answer in the absence of errors and omissions. In practice, measurement limitations mean that these approaches produce different figures that must be reconciled to produce a single estimate of GDP.

As already noted, the difference between GVA and GDP concerns the price valuation. GVA is measured at what are known as basic prices while GDP is measured at prices including taxes.

GDP and GVA are related in the following way:

GDP = GVA + taxes on products - subsidies on products

GDP is a key indicator of the economy and one of the most commonly used measures of output.

■ GDP (and GVA) are measured consistently across many countries following the definitions given in the System of National Accounts 1993 (SNA93) and the European System of Accounts 1995 (ESA95)

■ GDP per head is a key indicator of the state of the economy and there are advantages to producing comparable productivity measures

■ GDP is used for producing International Comparisons of Productivity because purchasing power parities (PPP), which are also used, relate to GDP rather than GVA or total output (see above)

GDP, total output and GVA are all measured in the National Accounts and are described in greater detail, along with the links between them, in **Chapter 4**.

1.2.1.4 Deflators

When measuring output over a time period, it is essential to remove any increase in the value of output caused by inflation: to understand either changes in welfare or changes in efficiency, output should be measured in volume or real terms. Therefore, when producing productivity estimates, suitable price indices are required to deflate output, GDP or GVA.

More information about choosing deflators and related issues is given in **Chapter 4**.

1.2.1.5 Using output in productivity estimates

The output used when generating productivity estimates should, in theoretical terms, be either total output or GVA. The choice of which one to use is based on whether the productivity measure being created relates only to primary inputs (such as labour and capital) or also to intermediate inputs (such as materials, energy and business services).

Generally speaking, when only primary inputs are involved then GVA should be used as this does not include intermediate consumption. However, when intermediate inputs are included then total output should be used as it does include these inputs.

It is important to remember, however, that data suitability can mean rejecting a theoretically preferred approach. For example, it is difficult to get suitable total output data at the industry level. There is more about the different outputs in **Chapter 4**. Inputs are defined and considered below, and discussed in more detail in **Chapter 5**.

1.2.2 Input

Input can be measured in a variety of different ways. For example, labour input can be measured as number of jobs, workers or hours worked. There are also other forms of input such as capital and raw materials. It is usually the choice of input that indicates the type of productivity measure. For example, output per unit of labour input is usually referred to as labour productivity. Inputs are sometimes referred to as 'factors of production'. More details are provided in **Chapter 5**.

1.2.3 Productivity levels and growth rates

What is often referred to as the productivity level is really a ratio (output divided by input), usually expressed as an index number with base equal to 100 in a chosen year. However, while these levels can be interesting measures in their own right, the focus is usually on the change in productivity over time, that is, how much more or less productive the economy (or region or industry) has become within a certain period.

The simplest form of growth in a year (or quarter) to express in an equation is given below.

$$\text{Growth per annum} = \frac{\text{Productivity in year } t}{\text{Productivity in year } t\text{-}1}$$

Within this equation a growth rate is shown in the form of the multiplier from the previous year. For example a multiplier of 1.02 would represent an increase of 2 per cent.

This in turn can be shown as output and input changes:

$$= \frac{\text{Output in year t}}{\text{Output in year t-1}} \div \frac{\text{Input in year t}}{\text{Input in year t-1}}$$

where, again, the multipliers would be of the same form (for example, 1.03 for output and 1.01 for input). Therefore growth in productivity equals growth in output divided by growth in input.

However, productivity measures are most often published as annual (or quarterly) percentage growth rates. These published percentage rates can be roughly related to output and input percentage growth rates:

Productivity % growth rate $\approx$ Output % growth rate - Input % growth rate

---

Box 1.1: Relating productivity growth rates to output and input

If a growth rate (usually expressed as a percentage) is called R_X where X is the measure of which this is a growth rate, then:

$$R_P = \frac{\text{Productivity in year t - Productivity in year t-1}}{\text{Productivity in year t-1}}$$

$$R_O = \frac{\text{Output in year t - Output in year t-1}}{\text{Output in year t-1}}$$

$$R_I = \frac{\text{Input in year t - Input in year t-1}}{\text{Input in year t-1}}$$

Also (from the basic definition of productivity)

$$\text{Productivity in year t} = \frac{\text{Output in year t}}{\text{Input in year t}}$$

$$\text{Productivity in year t-1} = \frac{\text{Output in year t-1}}{\text{Input in year t-1}}$$

Using these equations it can be shown that:

$$R_P = \frac{R_O - R_I}{R_I + 1}$$

Because R_I is small (for instance 3 per cent would be 0.03), this means that

$$R_P \approx R_O - R_I$$

This means that the productivity growth rate is approximately the output growth rate minus the input growth rate.

This approximate relationship is explained in greater detail in **Box 1.1**.

1.3 Measures of productivity

Whether productivity is observed as a growth rate or a level, the general term still covers a wide range of measures. These measures are individually defined and named for the types of input and output data they are constructed from. The two most well-known productivity measures are labour productivity and multi-factor productivity. These two measures and various less-known measures are described in greater detail below.

1.3.1 Labour productivity

Labour productivity is output per unit of labour input. There are various different ways of measuring labour input, such as jobs, workers or hours worked. A labour productivity data series effectively shows changes in output over time for the same value or amount of labour input.

Changes in labour productivity could occur, for example, because of better or more capital equipment, new technology advances, organisational changes (such as, a new management structure) or increased efficiency. However, such causes cannot be identified from the basic labour productivity time series. Additionally, labour productivity will not normally indicate the extent to which productivity change results from experience or skill changes in the workforce, although this can be measured if quality-adjusted labour input (QALI) measures are used (See **Chapter 5**).

To some extent the question of why labour productivity has changed can be inferred by productivity measures. For example, comparing output per worker and output per hour worked might show whether output has increased because of the adoption of longer working hours.

The choice of which labour input measure to use depends on what question is being addressed and what data are available. Additionally, there is an established hierarchy of the order in which the types of labour productivity measures are preferred in terms of the information they provide to users. More details are given below.

1.3.1.1 Per hour worked

Measurement of productivity is a key element towards assessing standards of living. A simple example is per capita income, probably the most common measure of living standards: income per person in an economy varies directly with one measure of labour productivity, value added per hour worked. In this sense, measuring labour productivity helps to better understand the development of living standards (OECD, 2006).

In one sense the purest labour measure of labour productivity is to use hours worked as defined in the Organisation for Economic Co-operation and Development (OECD) *Productivity Manual.* This is because, when perfectly measured, it includes the greatest precision about the amount of labour that has been used. It is clear that if the same numbers of workers work for longer hours then there is more input, and usually more output, but note that the workers are not necessarily more productive.

The main flaw with this method, and equally with output per worker and per job, is that it assumes all workers are equal by not accounting for characteristics of the work force such as skills and experience. ONS also produces quality-adjusted labour input (QALI) measures which do allow for these characteristics (see **Chapter 5**).

However, per hour worked data are not always of the highest quality as they tend to depend on self-reporting of working times. If hours worked data are not available, or not of reasonable quality, then per worker data are generally preferred to per job data.

1.3.1.2 Per worker

The headline measure in the ONS *Productivity First Release* is GVA per worker. Per worker is preferred to the per job measurement of productivity because the number of workers available is the ultimate constraint on volumes of labour, with allowances for migration and globalisation. This measure does not, however, accurately reflect changes to input from workers moving from full- to part-time (or vice versa) or from other shifts in the number of hours worked. Additionally there are issues when assigning workers to industries (this is discussed in greater detail in **Chapter 5**). However, when hours worked data are not available or are considered not fully reliable, per worker provides the next-best alternative.

1.3.1.3 Per job

GVA per job is also published by ONS and is the easiest and most internally consistent measure of productivity to calculate because the output and job numbers come from the same business surveys. Therefore more detailed industry information is published for output per job than per worker

or per hour worked. However, because of multiple job holders it is regarded as the least informative measure of the three. An increase in the number of jobs may simply reflect a move to job sharing rather than any change in the amount of labour input required to produce output.

1.3.2   Output per person

In addition to the various forms of productivity for the workforce there is the related measure of output per person, usually GDP or GVA per head (also called per capita) of the total population. This output per head measure is usually seen as a prosperity statistic and is often produced for international and sub-national comparisons. While on paper this measure appears to be constructed in the same form as a productivity measure, it is not usually considered as one.

The main reasons for this are general variations in the population structure, such as the proportion of the resident population in the workforce (for example, areas with a large number of pensioners or children will have a small proportion of people in the workforce) and commuting workers. This means that estimates per person can match output unevenly with those producing it, making them unreliable or unsuitable for productivity measurement. The relationship between productivity and output per head is, instead, effectively the participation rate of the potential workforce in the economy. This is shown in **Box 1.2**.

Some users do consider this as a productivity measure, particularly for international comparisons, as it relates output to a measure of input that is not affected by international differences in working practices, working hours, time management or organisational structure. It is also, arguably, an indicator of welfare or potential welfare for the residents of the area. However, in general, GDP per capita is used as a productivity measure only when other estimates are unavailable.

1.3.3   Capital productivity

Capital productivity is output per unit of capital input, where capital input is measured either as capital stock employed or of the services that the capital stock provides. Industrial analysis by business has a long tradition of work on capital productivity, most of it conducted within the firm for commercial reasons. Understanding the volume of output that can be produced by industrial plant is a major item of study in the manufacturing industry.

Box 1.2: Relating output per person to productivity measures

Output per person		Productivity per hour worked		Hours per job		Employment rate		Commuting effect		Activity rate

Output	=	Output	x	Hours worked	x	Employment workplace	x	Labour force workplace	x	Labour force residence
Resident population		Hours worked		Employment workplace		Labour force workplace		Labour force residence		Resident population

Where:

Employment workplace is the number of jobs by place of employment.
Labour force workplace is the number of workers by place of employment.
Labour force residence is the number of workers by place of residence.

Benchmarking comparisons are also routinely undertaken within and between firms to identify, and spread, 'best practice' in plant operation, therefore improving the ratio between physical output of saleable product and capital equipment.

When considering capital productivity in economic analysis:

- it is usually taken into account by comparing output with capital input

- it is not the same as return on capital

- it is a volume, or physical, partial productivity measure

OECD analysis (OECD, 2001a) shows that capital productivity in many member states has in fact declined over the period 1995 to 2005, with capital services growing faster than output. How far this is because of increasing inputs of IT investment without corresponding increasing increases in output (the 1999 to 2001 IT investment 'bubble') is still a subject of debate.

ONS, like most national statistics offices, does not publish any capital productivity figures. However, the components required to estimate capital productivity are published and capital productivity can effectively be seen as an input to multi-factor productivity, similar to both materials productivity and energy productivity (see below).

Capital services is the measure of capital input that is suitable for analysing and modelling productivity. Being a direct measure of the flow of productive services from capital assets rather than a measure of the stock of those assets, capital services essentially measures the actual contribution of the capital stock of assets to the production process in a given year. For example, capital services from computers refer to the service they provide rather than the value of the computers themselves.

The aggregate flow of capital services into the economy is obtained by weighting the flow of services from each type of asset by its share in total capital income. This means that, over recent years, the effects of short-life, high-return assets, such as IT equipment, have become increasingly important in determining capital inputs (Wallis, 2005). For a full discussion of the definition and importance of capital services, see **Chapter 5**.

Within the National Accounts, capital stock is measured as a value of the capital stock of assets, commonly known as net capital stock or wealth capital stock. On a national scale it is the current market valuation of a country or industry's capital assets. One purpose of calculating the net capital stock is to measure the depreciation or loss in value assets in the economy as they age. This is known as capital consumption, which is a component of GDP.

1.3.4 Materials productivity

Materials productivity analysis has also been a key topic in industrial analysis work. Many firms are keen to improve the relationship between output of saleable products and the volumes of raw materials and energy required to produce them. Optimisation of process yields is an important determinant of competitive position, and of productivity growth in many industries. One driver is change in technology, for instance miniaturisation increasing the numbers of semiconductor devices that can be produced from a square millimetre of silicon. Another is change in working practices such as better process control increasing the length of production runs and reducing lost material at the start and end of production.

In economic analysis of productivity, materials, energy and service inputs are often grouped together as 'other inputs' after the 'primary inputs', labour and capital. They come under the heading of 'intermediate inputs'. This takes account of the fact that firms make differing, and changing, choices over how much processing they do themselves, and how much they contract to suppliers.

This variation is what leads to the use of GVA as a preferred output measure for productivity analysis rather than total output. Increases in total output per employee achieved by purchasing part finished products and substituting them for raw materials do not necessarily represent productivity growth.

1.3.5 Energy productivity

Energy productivity is output per unit of energy used. It can be seen as a measure of efficiency in the use of energy or, arguably, of conservation. Like capital productivity and materials productivity, it is a measure rarely used in macroeconomics and ONS does not produce energy productivity figures. In contrast, again as with capital productivity and materials productivity, it is often measured at the firm level and seen as an important indicator within companies. Finally, like materials productivity, it can be seen as an intermediate input to multi-factor productivity.

1.3.6   Multi-factor productivity

Multi-factor productivity is useful in assessing an economy's underlying productive capacity (productive potential), itself an important measure of the growth possibilities of economies and of inflationary pressures (OECD Manual, 2001a).

Multi-factor productivity (MFP) is defined as the residual output growth of an industry or economy after calculating the contribution from all inputs (or factors of production). Put another way, it is the output growth which cannot be explained by increasing volume of inputs and is assumed to reflect increases in the efficiency of use of these inputs. Typically it is estimated indirectly as the residual after estimating the effect of the change in the volume of inputs. It is also sometimes called total-factor productivity (TFP), but will be consistently referred to as multi-factor productivity (MFP) within this publication.

Two forms of multi-factor productivity are most prevalent:

1. Labour-capital value added productivity

2. KLEMS total output productivity

Labour-capital value added productivity is where the growth of (gross) value added is accounted for by the growth of labour and capital (see **Chapter 7**).

The more detailed estimates employ the KLEMS approach, where the growth of real total output is accounted for by the growth of capital (K), labour (L), energy (E), materials (M) and business services (S). There is more information on the KLEMS project in **Chapter 12**.

Note that business services, as defined here, are an intermediate input and (unless exported) not an output. Business services productivity measures could be produced, similar to materials and energy productivity described above, but these are not to be confused with the services productivity described in **Chapter 8**. The latter is output services labour productivity, for instance services output per unit of labour input.

Both labour-capital value added productivity and KLEMS total output productivity tend to be used to analyse the contribution of specific industry sectors to growth. There is more about multi-factor productivity in the growth accounting section in **Chapter 3** and also in **Chapter 7**, which provides, alongside the theory, some multi-factor productivity estimates.

1.4   Conclusion

Measures of productivity can be used to monitor changes in living standards, in efficiency, or in competitiveness of the economy. The main measures described in this chapter are summarised in **Table 1.1** below (see also OECD, 2001a).

Table 1.1: Summary of productivity measures

Productivity measure	Output	Input
GVA per hour worked[1]	Gross value	Number of hours worked
GVA per worker[1]	added (GVA)	Number of workers
GVA per job[1]		Number of jobs
Labour-capital value added productivity (MFP)		Volume index of capital services (VICS) and quality-adjusted labour input (QALI)
GDP per person[2]	Gross domestic	Number of people
GDP per hour worked[1]	product (GDP)	Number of hours worked
GDP per worker[1]		Number of workers
KLEMS (MFP)	Total output	Capital, labour, energy, materials and business services

1. These are all labour productivity measures.

2. Also called GDP per capita – this is not usually regarded as a productivity measure but as an indicator of welfare.

Later chapters in this handbook explain the theory and data issues in more detail, as well as describing more fully the productivity measures available from ONS and plans for future development.

1.5   References

The Centre for the Study of Living Standards, Canada, available at: www.csls.ca/

OECD, (2001a) *Measuring Productivity: OECD Manual,* Organisation for Economic Co-operation and Development: Paris.

OECD (2006) OECD *Compendium of Productivity Indicators 2006,* Organisation for Economic Co-operation and Development: Paris.

HM Treasury (2000) *Productivity in the UK: The Evidence and the Government's Approach,* HMSO: London, available at: www.hm-treasury.gov.uk/media/D4A/E5/ACF1FBA.pdf

Wallis G (2005) 'Estimates of the volume of capital services', *Economic Trends* 624, pp 42–51, available at: www.statistics.gov.uk/downloads/theme_economy/ET624.pdf

Chapter 2

ONS Framework for Productivity

Policy users outside ONS monitor productivity for the UK, its industries and regions through analysis based on ONS National Statistics data. A framework for ONS productivity outputs must, therefore, include the statistical building blocks for these expert external users, as well as analysis published by ONS itself.

The framework outlined in this chapter has two main purposes. First, it describes ONS productivity outputs (both data and analysis) and streams of work more clearly. Second, it sets out ways of assessing the consistency and completeness of ONS productivity outputs in a way that can help form judgements on priorities to improve their coherence.

Presentation of the framework is in two parts. It begins with a description of levels within the economy at which productivity outputs are delivered and why those levels are used. It goes on to set out a summary of economic and labour market statistics required by users to analyse policy and evaluate productivity outcomes, where possible being consistent with National Accounts.

Established and New Productivity Frameworks

ONS works within established economic frameworks for productivity, and the theoretical background and assumptions required to sustain them. The most authoritative set of productivity definitions is provided by the Organisation for Economic Co-Operation and Development (OECD, 2001a) and the most commonly used theoretical framework is that originally set out by Robert Solow (Solow, 1957).

Because the ONS productivity framework is mostly associated with data and very broad definitions of productivity, more than one economic theory can be accommodated within it. The benefit is that this framework can apply to many different analyses.

2.1   Key users

The most intensive government policy users for productivity statistics include the following.

HM Treasury (HMT) uses assessments of trends in productivity growth to estimate future economic output, employment, and the capacity of the economy to support government spending. Together with other government departments it also has a close interest in the effectiveness of public services. HM Treasury is also jointly responsible with the Department for Trade and Industry for achieving national productivity targets.

The Bank of England (BoE) uses productivity analysis to understand current and future inflationary pressures in the economy.

Department for Trade & Industry (DTI) is responsible for achieving national and regional productivity targets, for managing drivers of productivity growth (investment, innovation, skills, enterprise formation and competition) and for improving industry competitiveness in the market sector.

Department for Work and Pensions (DWP) is concerned mainly with policies for productivity improvement as they affect welfare and income distribution.

Department for Education and Skills (DfES) is interested in assessing productivity and welfare effects associated with education and skills.

Regional government is interested in assessing regional productivity measures as they affect regional living standards and welfare.

National Accounts define **market sector activity** as that which is undertaken at prices that are economically significant and where the output is disposed of or intended for sale through the market. In ONS estimates, contribution to total gross value added (GVA) by the market sector is calculated using the production data underlying the whole economy quarterly output measure, GVA at basic prices. In other countries, such as the US and Canada, similar series are published under the name 'business sector output'. Definitions and practical measurement issues are given in greater detail in Herbert and Pike (2005) and Mahajan (2005 and 2006).

Productivity statistics are also used when forming international policy and guidance by Eurostat, OECD and others.

In addition, private sector analysts rely heavily on ONS data relating to productivity as part of their overall assessment of the UK economy and the ability of industries to compete internationally. The wider public also use this information to support their general understanding of economic performance and prospects.

In seeking to influence productivity through policy levers, users recognise that productivity can be influenced in a number of ways:

- macro productivity can be raised by improved efficiency in turning inputs to outputs across a broad range of firms and industries
- change in the mix of industries from lower to higher productivity activities

Raising productivity within an industry can be achieved through:

- more efficient use of inputs by existing firms to deliver the same, or higher value, outputs
- exit of low productivity firms, and their replacement by higher productivity firms

Raising productivity within a firm usually depends on:

- more efficient use of capital, labour and intermediate inputs thanks to better management or co-ordination
- new products or processes, which use inputs more effectively or meet new customer needs
- changes in quality of inputs, which may not be reflected in measurement

Labour productivity, around which many policy objectives are focused, may increase through all these mechanisms, and through increased investment in capital assets (known as capital deepening). For more detail see **Chapter 3**.

2.2 Productivity by activity

Productivity data are required by users, and presented by ONS, at five levels of aggregation, summarised in **Figure 2.1** below:

1. whole economy (GDP per worker/hour) for international comparisons, both of levels and of rates of change. Outputs and inputs associated with oil extraction are omitted for some analytical purposes, including assessment of trend productivity growth

2. market sector gross value added (MSGVA), again noting that:

    a. oil extraction, imputed owner-occupied and other rentals may be excluded from analysis using this concept

    b. this implies productivity for the non-market or government sector (by difference with GDP) using current National Accounts measures which may not truly reflect the value of non-market output because large parts of government activity are still measured in terms of inputs

    c. productivity performance of public services is more accurately assessed by measures which focus on the inputs and outputs associated with specific services (see **Chapter 9** for more details)

3. market sector activity split as a first broad division between production and services activities

4. these data subdivided again by industry (with the degree of disaggregation possible determined by available sample sizes of source data)

5. firm level data, used in microdata analysis, support the above to assess the impacts and interdependence of productivity drivers. This type of analysis allows productivity differences to be considered in terms of factors such as firm size, ownership, organisation, labour force characteristics and innovation activity (see **Chapter 10** for more details).

Figure 2.1: Disaggregation of productivity data by activity

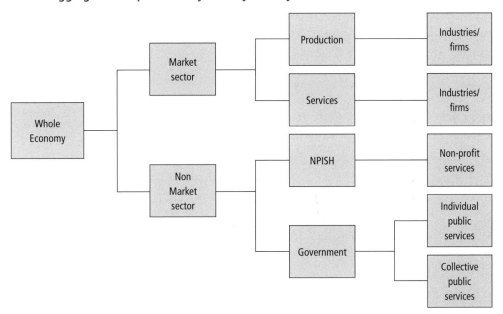

Figures related to the oil sector and rentals may be excluded from data presented for analysis of underlying productivity changes at these macroeconomic levels.

Aggregation is a summary of data providing information at a broader level than that at which the data were collected.

Disaggregation means breaking data down into its component sections. In this case, it involves breaking down data from general categories into detailed categories.

NPISH is an acronym for non-profit institutions serving households. Charities that provide services to older people or children are an example.

All the estimates above are derived through the National Accounts process, or from the microdata on which the National Accounts are based.

Productivity estimates for non-market activity are based on output or outcome measures and are split by institutional sector, and/or by type of service delivered to users. Such figures are increasingly being built through the work of the UK Centre for the Measurement of Government Activity (UKCeMGA), based on the principles of the Atkinson Review.

Non-market sector productivity may be implied by differences between whole economy and market sector GVA measures in National Accounts, but such calculations are sensitive to:

- continuing use of input measures as proxies for output in some areas of National Accounts in marketed services but more commonly in the government sector

- differences between market and non-market sector activity in the current treatment of quality as it contributes to measurement of output volume (see **Chapter 6** for more details).

The treatment of public sector output is one of the areas in which National Accounts currently differ between countries, which can give rise to differences in comparative productivity growth rates. For example, the USA continues to value public sector services output by inputs. This leads to distortions in growth rates compared to EU economies, most of which use direct methods related to services output.

UKCeMGA is the United Kingdom Centre for the Measurement of Government Activity. This is a division of ONS that coordinates and drives forward development programmes to produce better measures of government output and productivity.

The Atkinson Review (named after Sir Tony Atkinson, who carried out the review) is a one-off investigation into the measurement of productivity in the public sector. It produced a final report known as **Measurement of Government Output and Productivity for the National Accounts.** For more information, please see **Chapter 9**.

2.3   Productivity by region

Productivity statistics are also required by region, in terms that represent welfare (GDP or income per head of population) and in terms related to competitiveness (GVA/labour input in industries).

A significant part of productivity policy implementation through DTI and other government departments is regionally based, with the objective of improving relative economic performance of communities with productivity disadvantages. **Figure 2.2** below represents the disaggregation needed, which often reaches below NUTS 1 level, to urban/rural splits, and to specific industries by region.

NUTS is an acronym for Nomenclature of Units for Territorial Statistics. It is a code used to identify areas within and for the European Union. Used here, NUTS 1 refers to the nine Government Office regions in England and the three devolved countries and NUTS 2 refers to counties or groups of counties, depending on size. See **Chapter 11** for more information.

Figure 2.2: Disaggregation of productivity data by geography

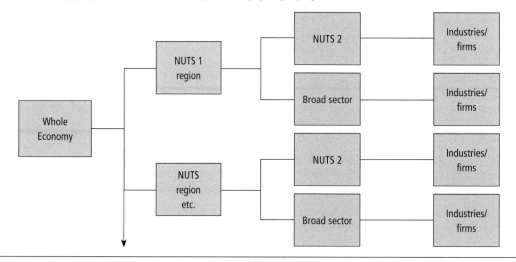

The level of geographic and industry disaggregation at which both output and input measures can be produced depends on survey samples and structure. In particular the attribution of output and employment to local units of multi-plant firms raises conceptual and practical issues (see **Chapter 5** for further details). ONS surveys mainly measure employment at the level of individual plants that make up multi-site reporting units, and output is usually imputed from employment data.

2.4   Measurements required in productivity statistics

A summary of the ONS current productivity portfolio is included as **Boxes 2.1** and **2.2** (presented at the end of this chapter), covering both the outputs from ONS, which are labelled as productivity, and the statistical building blocks for work by others.

Most ONS published productivity outputs have historically been labour productivity measures, the main exception being those produced by UKCeMGA

on government outputs that take account of capital and intermediate inputs where possible. However, multi-factor productivity estimates for the UK are now available on an experimental basis (see **Chapter 7**). Much of the work undertaken by other users centres on multi-factor productivity, and requires data on all inputs to the production process – capital, materials, services, ICT – not just labour. A framework to consider productivity should address both labour and multi-factor approaches, reflecting their interdependence and the need to build consistency. Therefore the simple framework in **Figure 2.3** shows the components of straightforward labour productivity estimates. These are based on GDP or GVA for the whole economy, for a broad sector or for a region, and are essentially welfare-focused measures. For example, in the EU structural indicators, they feature with the denominator per head of population, per worker, and per hour. The ratios between these indicators, for instance the percentage of the population in the labour force and the number of hours worked per person, are seen as levers for policy.

Figure 2.3: Labour productivity measures

	Current price Output/input	**Deflators**	**Volume measures**
Outputs	National GDP Regional GDP Industry total output or GVA	CPI (and PPPs in international analysis) PPIs for outputs and inputs	Real GDP change Real regional GDP 'Real' industry output
Inputs	Not required, as labour input directly measured in volume terms	Not required, as labour input directly measured in volume terms	Population (for welfare analysis) Workers/hours (for output analysis)

PPP is an acronym for purchasing power parities, a comparison of how much product you get for the same money in different countries. They are used across countries because they are regarded as being more appropriate than exchange rates for comparing productivity levels internationally. There is more information about PPPs in Chapter 12.

There are four individual producer price index (PPI) inquiries dealing with UK made or sold manufactured goods, UK exports of manufactured goods, imports of goods and manufactured goods and UK sold services.

From **Figure 2.3** it is clear that the main challenge for ONS in seeking to improve productivity measures is how far it is able to increase consistency in two respects: between input and output data series, and in measures of change over time. Ideally consistency is best assured by independent sources measuring outputs, inputs, and deflators on consistent definitions from populations (of enterprises and people) whose characteristics are well understood.

Multi-factor productivity measures cover changes in economic efficiency for manufacturing, marketed services or government output, at varying levels of disaggregation, and take account of a broader range of inputs. A best practice growth accounting framework for productivity is set out by Oulton (2004). This allows changes in GDP to be attributed to changes in the volume and quality of inputs, growth accounting is described in more detail in **Section 3.4**. **Figure 2.4** shows the range of outputs, inputs and deflators required to provide an integrated view.

Market sector output is ideally valued at market prices and deflated by price indices that take account of quality changes. Quality changes, in turn, should affect the volumes of both outputs and inputs used to derive productivity. See **Chapter 6** for further discussion of quality adjustment.

Non-market sector output is currently measured within National Accounts (and hence within GDP) by a mix of input cost and output measures, with output measures most common for those services delivered to individual citizens. UKCeMGA is developing, and consulting on, measures for government output that allow more explicitly for the range, mix, and quality of services delivered. See **Chapter 9** for further discussion of measuring public services.

For production sectors, output measurement methodology is well established: current price output measures, deflated by PPIs, give volume measures of output. For an increasing range of marketed intermediate

Figure 2.4: Multi-factor productivity measures

	Current price output/input	**Deflators**	**Volume measures**
Outputs	Production sectors sales value	PPIs => (quality adjusted)	Deflated revenue
	Market services sales value	⇔ (quality adjusted)	Deflated revenue or direct measures
	Government services input costs	<= (quality adjusted)	Direct measures
Inputs	Labour workforce FTEs labour hours labour cost	=> (quality or earnings adjusted)	'Real' measure of labour input QALI
	Capital stock	PPI deflators for investment; returns to 'price' capital services	VICS
	Materials/Services/ Energy	PPI SPPI deflators	'Real' measures of intermediate input

PPIs form one of a series of data sets on process changes for goods and services. There are three main indices used to deflate from expenditure to output – the consumer price index, producer price index and the services producer price index (previously called the corporate services price index).

QALI is an abbreviation for quality-adjusted labour input measures and VICS for volume index of capital services. (For more detailed information about QALI and VICS, please see **Chapter 5**.)

services, price indices can be constructed using the same approach (see Tily, 2006). However, for some marketed services and most of government, direct measures of output, adjusted for service quality, are regarded as giving the best approach to producing volume output data. Where this is the case, appropriate deflators can be derived for marketed services, but must be imputed for government output.

2.5   Consistency in productivity statistics

An important issue for multi-factor productivity analysis is consistency of output measures, and their deflators, with the economic approach used in growth accounting.

ONS National Accounts chained volume measures (CVM) of output measures are constrained to CVM expenditure measures (see Oulton, 2004), which reflect only expenditure deflators. This affects output measurement for both labour productivity and for multi-factor productivity estimates.

> A **chain index** is an index constructed by linking two or more index series of different base periods or different weights.
>
> **Chained volume measures** (CVM) are index numbers from a chain index of quantity. The index number for the reference period of the index may be set equal to 100 or to the estimated monetary value of the item in the reference period.

As a result, the ONS-published volume measures of industry output currently do not reflect price movements in both inputs and outputs and their effect on GVA (instead the difference between them is deflated by a price index for the output). Double deflation (which is described in **Chapter 4**) to achieve this is planned as part of the modernisation of National Accounts, but until this is finished there will not be complete consistency of input and output measures.

Some of the difficulties in achieving coherence and consistency for labour input measures and output have been discussed in Lindsay (2006). Conclusions of this work to improve the consistency of National Accounts output measures with compensation of employees, and total labour input, are being used as part of the modernisation of National Accounts. There is further discussion of these issues in Beadle (2007) and in **Chapters 5** and **13**.

Capital input to productivity estimation relies on a perpetual inventory model based on deflated investment.

Box 2.1: Expressing productivity outputs as labour productivity measures

Quarterly macro estimates:

- GVA/worker and GVA/hour for whole economy, (GVA at basic prices/LFS)
- manufacturing/services split on same measure, with manufacturing industry detail as National Statistics, but services as experimental data
- market sector GVA per worker and per hour (under development)

Annual measures:

- ABI based measures GVA/productivity job for 4 digit industries
- regional productivity, apportioning employees though Inter-Departmental Business Register (IDBR)
- international comparisons of GDP/worker and per hour worked, based on OECD data and converted to purchase power parities, with UK = 100 as a base

The UKCeMGA productivity programme (Education, Health and Social Care has been published for consultation so far) focuses on multi-factor productivity, using labour, capital and purchased inputs compared against volume measures of output, with estimates of quality based on outcomes.

Box 2.2: ONS data input for productivity analysis by others

- macro and industry level data
- National Accounts Supply and Use Tables data broken down into 57 industry categories
- capital services estimates, to support MFP work by the Bank of England and HM Treasury
- QALI measures to reflect labour characteristics in MFP work and the range of labour market data
- ABI in longitudinal form, which is part of the Annual Respondents' Database (ARD) to support analysis of market dynamics and productivity
- data from other business surveys, such as individual surveys for technology, skills, investment, to support analysis of productivity drivers
- output measures for public and other services

A longitudinal study or database associates all the data about one person or firm from as many different surveys as possible. Many different individual surveys are contained in the ARD. For more information about this, please see **Chapter 9**.

This is then used to calculate a capital service based on estimated rental rates for capital (see **Chapter 5** for details). Increasingly capital stock is calculated based on more detailed asset definitions – including intangible assets. These and other industry level intermediate inputs are based on National Accounts Supply and Use Tables analysis and therefore are consistant with output. For firm level analysis, and estimates of inputs depend directly on the ABI purchase survey (See **Chapter 10** for further details).

2.6   Further use of the framework

Oulton (2004) sets out a range of criteria for the coherence of output, input and price deflator data for productivity analysis. These will be considered within the frameworks set out above to set priorities for, and chart progress towards, fully consistent productivity data at industry level. The criteria include:

- double deflation of real value added

- better measures of services output and deflators, where possible removing 'assumed' productivity increases from estimates of output based on inputs

- improved measures of capital input, both by more detailed analysis of asset types and through more up-to-date estimates of asset lives, which determine capital services inputs

- enabling analysts to treat research and development as an asset (expected to be recommended as part of the international *System of National Accounts* after 2008) along the same lines as software analysis published in 2007 (Marrano, Haskel and Wallis, 2007)

- integrating statistics on employment, hours worked, output, prices and investment on a common industrial breakdown

The same requirements for consistency over time, and for coherence between inputs and outputs, apply to both industry and firm level work. In principle the criteria for improving the quality of data, and resulting analysis, should apply to both.

2.7   References

Atkinson A B (2005) *Atkinson Review: Final Report. Measurement of Government Output and Productivity for the National Accounts*, Palgrave Macmillan: Basingstoke, available at: www.statistics.gov.uk/about/data/methodology/specific/publicSector/atkinson/final_report.asp

Beadle J (2007) 'Modernising the UK's National Accounts', *Economic & Labour Market Review* 1, pp 27–32, available at: www.statistics.gov.uk/cci/article.asp?id=1737

Herbert R and Pike R (2005) 'Market Sector Gross Value Added – A new experimental National Accounts aggregate', *Economic Trends* 623, pp 15–19, available at: www.statistics.gov.uk/cci/article.asp?ID=1171

Lindsay C (2006) 'Review of methodologies for calculating National Accounts' Compensation of Employees', Office for National Statistics, available at: www.statistics.gov.uk/cci/article.asp?id=1609

Mahajan S (2005) Input-Output: Market Sector and Non-Market Sector Activity, 1992-2003, *Economic Trends* 623, pp 20-41, available at: www.statistics.gov.uk/cci/article.asp?id=1220

Mahajan S (2006) UK Input-Output Analysis, 2006 edition, Office for National Statistics: London, available at: www.statistics.gov.uk/input-output

Marrano M G, Haskel J and Wallis G (2007) 'What Happened to the Knowledge Economy? ICT, Intangible Investment and Britain's Productivity Record Revisited', Queen Mary, University of London Working Paper, available at: www.econ.qmul.ac.uk/papers/wp.htm

OECD (2001a) *Measuring Productivity – OECD Manual*, Organisation for Economic Co-operation and Development: Paris.

Oulton N (2004) 'A Statistical Framework for the Analysis of Productivity and Sustainable Development' *(for Allsopp Review)*, Centre for Economic Performance, London School of Economics: London, available at: www.hm-treasury.gov.uk/media/FD6/5F/allsopp_oulton_140.pdf

Solow R (1957) 'Technical change and the Aggregate Production Function', *Review of Economics and Statistics* 39, pp 312–320.

Tily G (2006) 'Improvements to timely measures of service sector output', *Economic Trends* 630, pp 29–32, available at: www.statistics.gov.uk/cci/article.asp?id=1555

Chapter 3

Productivity Theory and Drivers

Measuring aggregate productivity accurately and consistently is an important objective for a National Statistical Institute (NSI). Users, however, also want to look behind the statistics to understand the dynamics and determinants of productivity growth.

Increasing productivity is generally considered to be the only sustainable way of improving living standards in the long term. Statistical evidence to help policy makers understand the routes to productivity growth, especially those which can be influenced by government, can help lead to better policy.

This chapter introduces the main determinants – or 'drivers' – of productivity growth. It then explains how productivity statistics can be compiled and presented in a way that helps illuminate some of the key determinants. In particular, this chapter gives details of the growth accounting framework that decomposes economic growth into the contributions of capital, labour and other inputs. It does this both for the economy as a whole and for sectors of industry.

The Relationship between Productivity Theory and Policy

Productivity theory starts with the simple concept of output per unit input to produce the growth accounting framework and many more detailed approaches. A great deal of work and analysis has been carried out in this area by experts around the world.

ONS produces a wide range of productivity estimates. Users, such as other government departments, require this information because it helps them to understand and then design policies to improve productivity within the UK. Productivity is key to living standards (see **Section 1.1**) and therefore government policies aim to ensure UK productivity growth is strong, particularly in comparison with other developed countries.

3.1   The importance of productivity and competitiveness

Over the long term, increased productivity is the key determinant of economic growth, and together with higher employment is the primary route to higher living standards. Prosperity is usually measured by gross domestic product (GDP) per person: the total output of the economy relative to the UK population. There are essentially two ways of increasing GDP per person:

1. to have a higher level of employment or hours, so that the total labour input in the economy increases

2. to increase the amount of output each person produces: that is, increase their productivity

Given potential limitations on the rise of the UK's labour force, boosting UK productivity growth is generally accepted as the primary route to improving our future standard of living in the long term.

The Government has therefore, for some years, targeted improved UK productivity and competitiveness performance, and currently does so through the joint HM Treasury (HMT) and Department of Trade and Indstry (DTI) public service agreement:

> Demonstrate progress by 2008 on the Government's long-term objective of raising the rate of UK productivity growth over the economic cycle and improving competitiveness and narrowing the productivity gap with the US, France and Germany.

The emphasis on increasing productivity has been given further focus by recent increased globalisation of the world economy. Strong productivity growth is essential if UK companies are to be competitive and make the most of opportunities from globalisation – exploiting emerging markets and attracting foreign direct investment. Increased flexibility will also help to facilitate adjustment as globalisation intensifies economic structural change.

3.2   The Government's five driver framework

Analysis of the underlying components of economic performance suggests that certain factors are critical for determining productivity growth. The Government's productivity framework identifies five drivers that interact to underlie long-term productivity performance: investment, innovation, skills, enterprise and competition.

Investment is in physical capital – machinery, equipment and buildings. The more capital workers have at their disposal, generally the better they are able to do their jobs, producing more and better quality output.

Innovation is the successful exploitation of new ideas. New ideas can take the form of new technologies, new products or new corporate structures and ways of working. Such innovations can boost productivity, for example as better equipment works faster and more efficiently, or better organisation increases motivation at work.

Skills are defined as the quantity and quality of labour of different types available in an economy. Skills complement physical capital, and are needed to take advantage of investment in new technologies and organisational structures.

Enterprise is defined as the seizing of new business opportunities by both start-ups and existing firms. New enterprises compete with existing firms by new ideas and technologies increasing competition. Entrepreneurs are able to combine factors of production and new technologies forcing existing firms to adapt or exit the market.

Competition improves productivity by creating incentives to innovate and ensures that resources are allocated to the most efficient firms. It also forces existing firms to organise work more effectively through imitations of organisational structures and technology.

Policies designed to increase productivity are often targeted at these drivers (see **Chapter 10** for more details of research work in this area). However, to determine the success of such action, the accurate measurement of productivity is vital.

3.3   Multi-factor productivity

As stated in **Chapter 1**, multi-factor productivity (MFP) is the residual contribution to output growth of an industry or economy after calculating the contribution from all its factor inputs. The MFP measure produced within ONS is labour-capital value added productivity. An explanation of this form of MFP, along with a set of estimates, is given in **Chapter 7**.

MFP is effectively defined from the growth accounting framework. Therefore, to explain MFP fully, an explanation of growth accounting and its history is required.

> Primary inputs (or primary factor inputs) are resources that go into producing something but are treated as outside (or sometimes described as exogenous to) the production process. This includes labour and capital and may also be called direct inputs.

3.4   The growth accounting framework

> Growth accounting decomposes growth, but does not explain the process of technological change (HMT, 2006).

The growth accounting framework acts as a mechanism for breaking down the sources of economic growth into the contributions from increases in capital, labour and other factors. When these factors have all been accounted for, what remains is usually attributed to technology. This remainder is often called the Solow residual and, in theory, if all the factors contributing towards productivity were identified and measured correctly then this residual would be zero. There is more information about this residual in the section on MFP in **Chapter 7**.

When using growth accounting it is important to be aware of its limitations as well as its uses. As identified in the quote above, while this decomposition identifies factors that change productivity growth, it is not an explanation in itself of how those factors work.

Growth accounting is a specific, useful way of observing the changing structure of the economy, and assessing the contribution of each sector or industry to the whole. It also provides a very useful framework for the collection of economic statistics. This approach might be called 'joined up statistics' because it links various economic growth

and labour measures together to provide a more detailed picture of the economy.

The growth accounting framework is the main framework used internationally and is now more than fifty years old. More on the history of growth accounting is given towards the end of this chapter. The growth accounting approach has been codified in two Organisation for Economic Co-operation and Development (OECD) manuals – OECD (2001a and 2001b) – and is now the primary approach to MFP within National Statistical Institutes (NSIs) across the world. Below is an informal treatment.

3.4.1   The aggregate framework

As stated above, the growth accounting framework decomposes economic growth into the contributions from labour, capital and other factors. This amounts to relating growth in GDP to growth in employment and growth in the various capital services (from buildings, vehicles, computers, and other resources). It also allows for any other factors, such as, for example, technical change. This is easiest to show through equations.

The starting point is the aggregate growth accounting equation:

Growth of GDP = [Capital's share **times** growth of   (1)
                        capital input]

plus [Labour's share **times** growth of labour input]

plus growth of Multi-Factor Productivity (MFP)

where GDP, capital and labour are all chain indices of their respective components.

Labour input is a weighted average of the growth rates of the different types of labour, where the weights are the shares of each type in the aggregate wage bill. There is more about defining and estimating the different types of labour input in **Chapter 5**; the labour input series here is effectively a quality-adjusted labour input (QALI) measure.

Capital input is defined as aggregate capital services, not capital stock. In this definition, capital services are a direct measure of the flow of productive services from capital assets rather than a measure of the stock of those assets. For example, capital services from computers refer to the service they provide rather than the value of the computers themselves. The treatment of capital is therefore analogous to the treatment of labour, where each type of labour input is measured by the flow of labour services, for instance hours worked. There is more about defining and estimating capital services in **Chapter 5**.

Labour's share is the proportion of GDP attributable to labour. The largest component of this is the wage bill but it actually comprises all compensation made to labour.

Capital's share is the remainder of GDP (ie. attributable to capital).

Note that:

Labour's share plus **Capital's share** = 1

Labour input grows **either** if hours worked increase **or** if the quality of labour increases; the latter occurs if the composition of the labour force shifts towards better paid workers (Bell, Burriel-Llombart and Jones (2004)). Also see **Chapter 5** for more details on increasing labour input for a QALI measure. Likewise **capital input** grows if the amount or the quality increases.

MFP growth is calculated as a residual in this equation. It is often regarded as a representation of technology change but, realistically, includes any factors not represented by the **labour input** or **capital input** series. The contribution to growth of improved management structures or practices might be a part of this residual, for example. If technology could be expressed in a similar way to labour and capital then an extra term could be added to the aggregate growth accounting equation. Therefore, if all the factors that affect productivity could be included then the residual would equal zero.

Equation (1) can be rearranged in per hour worked terms as

Growth of GDP
per hour worked = Capital deepening   (2)
           plus Labour quality contribution
           plus MFP growth

where
Capital deepening = [Capital's share **times** growth of capital input per hour worked]

Labour quality contribution = [Labour's share **times** growth of labour input per hour worked]

Rearranging (1) and (2), MFP can be seen as:

Growth of MFP =   growth of GDP   (3)
           minus [Capital's share **times** growth of capital input]
           minus [Labour's share **times** growth of labour input]

Growth of MFP   (4)
per hour worked = growth of GDP per hour worked
           minus Capital deepening
           minus Labour's quality contribution

Equation (3) shows that MFP is the contribution to GDP growth unexplained by the contribution of capital and labour inputs growth.

3.4.1.1 Intermediate inputs

The equations above consider MFP only in terms of the primary inputs, labour and capital, of GDP. Primary inputs are those which are treated as outside (sometimes described as exogenous to) the production process. However it is also common for MFP to be considered in terms of intermediate inputs (materials, energy, business services) of GDP, where intermediates are those inside or used up by the production process. Alternatively, MFP can be considered in terms of direct inputs of GVA.

To describe MFP in terms of primary and intermediate inputs of GDP:

Growth of MFP =   growth of GDP   (5)
           minus [share of direct inputs **times** growth of direct inputs]
           minus [share of intermediate inputs **times** growth of intermediate inputs]

To describe MFP in terms of primary inputs of GVA:

Growth of MFP =   growth of GVA   (6)
           minus [Capital's share **times** growth of capital input]
           minus [Labour's share **times** growth of labour input]

3.4.2 Building up from the industry level

Having considered the growth accounting framework and, consequently, MFP for the whole economy, the next step is to consider how the framework is seen at the industry level. This can be demonstrated by moving from the equations (1) or (2) to corresponding relationships at the industry level.

Measuring the growth of MFP in each industry requires industry data. These data are the price and quantity of total output and the prices and quantities of inputs and outputs for a set of industries covering the whole economy. Using these data, further equations can be produced. Here both primary and intermediate inputs are considered.

For the *i*th industry:

Growth of MFP
in industry i = Growth of total output in industry *i*   (7)
              minus cost-share-weighted growth
              of capital services, labour and
              intermediate input

3.4.3 Aggregation

The crucial link between the industry MFP rates given by **equation** (7) and the aggregate MFP growth rate given by **equation** (5) is provided by the concept of **Domar aggregation** (Domar 1961), named after its creator. This is defined as follows:

Aggregate MFP growth rate = Domar-weighted sum of industry MFP growth rates

where the **Domar weight** for industry i is

Nominal total output of industry *i*
——————————————————————
Nominal GDP

> **The difference between a 'real' variable and a 'nominal' variable:**
>
> A real variable (for example, the real interest rate) is one where the effects of inflation have been factored in.
>
> A nominal variable is one where the effects of inflation have not been accounted for.
>
> Nominal output, or GDP, refers to output or GDP at current prices.

The Domar weights will sum to more than one, reflecting the fact that each industry makes a double contribution to aggregate MFP, once in its own right and once through reducing the costs of industries that buy from it.

> **Box 3.1: The dual approach**
>
> MFP growth can also be calculated using prices rather than quantities. This is the so-called dual approach because the framework is seen in terms of prices instead of quantities.
>
> Using this alternative, equation (1) has an equivalent:
>
> Growth of output price = [capital's share **times** growth   (1a)
>   of rental price]
>   **plus** [Labour's share **times** growth
>   of wages]
>   **minus** growth of multi-factor
>   productivity (MFP)
>
> Therefore equation (3) also has an equivalent:
>
> Growth of MFP = [capital's share **times** growth of   (3a)
>   rental price]
>   **plus** [Labour's share **times** growth of wages]
>   **minus** growth of output price
>
> In other words, MFP can also be viewed as the unexplained difference between the growth in cost of the inputs and the growth in cost of the output.
>
> The industry equation can equally be constructed in price terms:
>
> Growth of MFP   (7a)
> in industry *i* =   [growth of price of total output of *i*]
>   **minus** [cost-share-weighted growth of prices of
>   capital services, labour and intermediate input]
>
> Provided that the accounting system is consistent, the dual approach of this (7a) must yield exactly the same answer as the one above (7) that uses quantities.

The important element to understanding the Domar weight is considering the ratio between the output of a particular industry and GDP.

This equation can be shown to hold exactly if any given input (for instance university-educated female workers aged 30–34) is paid the same wage in all industries. If this is not the case, then the equation for aggregate MFP growth also contains terms reflecting the reallocation of capital and labour towards or away from higher value uses (Jorgenson *et al* (1987)). But the Domar-weighted sum can still be regarded as the best measure of underlying productivity growth at the aggregate level. Therefore the sources of aggregate MFP growth rates can be traced to their industries of origin. Changes in aggregate MFP can be assigned either to changes in the underlying industry rates or to structural change (changes in the Domar weights).

3.4.4   The history of growth accounting

The pioneering growth accounting studies were at the whole economy level. The growth accounting framework was first formalised by Solow (1957), although the earliest empirical applications preceded his seminal paper as shown by Hulten (2000). Subsequently, the framework has been deepened by Jorgenson and his various collaborators (including Domar (1961), Jorgenson and Griliches (1967), Hulten (1978), Jorgenson, Gollop and Fraumeni (1987) and Jorgenson (1989)).

Work has been carried out at the sectoral and industry level as this more closely reflects the interests of policy makers. Consequently, through the work of Domar (1961), Hulten (1978) and Jorgenson *et al* (1987), the growth accounting framework has been extended to the industry level. 'Best practice' in this area is the Jorgensonian growth accounting framework, now enshrined in two OECD manuals (OECD (2001a) and (2001b)).

Growth accounting analyses have been employed to inform the UK policy debate (O'Mahony (1999)) and to analyse the failure of Europe or the UK to experience a similar productivity acceleration to the US (Colecchia and Schreyer (2002); van Ark *et al* (2002); O'Mahony and van Ark (2003); Basu *et al* (2003); European Commission (2003)). They have also been very influential in the ongoing debate about the US productivity acceleration of the 1990s, such as in Oliner and Sichel (2000) and Jorgenson and Stiroh (2000a) and (2000b). However, the System of National Accounts 1993 (SNA93) does not refer to growth accounting, probably because SNA93 is not directly concerned with productivity measurement. Where productivity is referred to, it is in terms of labour productivity rather than MFP.

It may seem that growth accounting, being based on the idealistic assumption of perfect competition, is too simplistic to represent the real-life economic picture. But if the data and methods required for growth accounting are not available then it is unlikely that supposedly more sophisticated analyses could be carried out either.

Also, the statistics required for growth accounting can be used as a basis for testing more complex hypotheses going beyond those required for growth accounting itself (for instance as is done by Oulton and Srinivasan, 2005). Another advantage of the growth accounting framework is that implementing it imposes an important discipline: more tests are imposed on the consistency and coherence of the National Accounts than is the case under our present system. There is more about consistency both within and between output and input in **Chapters 4** and **5**.

3.5   Future work

ONS does not currently use the growth accounting framework formally and has not previously produced MFP estimates on a regular basis, although various ad hoc analyses have been carried out (MFP figures are given in **Chapter 7**). However, ONS aims to include the growth accounting framework within the new National Accounts system (there is more information on this in **Chapter 13**). As part of this, MFP estimates will be produced on a regular basis, will be produced, primarily as a diagnostic tool for ensuring that National Accounts and labour market statistics are consistent.

Acknowledgement

ONS is grateful to Nicholas Oulton for agreeing to allow this chapter to be written with extensive reference to 'A Statistical Framework for the Analysis of Productivity and Sustainable Development' (Oulton, 2004).

3.6　References

van Ark B, Inklaar R and McGuckin R (2002) 'Changing gear': productivity, ICT and service industries: Europe and the United States, Groningen Growth and Development Centre, Research Memorandum GD-60: Groningen.

Basu S, Fernald J, Oulton N and Srinivasan S (2003) 'The case of the missing productivity growth: or, does information technology explain why productivity accelerated in the United States but not in the United Kingdom?', NBER Macroeconomics Annual, MIT Press: Cambridge, MA.

Bell V, Burriel-Llombart P and Jones J (2005) 'A quality-adjusted labour input series for the United Kingdom (1975–2002)', Bank of England Working Paper No. 280, Bank of England: London.

Colecchia A and Schreyer P (2002) 'ICT investment and economic growth in the 1990s: is the United States a unique case? A comparative study of nine OECD countries', Review of Economic Dynamics 5(2), pp 408–442.

Department of Trade and Industry and Her Majesty's Treasury (2004) Productivity in the UK 5: Benchmarking UK productivity performance, HMT, HMSO: London.

Domar E D (1961) 'On the measurement of technological change', Economic Journal, Vol. LXXI, pp 709–729.

European Commission (2003) 'Choosing to Grow: Knowledge, Innovation and Jobs in a Cohesive Society'. Report to the Spring European Council, 21 March 2003 on the Lisbon strategy of economic, social and environmental renewal, European Communities: Luxembourg.

HM Treasury (2006) Productivity in the UK 6: Progress and New Evidence, HMSO: London, available at: www.hm-treasury.gov.uk

Hulten C R (1978) 'Growth accounting with intermediate inputs', Review of Economic Studies 45, pp 511–518.

Hulten C R (2000) 'Total factor productivity: a short biography', NBER Working Paper No. 7471, NBER: Cambridge, MA.

Jorgenson D W (1989) 'Capital as a factor of production', in D W Jorgenson and R Landau (eds), Technology and capital formation, The MIT Press: Cambridge, MA.

Jorgenson D W and Griliches Z (1967) 'The explanation of productivity change', Review of Economic Studies 34, pp 249–283.

Jorgenson D W, Gollop F M and Fraumeni B M (1987) Productivity and US Economic Growth, Harvard University Press: Cambridge, MA.

Jorgenson D W and Stiroh K J (2000a) 'US economic growth at the industry level', American Economic Review, Paper and proceedings 90, pp 161–168.

Jorgenson D W and Stiroh K J (2000b) 'Raising the speed limit: US economic growth in the information age', in Brainard W C and Perry G L, Brookings Papers on Economic Activity 1, Brookings Institution Press: Washington, pp 125–211.

OECD (2001a) Measuring Productivity: OECD Manual, Organisation for Economic Co-operation and Development: Paris.

OECD (2001b) Measuring Productivity: OECD Manual, Organisation for Economic Co-operation and Development: Paris.

Oliner S D and Sichel D E (2000) 'The resurgence of growth in the late 1990s: is information technology the story?', Journal of Economic Perspectives 14, Fall, pp 3–22.

O'Mahony M (1999) 'Britain's Productivity Performance 1950–1996: An International Perspective', National Institute of Economic and Social Research: London.

O'Mahony and van Ark B (ed.) (2003) 'EU Productivity and Competitiveness: An Industry Perspective: Can Europe Resume the Catching-Up Process?', Office for Official Publications of the European Communities: Luxembourg.

Oulton N (2004) 'A Statistical Framework for the Analysis of Productivity and Sustainable Development (for Allsopp Review)', Centre for Economic Performance, LSE: London, available at: www.hm-treasury.gov.uk/media/FD6/5F/allsopp_oulton_140.pdf

Oulton N and Srinivasan S (2005) 'Productivity growth in UK industries, 1970–2000: structural change and the role of ICT', Bank of England Working Paper No. 259, Bank of England: London.

Solow R (1957) 'Technical change and the Aggregate Production Function', Review of Economics and Statistics 39, pp 312–320.

UN, OECD, IMF, EU Council Regulation (EC) No. 1467/97 (July 1997) System of National Accounts (Stability and Growth Pact), Official Journal of the European Communities L 209/6: Luxembourg.

Chapter 4

Output Measures: UK National Accounts

Productivity measures are constructed from output and input data. This chapter focuses on output measures produced within the UK National Accounts. The basic framework of the UK National Accounts is provided alongside an explanation of how they are constructed.

A detailed description of gross domestic product (GDP) is given and compared with gross value added (GVA). As part of this, the three approaches to measuring GDP (income, production and expenditure) are explained and compared, as are the processes used to generate measures of output.

This chapter also outlines the Input-Output Supply and Use Tables as they are produced in the UK and how they are used as a framework to reconcile the three different approaches to measuring GDP. The industry analyses produced through the supply and use framework provide the key output data to work on productivity for a range of users.

Creating Consistent Output Data

Producing good quality estimates of productivity requires consistent and coherent estimates of outputs and inputs. The data on outputs used in productivity work are derived from various parts of the UK National Accounts.

As stated in **Chapter 1**, productivity estimates tend to use one of three different measures of output:

1. total output

2. gross value added (GVA)

3. gross domestic product (GDP)

Total output, or output, is the value of the goods and services produced. It broadly equals the value of the sales plus any increase in the value of the inventory of finished goods not sold and work-in-progress.

In contrast, the other two measures are net of inputs used, meaning that they equal the value of production **less** the value of intermediate inputs and, therefore, are both value-added measures.

GDP and GVA are both compiled from the National Accounts. Therefore, in order to fully understand these measures, how they are constructed and the difference between them, an explanation of the UK National Accounts is required.

The Input-Output Supply and Use Tables are also covered as these tables provide the natural framework which links the inputs used, GVA and the outputs produced on a consistent basis. In the UK, these tables underpin the single estimate of annual current price GDP as derived from the production, income and expenditure approaches.

4.1   The basic framework of the UK National Accounts

The accounting framework provides for a systematic and detailed description of the UK economy, and the structure of the framework is laid out as in the *United Nations System of National Accounts 1993* (SNA93). This then forms the basis of the *European System of Accounts 1995* (ESA95), as used by all Member States.

This framework includes:

- the sector accounts, which provide, by institutional sector, a description of the different stages of the economic process from production through income generation, distribution and use of income to capital accumulation and financing

- the Input-Output framework, which describes the production process in more detail

The framework contains all the elements required to compile aggregate measures such as GDP, gross national income (GNI), saving and the current external balance (the balance of payments).

The economic accounts provide the framework for a system of volume and price indices, so that chained volume measures of aggregates such as GDP can be produced. It should be noted that, in this system, GVA, from the production and income approaches, is measured at basic prices (including other taxes **less** subsidies on production but not on products). Factor cost (which excludes all taxes **less** subsidies on production) is not used, nor is GDP, which is valued at market prices. The system also encompasses measures of population and employment to allow for derived analyses such as productivity.

The whole economy is subdivided into institutional sectors. In the UK National Accounts, there are seven main institutional sectors:

- central government

- local government

- public corporations

- private financial corporations

- private non-financial corporations

- households

- non-profit institutions serving households (NPISHs)

For each sector, current price accounts run in sequence from the production account through to the balance sheet. The accounts for the whole UK economy and its counterpart measure – the rest of the world – follow a similar structure to the UK sectors, although several of the rest of the world accounts are collapsed into a single account because they can never be complete when viewed from a UK perspective. Furthermore because of limits to data quality, the NPISHs sector is not shown separately but combined with the households sector.

The UK National Accounts also have an industrial dimension and use the *Standard Industrial Classification 2003* (SIC (2003)), which is in line with the UN NACE Rev. 1.1 classification. The present UK Input-Output Supply and Use Tables show 123 industries and products covering the whole economy.

4.1.1   What are the economic accounts?

The integrated economic accounts of the UK provide an overall view of the economy and the sequence of accounts follow that laid out in the SNA93 and ESA95.

An account records and displays all of the flows and stocks for a given aspect of economic life. In each account, the sum of resources is equal to the sum of uses with a balancing item to ensure this equality. Normally the balancing item will be an economic measure which is itself of interest.

By employing a system of economic accounts, the accounts can be built up for different areas of the economy which highlight, for example, production, income and financial transactions. In many cases, these accounts can be elaborated and set out for different institutional units and groups of units (or institutional sectors). Usually a balancing item has to be introduced between the total resources and total uses of these units or sectors and, when summed across the whole economy, these balancing items constitute significant aggregates.

The accounting structure is uniform throughout the system and applies to all units in the economy, whether they are institutional units, sub-sectors, sectors or the whole economy, though some accounts (or transactions) may not be relevant for some sectors.

The economic accounts are grouped into four main categories, and the sequence is as follows:

1. Goods and Services Account (not split by sector)
2. Current Accounts
3. Accumulation Accounts
4. Balance Sheets

The SNA93 and ESA95 provide much more detail describing each of these accounts and the links between them.

4.1.2   Overview of the UK National Accounts

The UK, like many other countries, gives priority to the production of a single estimate of GDP using data covering the *production, income* and *expenditure* approaches to measuring GDP. The income analysis is available only at

current prices, whereas the expenditure analysis is available at both current prices and chained volume measures. On the production side, analysis of GVA in chained volume measures is compiled quarterly, whereas the current price estimates are compiled annually through the production of Input-Output Supply and Use Tables.

A summary of the availability of the detailed components for each approach to measuring GDP is shown in **Figure 4.1**.

Figure 4.1: Availability of the detailed components of UK GDP

	Current prices		Chained volume measures	
Approach to GDP	Quarterly	Annual	Quarterly	Annual
Production	n/a	√	√	√
Income	√	√	n/a	n/a
Expenditure	√	√	√	√

Income, capital and financial accounts are also produced quarterly for each of the institutional sectors: non-financial corporations, financial corporations, general government and the households and NPISHs sectors. Detailed goods and services accounts and production accounts by industry and by sector are not produced quarterly.

The quarterly accounts produced are fully integrated, but with a statistical discrepancy, known as the statistical adjustment, shown for each sector account. This adjustment reflects the difference between the sector net borrowing or lending from the capital account and the identified borrowing or lending in the financial accounts which should theoretically be equal. Financial transactions and balance sheets are also produced for the rest of the world sector in respect of its dealings with the UK.

UK Input-Output Supply and Use Tables are produced annually, and only at current prices, integrating various parts of the accounting framework. The *production, income* and *expenditure* approaches to GDP are wholly integrated in the Input-Output Annual Supply and Use Tables framework. In the UK, consistent income-based totals can be derived in three ways: by industry, by institutional sector and by category of income.

When balanced, the UK Input-Output Annual Supply and Use Tables provide a coherent, consistent and wholly integrated story for a single year, including:

- a single annual estimate of GDP at current market prices, which is underpinned with components of the *production, income* and *expenditure* approaches to measuring GDP

- full and detailed Goods and Services Accounts

- production accounts by industry and by sector

- generation of Income Accounts by industry and by sector

4.1.3   Groupings of sectors

It is important to distinguish that there are different groupings of sectors which meet various user needs. Although the classification and coverage of the sectors are determined by international guidelines, various users are interested in the individual sectors as well as particular groupings of the sectors. For example, the private sector and public sector composition differs from the market sector and non-market sector. These sectors are defined below.

In the UK, there is much interest in market sector based measures, which provide useful indicators for assessing macroeconomic activity and productivity trends, and play a key role in assessing demand pressures and the impact on price inflation. Consequently, ONS recently began regular production and publication of a market sector productivity measure (see **Chapter 8**). The Bank of England and HM Treasury are key users of different sectoral analysis to help them manage various aspects of monetary and fiscal policy.

4.1.3.1 Private and public sectors

The seven institutional sectors used throughout the UK National Accounts are classified to the private sector and public sector, as follows:

Private sector:

- private non-financial corporations

- private financial corporations

- households

- NPISHs

Public sector:

- central government

- local government

- public corporations (financial and non-financial)

Financial Intermediation Services Indirectly Measured (FISIM) is not currently allocated to either private sector or public sector.

> **Financial Intermediation Services Indirectly Measured**
>
> The output of many financial intermediation services is paid for not by charges, but by an interest rate differential. FISIM imputes charges for these services and corresponding offsets in property income. Guidance on using FISIM was introduced in the UN's System of National Accounts 1993 (a set of worldwide standards for National Accounts calculations) and is soon to be incorporated into the UK National Accounts.

4.1.3.2 Market sector and non-market sector

The role and purpose of the market sector and the non-market sector, and their impact on the economy, differ substantially.

The institutional sectors that form the market sector are:

- private non-financial corporations

- private financial corporations

- households

- public corporations (financial and non-financial)

The remaining institutional sectors form the non-market sector, and are:

- central government

- local government

- NPISHs

FISIM is not currently allocated to either market sector or non-market sector.

The different roles, coverage, definitions and treatment of the market sector and the non-market sector in the National Accounts are explained in Mahajan (2005).

4.1.4   Economic activity: what is included and excluded from the production boundary?

GDP is defined as the sum of all economic activity taking place in the UK territory. Having defined the economic territory it is important to be clear about what is defined as economic activity.

In its widest sense, it could cover all activities resulting in the production of goods or services and so encompass some activities which are very difficult to measure. For example, since the 2001 edition, the UK National Accounts *Blue Book* has included estimates of the smuggling of alcoholic drink and tobacco products, and the production, income and expenditure directly related to it.

On the other hand, the UK National Accounts do not include estimates for illegal activities such as narcotics and prostitution.

In practice, the production boundary under SNA93 and ESA95 is defined as that inside which all the economic activities are taken to contribute to economic performance. This economic production may be defined as activity carried out under the control of an institutional unit that uses inputs of labour or capital and goods and services to produce outputs of other goods and services. They are all activities where an output is owned and produced by an institutional unit, for which payment or other compensation has to be made to enable a change of ownership to take place. This omits purely natural processes.

The decision whether to include a particular activity within the production boundary takes into account the following:

- does the activity produce a useful output?
- are the products or activity marketable and does it have a market value?
- if the product does not have a meaningful market value can a market value be assigned (for instance, can a value be imputed)?
- would exclusion (or inclusion) of the product of the activity make comparisons between countries or over time more meaningful?

In practice, the ESA95 production boundary can be summarised as follows:

The production of all goods, whether supplied to other units or retained by the producer for own final consumption expenditure or gross capital formation, and services only in so far as they are exchanged in the market and/or generate income for other economic units (ESA95).

For households, this has the result of including the production of goods on own-account, for example the produce of farms consumed by the farmer's own household. (However, in practice, produce from gardens or allotments has proved impossible to estimate in the UK so far.) There are further details of exclusions in **Box 4.1**.

As said in **Chapter 1**, it should be noted that GDP is a measure of economic activity, and does not measure human wellbeing and thereby is only an indicator of welfare. Also, GDP does not reflect the impact of economic activity on the environment.

Box 4.1: Exclusions from the production boundary

The present production boundary excludes:

- domestic and personal services produced and consumed within the same household, for example: cleaning, decoration and maintenance of the dwelling; cleaning, servicing and repair of household durables; preparation and serving of meals; care, training and instruction of children; care of sick or elderly people; and transportation of household members or goods

- volunteer services that do not lead to the production of goods, for example: caretaking and cleaning without payment

- natural breeding of fish in open seas

Although the production of some of these services does take considerable time and effort, the activities are self-contained with limited repercussions for the rest of the economy and, as the vast majority of household domestic and personal services are not produced for the market, it is very difficult to value the services in a meaningful way.

The ESA95 records all outputs that result from production within the production boundary. However, there are two notable exceptions:

- outputs of ancillary activities are not recorded; all inputs consumed by an ancillary activity, for example, materials, labour and consumption of fixed capital, are treated as inputs into the principal or secondary activity which it supports

- outputs produced for intermediate consumption in the same local kind-of-activity unit are not recorded. However, all outputs produced for other local kind-of-activity units belonging to the same institutional unit are to be recorded as output

4.2   Prices used to value the products of economic activity

In the UK a number of different prices may be used to value inputs, outputs and purchases, with prices being different depending on the perception of the bodies engaged in the transaction. For example, the producer and user of a product will usually perceive the value of the product differently, with the result that the output prices received by producers can be distinguished from the prices paid by purchasers.

These different prices – basic prices, producers' prices and purchasers' prices – are looked at in turn below. They differ as a result of the treatment of taxes on products less subsidies on products, and trade and transport margins.

4.2.1   Basic prices

Basic prices are the preferred method of valuing output and GVA in the accounts. This price basis reflects the amount received by the producer for a unit of goods or services, minus any taxes payable, and plus any subsidy receivable on that unit as a consequence of production or sale (for instance, the cost of production including subsidies).

As a result, the only taxes included in the price will be taxes on the output process – for example, in the UK these include business rates and vehicle excise duty – which are not specifically levied on the production of a unit of output. Basic prices exclude any transport charges invoiced separately by the producer. When a valuation at basic prices is not feasible then producers' prices may be used. The basic price valuation is used to construct the Input-Output Analytical Tables.

4.2.2   Producers' prices

Producers' prices may be thought of as the prices of goods and services 'at the factory gate'. This valuation includes all taxes on production and some taxes on products, for example excise duties.

Producers' prices =   basic prices
         plus those taxes paid per unit of output (other than taxes deductible by the purchaser, such as Value Added Tax (VAT), invoiced for output sold) **less** any subsidies received per unit of output.

4.2.3   Purchasers' prices or market prices

Purchasers' prices are those prices paid by the purchaser and include transport costs, trade margins and taxes (unless the taxes are deductible by the purchaser).

Purchasers' prices = producers' prices
         plus any non-deductible VAT or similar tax payable by the purchaser **plus** transport costs paid separately by the purchaser and not included in the producers' price.

Purchasers' prices are sometimes referred to as market prices, for example, GDP is valued at market prices and not purchasers' prices. This is a minor distinction between the purchasers' price and market price valuation of GDP. This is because of the valuation of imports, which are recorded as free on board and not as purchasers' prices (which will include taxes [**less** subsidies] on imports) when deducted from the expenditure approach. A balance is achieved as these taxes (**less** subsidies) are added in the production approach. Therefore the valuation of GDP is referred to as market prices and not as purchasers' prices.

4.3   Gross domestic product (GDP)

As mentioned earlier, priority is given in the UK to measuring GDP. This forms the major component of GNI, which in turn forms one of the key measures used to estimate the UK contribution to the European Union. The GDP measure is sometimes used for calculating productivity, particularly when constructing international comparisons of productivity, see **Chapter 12**.

4.3.1   Different approaches to measuring GDP

The three approaches and the need for balancing GDP, arguably the most important aggregate or summary indicator for purposes of economic analysis, and comparisons over time are detailed below.

All three approaches also form the basis of estimating UK GDP both quarterly and annually. The use of three different methods which, as far as possible, use independent sources of information avoids sole reliance on one source and allows greater confidence in the overall estimation process.

4.3.1.1 Production

The *production* approach looks at the contribution of each economic unit by estimating the value of their output **less** the value of goods and services used up in the production process to produce their output, this is also known as GVA. The estimation and coverage of output is described in detail in the SNA93 and ESA95 but in broad terms is turnover (excluding VAT) adjusted for changes in inventories.

Using the *production* approach:

GDP =   the sum of gross value added of the institutional sectors or of the industries, **plus** taxes on products and imports and **less** subsidies on products (which are not allocated to sectors and industries).

Where:

GVA =   the total value of output of goods and services produced **less** the intermediate consumption (goods and services used up in the production process in order to produce the output).

GDP is also the balancing item in the whole economy production account.

The above treatment for GDP is applied to producing units classified to the market sectors and it is important to note that the treatment differs for producing units classified to the non-market sectors.

The estimate of output for producing units in the non-market sector is derived by summing their costs, for example intermediate consumption, compensation of employees, taxes (**less** subsidies), on production and consumption of fixed capital. GVA is the sum of compensation of employees, taxes (**less** subsidies) on production and consumption of fixed capital.

The *production* approach to GDP, and the estimates of GVA, can be analysed by using an industry dimension or by a sector dimension as presented in the 2000 edition of *UK Input-Output Analyses*.

GVA is the variable used when producing labour productivity estimates, in particular the headline measure in the UK Productivity First Release. Also, output per worker uses GVA as the output measure, see **Chapter 1**.

Annual current price estimates of GVA by industry and by sector are produced through the process of producing annual Input-Output Supply and Use Tables (see **Section 4.6**). However, quarterly estimates of chained volume measures

of GVA by industry are produced using an output based approach (see **Section 4.3.6**).

4.3.1.2 Income

The *income* approach measures the incomes earned by individuals and corporations in the production of goods and services.

Using the *income* approach:

GDP =   the sum of uses in the whole economy generation of income account (compensation of employees, taxes on production and imports **less** subsidies, gross operating surplus and gross mixed income of the whole economy) **plus** taxes on products and imports **less** subsidies on products.

The *income* approach provides estimates of GDP and its income component parts at current market prices. The sources and methods of this approach are described in detail in Chapter 14 of *Concepts, Sources and Methods* (ONS 1998).

As it suggests, the *income* approach adds up all income earned by resident individuals or corporations in the production of goods and services and is therefore the sum of uses in the generation of income account for the total economy (or alternatively the sum of primary incomes distributed by resident producer units). See **Box 4.2** for exclusions to this approach.

Box 4.2: Exclusions from the income approach

Some types of income are not included, for example, transfer payments such as unemployment benefit, child benefit or state pensions. Although they do provide individuals with money to spend, the payments are made out of, for example, taxes and national insurance contributions.

Transfer payments are a redistribution of existing incomes and do not represent any addition to current economic activity. To avoid double counting, these transfer payments and other current transfers, for example taxes on income and wealth, are excluded from the calculation of GDP although they are recorded in the secondary distribution of income account.

In the UK, the income measure of GDP is obtained by summing together:

- gross operating surplus

- compensation of employees

- taxes on production and imports less any subsidies on production

- taxes on products and imports less any subsidies on products

Gross operating surplus excludes holding gains but includes:

- self-employment income (mixed income and quasi-corporations)

- gross trading profits of private financial corporations

- gross trading profits of private non-financial corporations

- gross trading surplus of public corporations (financial and non-financial)

- rental income

- non-market consumption of fixed capital

- FISIM

The *income* approach to GDP can be analysed either by industry, by sector or by type of factor income as presented in the 2006 edition of the *UK Input-Output Analyses*.

The *income* approach cannot be used to calculate chained volume measures directly because it is not possible to separate income components into prices and quantities in the same way as for goods and services. However, a chained volume measure of the income-based total is obtained indirectly. The expenditure-based GDP deflator at market prices (also known as the index of total home costs) is used to deflate the current market price income based total estimate to provide a chained volume measure of the total income component of GDP for balancing purposes.

4.3.1.3 Expenditure

The *expenditure* approach measures the final expenditures or uses by consumers and producers of goods and services produced within the domestic economy.

Using the *expenditure* approach:

GDP =   the sum of final uses of goods and services by resident institutional units (actual final consumption expenditure and gross capital formation)
plus exports of goods and services and **less** imports of goods and services.

The total is obtained from the sum of final consumption expenditure on goods and services by households, NPISHs and government, gross capital formation (gross fixed capital formation on tangible and intangible fixed assets, changes in inventories and acquisitions less disposals of valuables) and net exports of goods and services. This can be represented as:

- households final consumption expenditure

- NPISHs final consumption expenditure

- central government final consumption expenditure

- local government final consumption expenditure

- gross fixed capital formation

- changes in inventories

- acquisitions less disposals of valuables

- exports of goods and services

- **less** imports of goods and services

The data for these categories are estimated from a wide variety of sources including business surveys, expenditure surveys, the government's internal accounting system, surveys of traders and the administrative documents used in the importing and exporting of goods.

To avoid double counting in this approach it is important to classify consumption expenditures as either final or intermediate.

Final consumption *expenditure* involves the consumption of goods purchased by or for the ultimate consumer or user. These expenditures are final because the goods are no longer part of the economic flow or being traded in the market place. Intermediate consumption, on the other hand, is consumption of goods and services that are used or consumed in the production process. Gross capital formation is treated separately from intermediate consumption as the goods (or services) involved are not used up within the production process in an accounting period, except for depreciating over time.

Exports include all sales to non-residents, and exports of both goods and services have to be regarded as final consumption expenditure, since they are final as far as the UK economy is concerned.

Imports of goods and services are deducted because, although they are included directly or indirectly in final consumption expenditure, they are not part of domestic production.

The *expenditure* approach is used to estimate chained volume measures of GDP. The chained volume measure shows the change in GDP after the effects of inflation have been removed (see **Section 4.3.6**).

4.3.2   GDP: Difference between the concept of net and gross

The term gross refers to the fact that when measuring domestic production, this does not allow for an important phenomenon: capital consumption or depreciation of capital assets. Capital goods are different from the materials and fuels used up in the production process because they are not used up in the period of account but are instrumental in allowing that process to take place. However, over time capital goods do wear out or become obsolete, and in this sense GDP does not give a true picture of value added in the economy.

In other words, in calculating value added as the difference between output and intermediate consumption, a current cost should be included as the part of capital goods used up in the production process; that is, the depreciation of the capital assets.

Net in National Accounts terms means net of this capital depreciation, for example:

> **Gross domestic product** at market prices
> **less**   Consumption of fixed capital
> **equals** **Net domestic product** at market prices

However, because of the difficulties in obtaining reliable estimates of the consumption of fixed capital (depreciation), GDP remains the most widely used measure of economic activity.

4.3.3   UK GDP

The resulting estimates, however, like all statistical estimates, contain errors and omissions. The best estimate of GDP is attained by reconciling the estimates obtained from all three approaches: *production, income*

and *expenditure*. See **Box 4.3** for details of discrepancies between the different approaches and the definitive estimate of GDP.

On an annual basis, this reconciliation is carried out through the construction of the Input-Output Supply and Use Tables for the years for which data are available, and for subsequent periods by carrying forward the level of GDP set by the annual balancing process by using the quarterly movements in production, income and expenditure indicators.

Box 4.3: Statistical discrepancy

For years in which no balance has been struck through the Input-Output Supply and Use Tables, a statistical discrepancy exists between estimates of the total expenditure components of GDP and the total income components of GDP after the balancing process has been carried out. This statistical discrepancy is made up of two components shown in the accounts, namely:

- the expenditure statistical discrepancy, which is the difference between the sum of the expenditure components and the definitive estimate of GDP. The expenditure adjustment is allocated to the estimate of changes in inventories component

- the income statistical discrepancy, which is the difference between the sum of the income components and the definitive estimate of GDP (with sign reversed). The income adjustment is allocated to the estimate of gross operating surplus (profits) component for the private non-financial corporations sector

---

4.3.4   Valuation of GDP and GVA

The figure below shows the link between GDP and GVA as well as the distinction between market prices, basic prices and factor cost measures in the UK:

> **GVA at factor cost**
> **plus**   taxes on production other than taxes on products
> **less**   subsidies on production other than subsidies on products
> **less**   FISIM
> **equals** **GVA at basic prices**
> **plus**   value added taxes on products
> **plus**   other taxes on products
> **less**   subsidies on products
> **equals** **GDP at market prices**

GDP at market prices includes other taxes (**less** subsidies) on production and products, while GVA at basic prices includes only those other taxes (**less** subsidies) on production, such as business rates which are not taxes on products and GVA at factor cost excludes all taxes (**less** subsidies) on production and products.

A brief explanation of taxes and subsidies is given below and much more detail covering those taxes and subsides within the UK production boundary can be found in an article in the October 2006 Economic Trends, 'Taxes and subsidies within the production boundary, 1992–2004', in the October 2006 edition of *Economic Trends*.

4.3.4.1 Taxes on production and products

Taxes on production and imports including taxes on products, along with subsidies, make up the factor cost adjustment which represents the difference between GDP at market prices (sum of final expenditures) and GVA at factor cost (sum of incomes).

Part of this adjustment in the UK National Accounts has to be added to the sum of incomes to obtain GDP at market prices. The basic price adjustment, which is the sum of taxes on products **less** subsidies on products, is the difference between GVA at basic prices and GDP at market prices. It should be noted, prior to the introduction of the ESA95, the factor cost valuation was applied to both GVA and GDP for the UK.

Taxes on production and imports are taxes paid during the production or import of goods and services. They are paid irrespective of whether profits are made. They comprise taxes on products and other taxes on production.

Taxes on products are taxes paid per unit of good or service produced, sold, leased, transferred, exported or imported. They are included in the prices paid to suppliers of goods and services, so they are included in intermediate consumption at purchasers' prices, except for deductible VAT.

> **Deductible VAT** differs from other taxes on products. It is levied like other taxes on products but producers are reimbursed by government for the amount they pay when goods and services are bought. Intermediate consumption at purchasers' prices is the price paid less deductible VAT refunded. The value of sales or production at producers' prices also excludes any deductible VAT charged.

Suppliers are required to pay to government any taxes on products included in their prices. So the supplier's net revenue from selling the good is the selling price **less** the taxes on products included in the selling price. This is the basic price. It is the price at which market output is measured since it represents the producers' actual revenue.

Other taxes on production are taxes which producers have to pay but they are not paid when goods and services are bought and therefore not included in intermediate consumption. They are levied separately and are usually linked to the use of fixed capital or to the right to undertake certain regulated activities.

4.3.4.2 Subsidies on production and products

Whenever taxes on production or taxes on products are referred to, subsidies should be considered at the same time but treated in reverse, for example where taxes are added, subsidies are deducted and vice-versa.

Subsidies are current unrequited payments which general government or the Institutions of the European Union make to resident producers, with the objective of influencing their levels of production, their prices or the remuneration of the factors of production.

Other non-market producers can receive other subsidies on production only if those payments depend on general regulations applicable to market and non-market producers as well. By convention, subsidies on products are not recorded on other non-market output.

4.3.5   Headline GDP

The chained volume measure of GDP at market prices provides the key indicator of the state of the economy; this is sometimes called 'headline' GDP. The chained volume measure of GVA at basic prices, another useful short-term indicator of growth in the economy, is the headline measure for the *production* approach. It is compiled in a way which is relatively free of short-term fluctuations because of uncertainties of timing.

4.3.6   UK GDP chained volume measure

When looking at the change in the economy over time, the main concern is usually whether more goods and services are actually being produced now than at some time in the past. With productivity, however, the point of interest is whether this capital is increasing relative to the inputs.

Over time, changes in current price GDP show changes in the monetary value of the components of GDP and, as these changes in value can reflect changes in both price and volume, it is difficult to establish how much of an increase in the series results either from increased activity in the economy or an increase in the price level; only the former should be included in productivity measures. It is therefore useful to measure GDP in real terms, meaning excluding price effects, as well as at current prices. In most cases, the revaluation of current price data to remove price effects (known as deflation) is carried out by using price indices such as component series of the retail prices index or producer price index to deflate current price series at a detailed level of disaggregation.

In the 2003 edition of the *Blue Book* a new method of measuring GDP in real terms, annual chain-linking, was introduced to replace fixed base chain-linking, which was used in previous editions. The real GDP time series produced by annual chain-linking are referred to as chained volume measures.

- In the UK economic accounts, the *expenditure* approach is used to provide current price and chained volume measures of GDP

- Because of the difficulties in accounting for changes in labour productivity it is not possible to obtain direct chained volume measures of GDP from the *income* data. However, an approximate aggregate income measure is calculated by deflating the current price estimates using the GDP deflator derived from the *expenditure* approach for balancing purposes

- The quarterly *production* approach to estimating the chained volume measure of UK GDP is largely based on output indicators, and in the UK is often referred to as the output approach

There are two main methods used to remove the effects of inflation to obtain these chained volume measures. For some series, price indices for particular goods and services are used to deflate the current price series, such as:

- components of the:
  - ○ consumer price index (CPI)
  - ○ retail prices index (RPI)
  - ○ producer price index (PPI)
- corporate services price indices (CSPI)
- import prices
- export prices

For other series, chained volume measures are assumed to be proportional to the volume of goods or services. The calculation of these chained volume measures are explained in **Box 4.4**.

The reference year for **the chained volume measure series** in the 2006 edition of the *Blue Book* is 2003; the chained volume measure of GDP for 2003 is referenced to, and therefore equal to, the annual current price estimate of GDP for 2003. The price indices also make allowances for quality changes over time and the use of hedonic adjusted price deflators are applied in industries producing high-technology type products such as computers.

The year 2003 is the latest base year for chained volume measures published in the 2006 edition of the *Blue Book*. Therefore estimates for 2004, 2005 and the early periods of 2006 are based on 2003 prices, estimates for 2003 are based on 2002 prices and so on. These previous years' prices data are chain-linked to produce continuous time series called chained volume measures, in a similar fashion to the fixed-based chain-linking described earlier. As 2003 is the latest base year, current price data therefore equals chained volume measures annually in 2003.

Chained volume measures prior to 2003 are non-additive in the 2006 edition of the *Blue Book*.

The Eurostat Handbook on Prices and Volume Measures in National Accounts presents preferred methods, and alternatives, to deflate various components of the National Accounts and also describes how to handle quality change type issues. Quality adjustments and related issues are covered in more detail in **Chapter 6**.

Box 4.4: Calculating chained volume measures

In theory, chained volume measures of GVA should be estimated by double deflation. As it is hard to get reliable information from companies, in the UK double deflation is only used in the estimation of output for the agriculture and electricity industries. So, for most industries' movements, the chained volume measures for GVA are estimated by the use of output series only.

This approach assumes stable relationships between variables such as intermediate consumption, GVA and output over the short-term. For example, current price turnover is used as a proxy for output, and, in turn, when deflated forms a proxy for the chained volume measure of GVA. In other cases, direct indicators of the volume of output are used as a proxy to produce the chained volume measure of GVA.

Double deflation is planned as part of the future production of GVA methodology through the Input-Output Supply and Use Tables in both current prices and chained volume measures, see **Chapter 13** for more details.

For industries whose outputs are mainly goods, output can be estimated from the physical quantities of goods produced or from the value of output deflated by an index of price. Examples include alcohol, motor vehicles and some energy producing industries.

Apart from the use of output to estimate

chained volume measures of GVA, which accounts for around 90 per cent of the total of the production measure, a number of other kinds of indicator might be used as a proxy for the change in GVA. For example, they may be estimated by changes in inputs, where the inputs chosen may be materials used, employment or some combination of these.

In the short-term, it is assumed that movements in GVA can be measured this way. However, changes in the ratio of output and inputs to GVA can be caused by many factors: new production processes, new products made and inputs used; and changes in inputs from other industries will all occur over time. Aggregated over all industries, the impact of these changes will be lessened. In the longer term all indicators are under constant review, with more suitable ones being used as they become available.

Again, it is worth noting that non-market dominated industries are treated differently from the market sector dominated industries. In many cases, direct volume measures are used for deflating non-market output. Collective services such as defence in chained volume measures are measured according to the traditional convention whereby output is equal to the total value of the inputs.

The estimate of GVA for all industries, the proxy for the quarterly *production* measure

of GDP in chained volume terms, is finally obtained by combining or weighting together the estimates for each industry according to its relative importance in terms of GVA as established in the Input-Output Supply and Use Tables for the reference year.

For each year, these GVA weights are based on the Input-Output Supply and Use Tables for the immediately preceding year, except for the most recent years. For example, in the 2006 *Blue Book*, GVA weights are derived from the Input-Output Supply and Use Tables for 2003, and the years 2004 and 2005 will also be based on these weights. This process occurs annually on a rolling basis.

Although Input-Output Supply and Use Tables for 2004 were produced for the first time in the 2006 *Blue Book*, these tables are considered as provisional and become much more firmly based after the first annual revision to these tables, therefore the GVA weights for 2004 are not taken on at this stage. This situation reflects the basis and quality of the survey and administrative source data as well as past revisions performance of the data used to populate these tables.

This use of previous years' weights is a feature of the move to annual chain-linking, introduced in the UK National Accounts in the 2003 edition of the *Blue Book*.

Double deflation is a method to estimate real GVA by deflating output and intermediate inputs separately before subtracting the latter from the former. This is in contrast to the single deflation method whereby the subtraction is done at current prices and the difference (GVA at current prices) is deflated using an output deflator to arrive at real GVA estimates. This means that an industry's total output is deflated by the price of its output, while each input is deflated by its own price index.

4.4 Annual chain-linking

The fixed-base chain-linking method, which was used in editions of the *Blue Book* prior to 2003, produced constant price estimates of GDP whereby the price structure prevailing in 1995 was used to compile data from 1994 onwards. For years prior to 1994, more appropriate pricing structures were used and, in order to link all of the constant price estimates to produce continuous time series, a process of chain-linking was used whereby blocks of constant price data with different price bases were linked together.

In the link years, figures were calculated with reference to two consecutive base years to obtain a linking factor so that the whole time series could be shown with reference to the latest base year. This system of fixed-base chain-linking is described later in this section.

In the 2003 edition of the *Blue Book*, the fixed-base chain-linking method was replaced with an annual chain-linking process which produces chained volume measures of GDP. Chained volume measures are calculated by applying the price structure prevailing in the previous year for each year, except the most recent year(s), 2004 and 2005, where chained volume measures are calculated by applying the price structure prevailing in 2003.

These chained volume measure series are shown in £ million and referenced onto the latest base year. The process of annually chain-linking previous years' prices data onto a continuous time series referenced onto the latest base year results in a loss of additivity in the annual data prior to the latest base year. Each year the latest base year and therefore the reference year will move forward by one year.

In the *expenditure* measure of GDP all of the components are annually chain-linked, as described above, and the chained volume measure of total GDP is aggregated from these components. The *production* (output) approach involves weighting together the detailed components using the contribution to current price GVA (or weight) in the immediately preceding year and annually chain-linking to produce a continuous time series. The application of annual chain-linking to the *production* (output) measure of GDP is described in detail in Reed and Tuke (2001).

Annual chain-linking provides more accurate measures of growth in the economy than that provided by the old method of fixed-base chain-linking because more up to date, and therefore more appropriate, price structures are used. The move to annual chain-linking is also consistent with international guidelines as laid down in SNA93.

4.5   Index numbers and price indices

Some chained volume measure series are expressed as index numbers in which the series are simply scaled proportionately to a value of 100 in the reference year. These index numbers are volume indices of the 'base weighted' or 'Laspeyres' form, see Chapter 2 of *Concepts, Sources and Methods* (ONS 1998).

Aggregate price indices are of the 'Paasche' or 'current-weighted' form. They are generally calculated indirectly by dividing the current price value by the corresponding chained volume measure and multiplying by 100. Examples are the GDP deflator and the households' consumption deflator.

Value indices are calculated by scaling current price values proportionately to a value of 100 in the reference year. By definition such a value index, if divided by the corresponding volume index and multiplied by 100, will give the corresponding price index.

4.6   Input-Output Annual Supply and Use Tables

The main aim of ONS's Input-Output work is to provide a framework for the detailed reconciliation of the components of the three approaches to measuring GDP, thereby agreeing a single annual estimate of current market price GDP.

The annual estimates prepared for the *Blue Book* incorporate the results of annual inquiries which become available in the first part of the year, although estimates for the latest year are still based largely on quarterly information. As new data are collected it is likely that revisions will be necessary.

The process of reassessing these estimates involves the preparation of Input-Output Supply and Use Tables. This Input-Output approach amalgamates all the available information on inputs, outputs, GVA, income and expenditure. Similarly the production of the consolidated sector and financial accounts requires the preparation of 'top-to-bottom' sector and sub-sector accounts to identify discrepancies in the estimates relating to each sector. The thorough and detailed nature of this estimation process takes time, and has often included large revisions to earlier years.

4.6.1   GDP and the balancing of the annual accounts

As discussed earlier, the three different approaches to estimating current price GDP should theoretically produce the same result. However, the different approaches are based on different surveys and administrative data sources and each produces estimates which, like all statistical estimates, are subject to errors and omissions.

A definitive GDP estimate can only emerge after a process of benchmarking components, balancing and adjustment.

ONS believes that the most reliable 'definitive' estimate of the current price level of GDP is that derived using the annual Input-Output Supply and Use Tables framework. Therefore, for the years when Input-Output Supply and Use Tables are available, GDP is set at the level derived from that year's balance. For periods subsequent to the latest Input-Output Supply and Use Tables, the level of GDP is carried forward using the quarterly movements in production, income and expenditure totals.

The annual balancing and compilation process is described in Mahajan (1997).

4.6.2   The Input-Output framework and GDP

The main National Accounts is primarily concerned with the composition and value of goods and services entering into final demand (for example, purchases by consumers) and the outputs and incomes generated in the production process. It does not display the inter-industry transactions which link these activities.

The UK Input-Output Supply and Use Tables, however, do include these intermediate transactions which form inputs into these processes, therefore providing an extra dimension. The Input-Output analyses are constructed to show a balanced and complete picture of the flows of products in the economy and illustrate the relationships between producers and consumers of goods and services.

On an annual basis Input-Output Supply and Use Tables are used to achieve consistency in the economic accounts' aggregates by linking the components of GVA, inputs, outputs and final demand. As the *production, income* and *expenditure* approaches to measuring GDP can all be calculated from the Input-Output Supply and Use Tables, a single estimate of GDP can be derived by balancing the supply and demand for goods and services and reconciling them with the corresponding GVA estimates.

4.6.3   Industrial analyses

The Input-Output Supply and Use Tables and other industrial based analyses produced in the ONS use the Standard Industrial Classification 2003 (SIC (2003)). This classification is applied to the collection and publication of a wide range of economic and industrial statistics. The current version, SIC (2003) is consistent with the NACE Rev. 1.1. The industrial dimension is also used in the range of productivity analyses and per head type analyses.

The Input-Output Supply and Use Tables use the SIC (2003) covering the whole economy based on 123 Input-Output groups which form a mix of 2-digit, 3-digit and 4-digit categories across the hierarchy of the classification. The annex to this section shows the Classification of 123 Input-Output industry/product groups by SIC (2003) and how they relate to the NACE Rev. 1.1 classification. The NACE Rev. 1.1 categories are shown at the Division, Sub-section and Section level whereas the SIC (2003) links to the 123 I-O groups by Division, Group or Class as appropriate. The 123 industry/product groupings are listed in **Appendix Table 4A** at the end of this chapter.

> **The Input-Output process,** which produces Input-Output Supply and Use Tables annually as well as benchmarking various components of GDP, has been speeded up considerably over the last few years. The result is that the UK produces the first GDP balance through the Input-Output framework for a year around eighteen months after the end of that year. These full Input-Output Supply and Use Tables, consistent with the National Accounts *Blue Book,* are published as a separate web-only publication at the same time as the *Blue Book.* The latest annual Input-Output publication covers the periods 1992 to 2004, with summary information provided in the *Blue Book* (Chapter 2) itself.

A more common, and widely used level of aggregation covers the 11-industry level as shown in **Box 4.5.**

4.6.4   Structure of the UK Input-Output Annual Supply and Use Tables

The Input-Output Annual Supply and Use Tables consist of two matrices, which bring together the production, income and expenditure measures of GDP. When balanced, they provide a single measure of annual current price GDP, which integrates the components of GVA, inputs and outputs, and final demands.

Box 4.5: 11-industry level classification

11 industry level	Classification I-O groups
Agriculture, forestry & fishing	1–3
Mining & quarrying	4–7
Manufacturing	8–84
Electricity, gas & water supply	85–87
Construction	88
Distribution & hotels	89–92
Transport & communication	93–99
Finance & business services	100–114
Public administration & defence	115
Education, health & social work	116–118
Other services	119–123

The Input-Output Annual Supply and Use Tables, as illustrated in the **Figure 4.2**, reflect the structure and availability of the data collected and the components needed to balance the three measures of UK GDP:

- The Input-Output Annual Supply and Use Tables show the supply and demand for products in terms of 123 industries (represented by columns) and 123 products (represented by rows). Industries are defined using the SIC (2003) and businesses are classified on the ONS Inter-Departmental Business Register (IDBR) to industries according to whatever product accounts for the greatest part of their output. See **Appendix Table 4A** for the classification of the 123 Input-Output groups and their links to SIC (2003).

- The Supply Table shows the output of each industry by type of product at basic prices. Industries, by definition, produce mainly the principal product of the industry to which they are classified. The off-diagonal products are secondary production or by-products of the production process. The Supply Table is published in summary form only because of disclosure rules prohibiting the publication of data that may be traced to a single contributor to ONS inquiries.

Figure 4.2: Structure of the Input-Output Supply and Use Tables framework

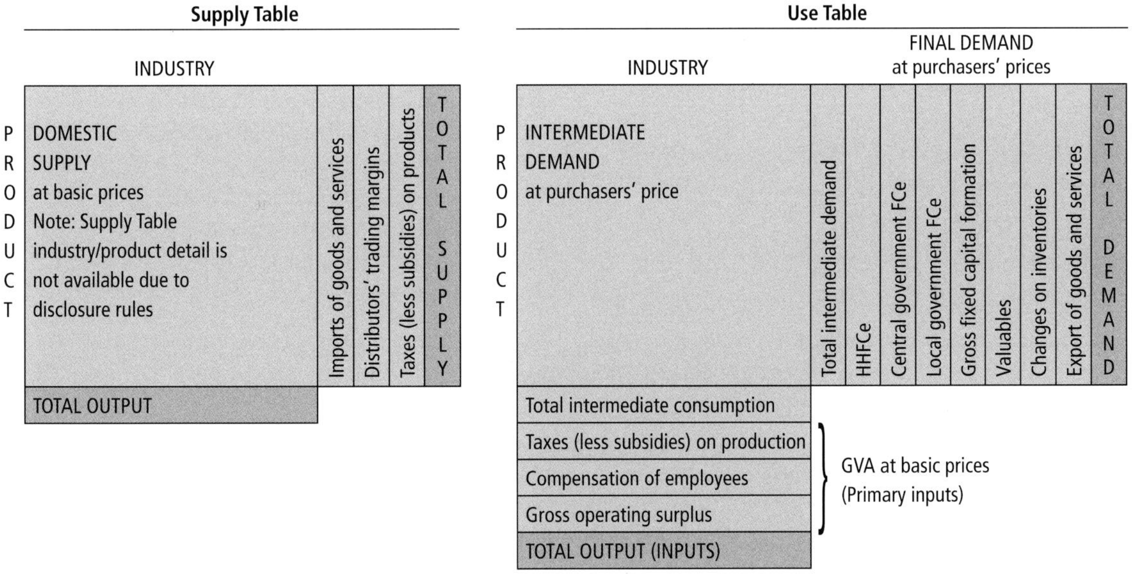

HHFCe represents Households final consumption expenditure.

NPISHs FCe represents Non-profit institutions serving households final consumption expenditure.

- The industrial dimension of the Use Table shows, for each industry, the costs incurred in the production process as intermediate consumption along with primary inputs (labour costs, taxes on production, profits, etc.). Note that productivity estimates use primary factors, for example labour and capital. These estimates are compared with GVA, for example the headline measure of GVA per worker. In addition, productivity can be measured with output matched to the sum of both primary and intermediate inputs, for example the KLEMS work, see **Chapter 12** for more detail.

- The product dimension of the Use Table shows intermediate demand and final demand and is valued at purchasers' prices, which represent the prices that purchasers actually pay.

- Estimates of consumption (both intermediate and final demand) include goods and services both domestically produced and imported.

Further details on the tables are given in Chapter 13 of *Concepts, Sources and Methods* (ONS 1998). A full description of the present methodology is given in the *Input-Output Balances Methodological Guide* (ONS 1997).

The Input-Output Supply and Use Tables are balanced, when:

For each industry:

> Total inputs (from the Use Table)
>
> **equals**
>
> Total outputs (from the Supply Table)

For each product:

> Supply (from the Supply Table)
>
> **equals**
>
> Demand (from the Use Table)

That is, when the data from the *production, income* and *expenditure* approaches used to fill these tables is balanced, all approaches produce the same estimate of current price GDP at market prices.

GDP at current market prices can be derived from the balances by taking the estimate of total GVA at basic prices (from the Use Table) and adding taxes on products and deducting subsidies on products (from the Supply Table).

This balancing process encompasses the validation of source data and benchmarking of various quarterly data onto the more comprehensive annual survey sources. Once the initial data estimates have been gathered, estimates of the components of supply and demand for products are prepared, together with the estimates of industry outputs and inputs and therefore GVA. The resulting *production* based estimates of current price GVA are then compared with the *income* and *expenditure* measures and checks, investigations and analyses are then carried out.

The coherence of these initial estimates is then assessed by:

- comparisons of GVA for each industry using the *income* and *production* based approaches, and

- comparisons of the components of supply and demand for each type of product (which effectively compare the *production* and *expenditure* approaches)

By analysing and reconciling these comparisons, a single GDP estimate is reached. Further details on the compilation and balancing process are available in Mahajan (1997).

4.7   Future plans

The development of new methods is planned following a high level review to look at the strengths and weaknesses of the UK National Accounts. This found that users' main concern is the evidence of bias in the early estimates of GDP leading to persistent upward revisions. The review recommended that the UK system should extend the use of the Input-Output Supply and Use Tables framework for the estimation of GDP and its components.

These planned changes will provide a robust foundation for supporting analysis of various dimensions of productivity and growth accounting. The Input-Output Supply and Use Tables framework, in particular, will do this by allowing output and value added elements of the economy to be presented alongside the inputs used in each industry.

In order to take full advantage of the current changes planned to the National Accounts systems, a structure for long-term productivity analysis will be included. This structure will be composed of National Accounts data sources along with checks and calculations to automatically produce detailed productivity estimates consistent with National Accounts. More details of this planned work are given in Beadle (2007) and in **Chapter 13**.

4.8   References

Atkinson A B (2005) *Atkinson Review: Final Report. Measurement of Government Output and Productivity for the National Accounts*, Palgrave Macmillan: Basingstoke, available at: www.statistics.gov.uk/about/data/methodology/specific/publicSector/atkinson/final_report.asp

Beadle J (2007) 'Modernising the UK's National Accounts', *Economic & Labour Market Review* vol 1, no 4, pp 27–32, available at: www.statistics.gov.uk/cci/article.asp?id=1737

Eurostat (1995) *European System of Accounts 1995* (ESA95), Office for Official Publications of the European Communities: Luxembourg.

Eurostat (2001) *Handbook on price and volume measures in national accounts*, Office for Official Publications of the European Communities: Luxembourg, available at: http://epp.eurostat.cec.eu.int/cache/ITY_OFFPUB/KS-41-01-543/EN/KS-41-01-543-EN.PDF

International Labour Organization (2004) Consumer Price Index Manual: Theory and Practice, Chapter 7, ILO: Geneva, available at: www.ilo.org/public/english/bureau/stat/guides/cpi/index.htm#manual

Mahajan S (1997) *Input-Output Methodological Guide*, 1997 edition, Office for National Statistics: London.

Mahajan S (1997) 'Balancing GDP: UK Annual Input-Output Balances', *Economic Trends* 519, pp 29–40.

Mahajan S (2005) 'Input-Output: Market sector and non-market sector activity', *Economic Trends* 623, pp 20–41, available at: www.statistics.gov.uk/StatBase/Product.asp?vlnk=11041

Mahajan S (2006) 'Development, Compilation and Use of Input-Output Supply and Use Tables in the UK National Accounts', Economic Trends 634, pp 28–46, available at: www.statistics.gov.uk/StatBase/Product.asp?vlnk=11041

Mahajan S (2006) 'Taxes and subsidies within the production boundary, 1992–2004', *Economic Trends* 635, pp 48–62, available at: www.statistics.gov.uk/StatBase/Product.asp?vlnk=11041

Mahajan S (2006) *UK Input-Output Analyses*, 2006 edition, Office for National Statistics, available at: www.statistics.gov.uk/inputoutput

Office for National Statistics (1995) UK ESA95 *Gross National Income Inventory of Methods*, available at: www.statistics.gov.uk/Statbase/Product.asp?vlnk=6392

Office for National Statistics (1998) *National Accounts Concepts, Sources and Methods*, TSO: London, available at: www.statistics.gov.uk/statbase/Product.asp?vlnk=1144

Office for National Statistics (2006) *United Kingdom National Accounts – The Blue Book*, 2006 edition, Palgrave Macmillan: Basingstoke.

Penneck S and Mahajan S (1999) 'Annual Coherence Adjustments in the National Accounts', *Economic Trends* 551, pp 27–32.

Reed G and Tuke A (2001) 'The effects of annual chain-linking on the output measure of GDP', *Economic Trends* 575, pp 37–53 available at: www.statistics.gov.uk/cci/article.asp?ID=87

Sharp P (1999) *Gross Domestic Product: Output Approach (Gross Value Added)*, 1999 edition, GSS Methodology Series no 15, Office for National Statistics: London.

United Nations Statistics Division (1993) *System of National Accounts* (SNA93), available at: http://unstats.un.org/unsd/sna1993/toctop.asp

11 level	Detail 123 level	Industry/product groups	Standard Industrial Classification (2003) Divisions Groups, Classes	NACE Rev.1.1 Industrial classification Division A60	Sub-section A31	Section A17	A6
Appendix Table 4A: Classification of Input-Output industry/product groups by Standard Industrial Classification (2003) and NACE Rev.1.1							
Agriculture	1	Agriculture, hunting and related service activities	01	01	A	A	
	2	Forestry, logging and related service activities	02	02			1
	3	Fishing, fish farming and related service activities	05	05	B	B	
Mining and quarrying	4	Mining of coal and lignite; extraction of peat	10	10			2
	5	Extraction of crude petroleum and natural gas; service activities incidental to oil and gas extraction	11 + 12	11 + 12	CA	C	
	6	Mining of metal ores	13	13	CB		
	7	Other mining and quarrying	14	14			
Manufacturing	8	Production, processing and preserving of meat and meat products	15.1	15	DA	D	
	9	Processing and preserving of fish and fish products; fruit and vegetables	15.2 + 15.3				
	10	Vegetable and animal oils and fats	15.4				
	11	Dairy products	15.5				
	12	Grain mill products, starches and starch products	15.6				
	13	Prepared animal feeds	15.7				
	14	Bread, rusks and biscuits; manufacture of pastry goods and cakes	15.81 + 15.82				
	15	Sugar	15.83				
	16	Cocoa; chocolate and sugar confectionery	15.84				
	17	Other food products	15.85 to 15.89				
	18	Alcoholic beverages - alcohol and malt	15.91 to 15.97				
	19	Production of mineral waters and soft drinks	15.98				
	20	Tobacco products	16	16			
	21	Preparation and spinning of textile fibres	17.1	17	DB		
	22	Textile weaving	17.2				
	23	Finishing of textiles	17.3				
	24	Made-up textile articles, except apparel	17.4				
	25	Carpets and rugs	17.51				
	26	Other textiles	17.52 to 17.54				
	27	Knitted and crocheted fabrics and articles	17.6 + 17.7				
	28	Wearing apparel; dressing and dyeing of fur	18	18			
	29	Tanning and dressing of leather; manufacture of luggage, handbags, saddlery and harness	19.1 + 19.2	19	DC		
	30	Footwear	19.3				
	31	Wood and wood products, except furniture	20	20	DD		
	32	Pulp, paper and paperboard	21.1	21	DE		
	33	Articles of paper and paperboard	21.2				
	34	Publishing, printing and reproduction of recorded media	22	22			

			Standard Industrial Classification (2003)	NACE Rev.1.1 Industrial classification			
Appendix Table 4A: Classification of Input-Output industry/product groups by Standard Industrial Classification (2003) and NACE Rev.1.1 (Continued)							
11 level	Detail 123 level	Industry/product groups	Divisions Groups, Classes	Division A60	Sub-section A31	Section A17	A6
Manufacturing continued	35	Coke, refined petroleum products and nuclear fuel	23	23	DF		
	36	Industrial gases, dyes and pigments	24.11 + 24.12	24	DG		
	37	Other inorganic basic chemicals	24.13				
	38	Other organic basic chemicals	24.14				
	39	Fertilisers and nitrogen compounds	24.15				
	40	Plastics and synthetic rubber in primary forms	24.16 + 24.17				
	41	Pesticides and other agro-chemical products	24.2				
	42	Paints, varnishes and similar coatings, printing ink and mastics	24.3				
	43	Pharmaceuticals, medicinal chemicals and botanical products	24.4				
	44	Soap and detergents, cleaning and polishing preparations, perfumes and toilet preparations	24.5				
	45	Other chemical products	24.6				
	46	Man-made fibres	24.7				
	47	Rubber products	25.1	25	DH		
	48	Plastic products	25.2				
	49	Glass and glass products	26.1	26	DI		
	50	Ceramic goods	26.2 + 26.3				
	51	Bricks, tiles and construction products in baked clay	26.4				
	52	Cement, lime and plaster	26.5				
	53	Articles of concrete, plaster and cement; cutting, shaping and finishing of stone; manufacture of other non-metallic products	26.6 to 26.8				
	54	Basic iron and steel and of ferro-alloys; manufacture of tubes and other first processing of iron and steel	27.1 to 27.3	27	DJ		
	55	Basic precious and non-ferrous metals	27.4				
	56	Casting of metals	27.5				
	57	Structural metal products	28.1	28			
	58	Tanks, reservoirs and containers of metal; manufacture of central heating radiators and boilers; manufacture of steam generators	28.2 + 28.3				
	59	Forging, pressing, stamping and roll forming of metal; powder metallurgy; treatment and coating of metals	28.4 + 28.5				
	60	Cutlery, tools and general hardware	28.6				
	61	Other fabricated metal products	28.7				
	62	Machinery for the production and use of mechanical power, except aircraft, vehicle and cycle engines	29.1	29	DK		
	63	Other general purpose machinery	29.2				
	64	Agricultural and forestry machinery	29.3				
	65	Machine tools	29.4				

Appendix Table 4A: Classification of Input-Output industry/product groups by Standard Industrial Classification (2003) and NACE Rev.1.1 (Continued)

11 level	Detail 123 level	Industry/product groups	Standard Industrial Classification (2003) Divisions Groups, Classes	NACE Rev.1.1 Industrial classification Division A60	Sub-section A31	Section A17	A6
	66	Other special purpose machinery	29.5				
	67	Weapons and ammunition	29.6				
	68	Domestic appliances not elsewhere classified	29.7				
	69	Office machinery and computers	30	30	DL		
	70	Electric motors, generators and transformers; manufacture of electricity distribution and control apparatus	31.1 + 31.2	31			
	71	Insulated wire and cable	31.3				
	72	Electrical equipment not elsewhere classified	31.4 to 31.6				
	73	Electronic valves and tubes and other electronic components	32.1	32			
	74	Television and radio transmitters and apparatus for line telephony and line telegraphy	32.2				
	75	Television and radio receivers, sound or video recording or reproducing apparatus and associated goods	32.3				
	76	Medical, precision and optical instruments, watches and clocks	33	33			
	77	Motor vehicles, trailers and semi-trailers	34	34	DM		
	78	Building and repairing of ships and boats	35.1	35			
	79	Other transport equipment	35.2 + 35.4 + 35.5				
	80	Aircraft and spacecraft	35.3				
	81	Furniture	36.1	36 + 37	DN		
	82	Jewellery and related articles; musical instruments	36.2 + 36.3				
	83	Sports goods, games and toys	36.4 + 36.5				
	84	Miscellaneous manufacturing not elsewhere classified; recycling	36.6 + 37				
Electricity, gas and water supply	85	Production, transmission and distribution of electricity	40.1	40	E	E	
	86	Gas; distribution of gaseous fuels through mains; steam and hot water supply	40.2 + 40.3				
	87	Collection, purification and distribution of water	41	41			
Construction Wholesale	88	Construction	45	45	F	F	3
	89	Sale, maintenance and repair of motor vehicles and retail trade and motor cycles; retail sale of automotive fuel	50	50	G	G	4
	90	Wholesale trade and commission trade, except of motor vehicles and motor cycles	51	51			
	91	Retail trade, except of motor vehicles and motor cycles; repair of personal and household goods	52	52			
	92	Hotels and restaurants	55	55	H	H	
Transport and communication	93	Transport via railways	60.1	60	I	I	
	94	Other land transport; transport via pipelines	60.2 + 60.3				
	95	Water transport	61	61			
	96	Air transport	62	62			

Appendix Table 4A: Classification of Input-Output industry/product groups by Standard Industrial Classification (2003) and NACE Rev.1.1 (Continued)

11 level	Detail 123 level	Industry/product groups	Standard Industrial Classification (2003) Divisions Groups, Classes	NACE Rev.1.1 Industrial classification Division A60	Sub-section A31	Section A17	A6
Transport and communication continued	97	Supporting and auxiliary transport activities; activities of travel agencies	63	63			
	98	Post and courier activities	64.1	64			
	99	Telecommunications	64.2				
Financial intermediation	100	Financial intermediation, except insurance and pension funding	65	65	J	J	5
	101	Insurance and pension funding, except compulsory social security	66	66			
	102	Activities auxiliary to financial intermediation	67	67			
	103	Real estate activities with own property; letting of own property, except dwellings	70.1 + 70.2(pt)	70	K	K	
	104	Letting of dwellings, including imputed rent	70.2 (pt)				
	105	Real estate activities on a fee or contract basis	70.3				
	106	Renting of machinery and equipment without operator and of personal and household goods	71	71			
	107	Computer and related activities	72	72			
	108	Research and development	73	73			
	109	Legal activities	74.11	74			
	110	Accounting, book-keeping and auditing activities; tax consultancy	74.12				
	111	Market research and public opinion polling; business / management consultancy activities; management activities of holding companies	74.13 to 74.15				
	112	Architectural and engineering activities and related technical consultancy; technical testing and analysis	74.2 + 74.3				
	113	Advertising	74.4				
	114	Other business services	74.5 to 74.8				
Public administration	115	Public administration and defence; compulsory social security	75	75	L	L	6
Education, health and social work	116	Education	80	80	M	M	
	117	Human health and veterinary activities	85.1 + 85.2	85	N	N	
	118	Social work activities	85.3				
Other services	119	Sewage and refuse disposal, sanitation and similar activities	90	90	O	O	
	120	Activities of membership organisations not elsewhere classified	91	91			
	121	Recreational, cultural and sporting activities	92	92			
	122	Other service activities	93	93			
	123	Private households employing staff and undifferentiated production activities of households for own use	95 to 97	95 to 97	P	P	

Chapter 5

Input Measures: Labour and Capital

Consistency within productivity estimates, for both labour and multi-factor measures, is of primary importance and requires coherent output and input data. For labour productivity this means labour input, workers, jobs or hours worked and for multi-factor productivity (MFP) this means both labour and capital inputs. These inputs are quality-adjusted labour input (QALI) measures and the volume index of capital services (VICS).

QALI measures not only hours worked as labour's input into production but also approximates workers' marginal productivity, using their characteristics to adjust hours worked. VICS captures the flow of services that stem from the physical capital stock and are used in the production process, taking account of changes in the mix of assets and their useful value. By taking account of known improvements in inputs, these measures produce more accurate estimates of productivity growth.

This chapter reviews current methodologies, and considers the importance of consistency within productivity estimates and the challenges that this provides. The chapter to describe how ONS ensures that coherent output and input measures are available. Specific attention is paid to ONS work to reconcile the estimates of labour input.

The chapter also describes the two new inputs ONS has developed for calculations – QALI and VICS.

The importance of labour and capital inputs

Productivity analysis requires measures of input from which output is produced. For the analysis to provide useful statistical or policy conclusions, inputs must be measured on the same basis as the outputs. Interpreting productivity levels and changes requires a good understanding of how inputs are defined, and how accurately they are measured.

For much of the analysis of past trends, and projections for the future, economists focus on the two primary inputs – labour and capital. The reason for this focus is simple. Policy makers wish to assess the potential for future output growth in the economy, and key levers available to do this are:

- to increase the supply of labour, through encouraging more people to enter the labour force

- increasing the skills of those already there

- increasing investment of various types

- improving the relationship between inputs and outputs

This chapter deals with the inputs used within ONS, namely labour, quality-adjusted labour input measures and the volume index of capital services. Information about the KLEMS project, mentioned in **Chapter 1**, which also uses intermediate inputs for productivity estimates, can be found in **Chapter 12**.

Since most ONS productivity measures focus on labour productivity, this chapter starts by discussing measures of labour input.

5.1   Labour input

ONS produces, on a quarterly basis, estimates of labour productivity measured in terms of output per worker, per job and per hour worked. Published in the ONS *Productivity First Release,* their quality depends directly on the quality of the underlying component data and how consistent these measures are with one another. In assessing ONS productivity data, it is important to understand the issues faced in measuring labour input. Considering some of the difficulties encountered in trying to produce consistent productivity measures, this section covers the ways in which ONS deals with and overcomes these problems.

Labour input can be assessed in two ways. Household surveys assess the supply of labour (measured by the number of workers and/or the number of hours they work), while business surveys ask firms and organisations how many people they employ, their earnings and hours of work. Practical issues govern how these are used. The most important of these are that:

- household surveys capture all types of labour input from UK residents, or at least those who would normally be captured in a census

- business surveys typically capture employed people, but not those who are self- employed or owner managers

- business surveys can capture short-term migrant labour supplied by people who are not normally resident in the UK

Because of the importance of self-employment in the UK economy, ONS takes the view that its major household survey, the Labour Force Survey (LFS), provides the best estimate of overall labour input into the economy. However, analysis shows that household surveys, in which individuals define for themselves the industries in which they work, are less reliable for detailed industry analysis than business surveys.

ONS has two other main surveys that cover employment: the Annual Business Inquiry (ABI), which asks about numbers of employees at each firm and is used in the workforce job series; and the Annual Survey on Hours and Earnings (ASHE), which is used for earnings analyses. These surveys provide estimates of labour input at firm or industry level.

5.1.1   Calculating labour productivity

To calculate whole economy labour productivity measures, ONS uses three different measures of labour: number of workers, number of jobs and number of hours worked.

The 'workers' measure, based on the LFS, is important because the number of workers in the economy reflects the overall 'employment rate' – the proportion of the UK working-age population engaged in paid work. One aim of government policy is to increase the employment rate, both to reduce the number of people excluded from work, and to raise the productive potential of the country. The headline figure in the ONS *Productivity First Release* is gross value added (GVA) per worker (see **Chapter 4** for a definition of GVA).

The 'jobs' measure is produced because policymakers need to understand productivity at the industry level, and take account of changes in the structure of the economy. To produce estimates by industry, one has to overcome the problem that an industry breakdown (for total production, detailed manufacturing and some service sectors) is only available on a GVA per job or per hour worked basis. This is mainly because there is currently no adequate mechanism available to allocate multi-job workers to specific industries on a completely consistent basis. 'Per job' productivity estimates use the data from business surveys, which identify numbers of employee jobs, and attempt to scale the labour input estimates using the LFS.

'Per hour' measures are considered by many analysts to provide the best basis for productivity estimates, because they take account of differences in working patterns between countries and industries, and the growing importance of part-time work. They also take account of short-term fluctuations in hours worked as firms respond to immediate changes in economic conditions and employees are asked to work overtime or shorter hours as demand goes up or down.

5.1.1.1 Estimates of worker numbers

The LFS is an ONS survey of households in the UK that collects information about people's employment status and conditions. It asks individuals about their current and previous jobs including which industries they work in, which jobs they hold within the industry and how many hours they work, whether employed or self-employed. It also enquires about related topics such as training and qualifications. The LFS Total Workers series groups workers into four classifications: employees, the self-employed, unpaid family workers and government supported trainees.

This survey provides ONS basic measures of labour input to the economy, based on a sample of 53,000 households, conducted in 'waves' on a quarterly basis. The survey has historically been designed to be consistent with Census definitions to allow scaling and benchmarking and therefore excludes people resident in the UK for less than six months. As the number of short-term migrant workers has increased with rising labour mobility in the EU, it has been necessary to find ways of overcoming this exclusion.

The LFS provides estimates of:

- the number of people in work, and whether they are employed or self-employed, for which there are few alternative sources

- their qualifications, pay, hours and industries in which they work

- the number of jobs they hold, with industry identified for the first two

There are alternative sources for some of these detailed breakdowns, which can be used in conjunction with LFS data.

The main issues of reliability and completeness for LFS overall total estimates are concerned with:

- overall population estimates, nationally and by region, to which LFS results are scaled

- coverage of workers, including temporary foreign workers, living in communal establishments

- coverage of temporary foreign workers living in private households

- the definition of self-employment, which can be affected by tax and employment legislation changes

The self employment definition issue is particularly important when it comes to making more detailed analysis of the structure of labour input. While there are alternative sources for information on employed people, the LFS, which relies on self-reporting, is the principle source for measuring the self-employed. Changes in the ways people respond to the LFS can, therefore, affect its reliability.

5.1.1.2 Estimates of job numbers

ONS produces a number of different, but related, estimates of jobs for different analytical purposes. The simplest is the measure of 'employee jobs'. This is the total number of organisation-based jobs in the economy – in the public and voluntary sector or in industry. They are measured using surveys of employers that are then summed and weighted across all firms. Because of the possibility that employees can work more than one job, they may be picked up and counted more than once in these surveys. This is why it is a measure of jobs rather than employees. It does not, however, distinguish between full-time and part-time jobs.

A broader measure using a similar approach is 'Workforce Jobs' (WFJ). This a measure of the number and type of jobs in the workforce, using data from business surveys, labour force surveys, and administrative sources. This is a more comprehensive measure of jobs in the UK economy.

However, for the purposes of estimating productivity, ONS compiles a measure of labour input on a 'jobs' basis consistent at the whole economy level with the LFS, considered to be the best measure of overall labour input in the economy as noted above. This is derived by taking the 'employee jobs' in the workforce, as defined and measured in employer surveys, scaled up to LFS totals. This scaled up total is apportioned to industries using employer sources on a reporting unit basis. A reporting, rather than local, unit basis is used to achieve consistency with the measurement of output in the National Accounts. This jobs series has been labelled 'productivity jobs' to distinguish it from the industry estimates available in the Workforce Jobs series which are on a local unit basis (**Section 5.1.2.5** contains further explanation of reporting and local units). The term 'productivity jobs' should not be confused with 'productive jobs' or the notion of 'productive hours' discussed below.

This measure of jobs used for productivity is a series of labour input, for which the industry distribution is consistent with a national measure, and so can be used to build up a national picture of productivity. This series has the definition at the bottom of this page.

Where RU = Reporting Unit (the level at which output is reported by firms in surveys), LFS = Labour Force Survey, i = an industry, and Scaling Factor = Total LFS Jobs/Total WFJ.

Employer surveys are preferred to the LFS for an industry split because self-reporting of industry – as in the LFS – is unreliable. For example, an area where self-reporting can be an issue is for agency workers. The industry to which they should allocate themselves is the industry of the agency to which they are contracted; in practice they report the industry of the workplace where they have been based.

5.1.1.3 Estimates of hours worked

Productivity measures based on hours worked have conceptual advantages over headcount productivity measures, which are based solely on the number of workers or jobs rather than the time people actually work.

Data on hours worked gives a better indication of the actual volume of labour input because a measure of hours worked allows accounting for differences in working patterns. For instance hours worked based productivity estimates differentiate between the working hours of full- and part-time workers.

To produce estimates of output per hour worked at industry level, the jobs data series used in productivity measurement is multiplied by the actual hours worked for the industry recorded in the LFS. This produces the hours worked series for productivity measurement:

$$\text{Hours Worked}_i = \text{Jobs}_i \times \text{LFS Hours Worked}_i$$

Where i = industry

Unlike the jobs series, the hours worked series is sensitive to the industry split used for the LFS. Specifically, the series will be affected if those who misreport their industry category work a consistently higher or lower number of hours each week than those who correctly report their industry category. However there are few alternative sources for hours, ASHE is a possibility but only records contracted hours, and so the LFS is currently used for this purpose.

5.1.1.4 Defining measures of hours worked

The number of hours people work is inherently difficult to measure accurately, and there is more than one way in which hours worked can be measured. For productivity purposes, hours actually worked is the key concept, rather than alternative definitions. ONS is involved in establishing international standards for hours actually worked (see **Box 5.1**).

Jobs data used for productivity measures $_{\text{Industry i}}$ =

Employee Jobs $_{\text{Industry i, RU based}}$ x Scaling Factor to LFS

+ Self Employed $_{\text{Industry i, LFS}}$

+ HM Forces $_{\text{Industry i}}$

+ Government Supported Trainees $_{\text{Industry i, LFS}}$

Box 5.1: International standards for hours actually worked

ONS is currently part of an international group developing a standard International Labour Organization (ILO) definition, which incudes the following:

Hours actually worked should include:

- productive hours
- hours spent on ancillary activities
- unproductive hours spent in the course of work
- short periods of rest

Hours actually worked should exclude:

- hours paid for but not worked (for example annual leave, sick leave)
- meal breaks longer than 30 minutes
- time spent on commuter travel between home and employment that is not actually time spent working, even if paid by the employer

As part of this, ONS has been involved in drafting a resolution that proposes that:

- statistics on working time should be measurable to account for all productive activities
- statistics prepared on number of hours worked should relate to the same reference period for the various groups of persons in employment

Data sources used to estimate the number of hours worked have different definitions that can vary somewhat from the concept of hours actually worked. Three main definitions of hours worked are typically used:

1. actual hours worked
2. usual hours worked
3. paid hours worked

The definition depends on the source used to obtain the data. Business surveys such as the ASHE are sent to employers who, since they have information on their workers' contracted hours, can readily provide it. In terms of productivity use, this definition does not measure the volume of labour input that is ideally needed because it excludes overtime hours worked. There are also effects that work in the opposite direction in that paid hours that are not actually worked will also be included.

Household surveys address this partly by asking for information that relates to both normal and actual hours

worked. The respondents are the workers, who may know more about the number of hours they worked than employers.

Estimates of GDP per hour worked are calculated by ONS for the *International Comparisons of Productivity, First Release* (see **Chapter 12**). There have been recent steps to improve comparability of hours worked data at international level.

As a ratio of National Accounts statistics produced by ONS and published measures of labour market data, productivity estimates can only be as timely or accurate as their source data. The strengths and weaknesses of various types of data are discussed below.

From National Accounts data – Like the National Accounts, productivity estimates are available on both a quarterly and an annual basis and are subject to revisions. These revisions occur as new data becomes available when firms return surveys to ONS that relate to a year for which data has already been published in quarterly form. Revisions to productivity estimates that originate from National Accounts are normally at their largest for the first two years after publication.

From labour market data – Productivity estimates are subject to census revisions. Every ten years, when census revisions feed into the LFS estimates, employment and productivity data are also revised. LFS estimates are also subject to revisions generated by mid-year population estimates, which are currently more significant because of migration related issues. LFS data are also seasonally adjusted.

5.1.2   Data source consistency

ONS headline measures of productivity are examples of single factor productivity that relate the measure of output to one factor of production: labour. The data sources and methodologies used to estimate the volume of output and labour input are very different. Estimates of GVA are produced primarily from business surveys, while labour input statistics are produced by ONS primarily from household surveys. Allocation of labour input to industries draws, however, on business surveys.

5.1.2.1 The need for consistency

Consistency between the measures of output and labour input is important in productivity analysis. The quality of productivity measures depends on three main criteria; all need to be addressed when constructing productivity estimates:

1. the quality of the underlying component data

2. the independence of the output and input measures

3. the extent to which they measure the same concept when gathered from different sources

Improving the coherence between different sources of macroeconomic statistics is a major issue in improving ONS's productivity measures. ONS is also examining consistency of individual productivity estimates and the wider use of labour market statistics as an input to National Accounts data. The major link between sources is in earnings figures, which bring together data collected via labour market statistics and sources used elsewhere in the National Accounts.

5.1.2.2 Assessing consistency

To assess the consistency of the various labour market statistics available with National Accounts estimates of GVA, it is necessary to pinpoint the areas where inconsistencies are likely to arise when the data series are confronted. Based on the literature and analysis of the data series, the following issues are fundamental to assessing the consistency of productivity ratios:

- industry classification
- sampling units
- weighting

This framework helps identify which of the currently available data sources are the most consistent for productivity use. However, it does not mean that the best source is completely consistent with the National Accounts data. This is further explained in the next part of the chapter.

5.1.2.3 Industry classification

The UK Standard Industrial Classification (UK SIC) is the basis that is used in the National Accounts to produce any industry level estimates of data, including estimates of GVA. The UK SIC classifies business establishments and other statistical units by the type of economic activity in which the establishment is engaged. This enables industrial

activities to be classified into a common structure. To produce consistent industry level productivity estimates, industry definitions and allocations of GVA and labour input need to be identical.

Box 5.2: The UK SIC (2003)

(Table 5A presents the industry definitions that are laid out in the UK SIC (2003), to which all National Accounts data adhere. UK SIC (2003) classifications are determined according to the principal activity of a unit. In order to produce consistent industry level estimates of productivity, it is necessary that the industry level estimates of labour input also comply with this framework. There needs to be a mechanism that produces consistent industry level estimates of the different measures of labour input.

Table 5A: The UK SIC (2003)

Section	Industry
A	Agriculture, Hunting and Forestry
B	Fishing
C	Mining and Quarrying
D	Manufacturing
E	Electricity, Gas and Water Supply
F	Construction
G	Wholesale and Retail Trade; Repair of Motor Vehicles and Personal and Household Goods
H	Hotels and Restaurants
I	Transport, Storage and Communication
J	Financial Intermediation
K	Real Estate, Renting and Business Activities
L	Public Administration and Defence; Compulsory Social Security
M	Education
N	Health and Social Work
O	Other Community, Social and Personal Services Activities
P	Private Households Employing Staff and Undifferentiated Production Households for Own Use

At present ONS produces industry labour productivity estimates on a regular basis for manufacturing (section D), total production industries (sections C, D and E) and on an experimental basis for total service industries (sections G to P inclusive).

In labour market statistics produced by ONS, the industry level detail inferred from business surveys, such as the ABI, is consistent with the UK SIC (2003) framework. Most ONS business surveys use the Inter-Departmental Business Register (IDBR) as the sampling frame. The IDBR is a register of legal units, which is the most comprehensive list of UK businesses available. Containing approximately 2.1 million businesses, it covers almost 99 per cent of economic activity within the UK. It also holds a wide range of information on business units, including the industry classification of each one.

As long as there is some linking mechanism in place that relates labour market statistics to the IDBR, it is possible to produce an industry breakdown consistent with that used within the National Accounts. This enables production of consistent industry level productivity estimates.

5.1.2.4 Accuracy of industry estimates

The LFS is the most comprehensive source for labour market statistics, but is recognised as less authoritative as an indicator of the industry in which workers are employed.

With household surveys, there is as yet no linking mechanism that allows a UK SIC (2003) code to be attached to a respondent's workplace; this would be required to produce more accurate estimates of the industry to which that measure of labour input should be allocated. Industry breakdowns from the LFS are subject to misclassifications caused by respondents giving an inaccurate description of the organisation for which they work. For example, as discussed above, LFS respondents may report their profession as opposed to the industry of their workplace.

Misreporting is increased when a respondent is not available at the time of the LFS interview. In that case, the interviewer will ask someone who shares residence to provide answers on that person's behalf. These answers, called proxy responses, account for approximately 30 per cent of all LFS responses, and are likely to be less accurate about some employment details, such as the industry in which the respondent works.

5.1.2.5 Sampling units

The term sampling units specifically refers to the consistency of the source data used for estimating measures of output and labour input. In this context, the sampling units are those from which data for

productivity analyses are collected at the reporting or local unit level.

Figure 5.1 outlines the structure of organisation according to the IDBR. All National Accounts data are based on reporting unit level data. Business surveys are sent to a reporting unit level of a firm, which can be the entire enterprise or a major activity within a larger business. This can be thought of as the head office of the organisation. Each reporting unit can consist of one or more local units, each of which can have its own industry associated with it. The local unit corresponds to a site such as a factory or shop.

Figure 5.1: Reporting and local unit

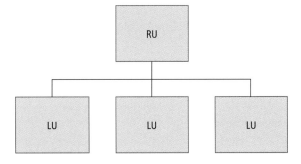

RU = Reporting Unit, which is consistent with the jobs data series for productivity measurement.

LU = Local Unit, which is consistent with the WFJ data series

For productivity analyses, labour market statistics should ideally be collected at the reporting unit level, since this is the level at which the estimates of GVA are collected. This is one of the reasons for having a specific jobs data series for productivity measurement. It is very similar to the WFJ series, but one fundamental difference between these two sets of data is the level that the employee jobs data represent. Data for both series are collected from the reporting unit level, but the WFJ series represents local unit level data and is apportioned to local units based on their relative size. WFJ is useful for regional productivity (for which reporting unit data need to be split) but the jobs series used for productivity is more consistent to use for producing estimates of output per job at both the economy and industry level.

5.1.2.6 Weighting

Weighting of labour market statistics affects consistency because it determines how well the estimates of employment are capturing the input of labour into productivity estimates. All of the labour market statistics available for productivity use are grossed up from survey data using population estimates. This means the quality and reliability of population estimates affect the quality and consistency of any productivity numbers that are produced.

> **Weighting** refers to the grossing up of sample data to the population level. This is done by assigning a weight to each item or subgroup within a sample, which is based on the ratio of the population total to the sample total for that item or subgroup. The weights will then be adjusted to account for the degree of non-response.

A key question about the methodology is whether population level estimates truly represent both the economy and industry level. The issues are whether an adequate population benchmark has been used to gross the survey data up and whether the grossing methodology takes into account varying degrees of non-response across sample subgroups.

The most consistent labour market statistics will use the most comprehensive census-type information available to gross up their survey data. These will either be information available from the Population Census or the IDBR, depending on whether the survey is household- or business- based.

Using the most appropriate population benchmark does not neccessarily mean that the industry breakdown of the resulting labour market data will represent the population composition. This is because there are varying degrees of non-response to all surveys across population subgroups. If not accounted for properly, subgroups that have a higher response rate will be overrepresented. The grossing weights that are used need to compensate for this by attributing a higher weight to subgroups that have a lower response rate and vice-versa. If this is not captured by the design of the weights, there are likely to be implications in terms of the consistency of any industry level productivity estimates that are produced.

5.1.2.7 Overview of the consistency arguments
Based on the consistency based analysis that has been summarised so far, the LFS is currently the most appropriate source to use for productivity analysis, in particular when measuring its quality as a source against

all three important factors:

1. the quality of underlying component data
2. coherence of the output and input measures and
3. the independent, while coherent, measurement of output and inputs (as opposed, for example, to measuring output from inputs as has happened when suitable output indicators are not available)

The main concern when the using the LFS to measure productivity remains the reliability of the industrial classification. A possible solution is the LFS-IDBR linking project, which is designed to link LFS responses to an accurate IDBR identifier. This work may provide the opportunity of using the LFS to produce consistent industry level productivity estimates, and would create industry level consistency between the LFS data and National Accounts.

5.1.3   Challenges and difficulties
The previous section of this chapter identified many of the issues that are prominent in the discussion of consistency between the National Accounts and labour market statistics. Two issues that need to be discussed further include:

1. Consistency across productivity measures
2. Reconciling labour market statistics

5.1.3.1 Consistency across productivity measures
Despite issues relating to its coverage, the LFS is the most comprehensive source of the number of workers in the economy and therefore the most accurate source for the headline measure of GVA per worker. It is important to use LFS data to ensure consistency across the three main types of productivity estimates (workers, jobs and hours worked).

The methodology employed constrains the jobs series created for productivity purposes to the LFS jobs series. By doing this output per worker and output per job measures will remain consistent.

Figure 5.2: Whole economy jobs

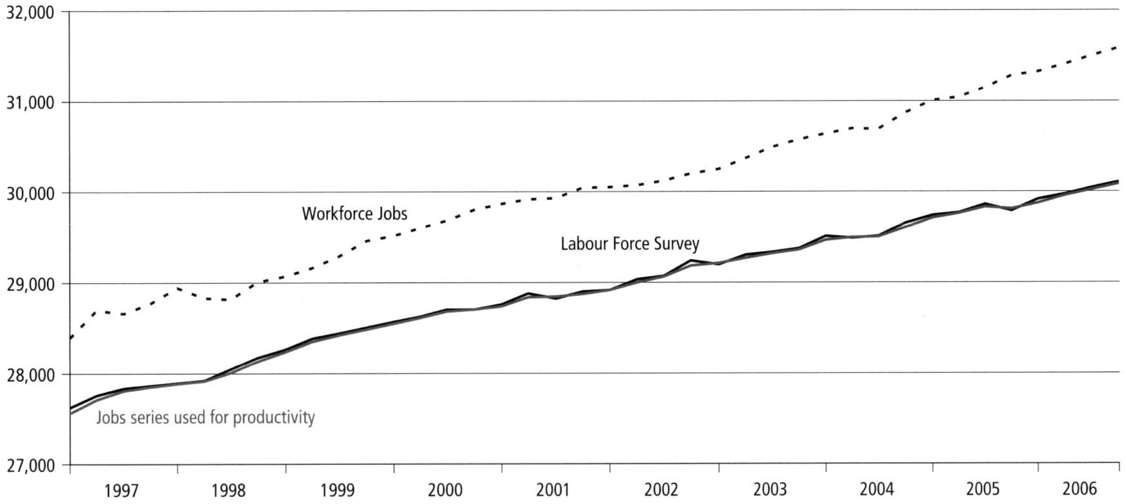

The effect of this can be seen (**Figure 5.2**) when comparing the WFJ series with the jobs series used for productivity measurement at the whole economy level. The level difference seen between these two series is driven by the fact that the jobs series used for productivity measurement is constrained to the LFS, so this series is reporting one million fewer jobs in the UK.

5.1.3.2 Reconciling labour market statistics

Employment is inherently difficult to measure, because of the variety of the labour market, and the difficulty of securing complete coverage through the LFS. Where gaps in coverage are known, alternative data sources are required to estimate the measures of employment that are not covered. The published LFS data series as it currently stands will be biased downwards because the coverage of the LFS falls short of the whole population. ONS recognises this and currently produces reconciled estimates of labour input that are conceptually more consistent with output data from the National Accounts.

The rest of this section explores estimates of labour input, making use of alternative data sources to estimate these gaps in the coverage of the LFS. This would provide a conceptually more consistent measure of labour input to use for productivity purposes.

5.1.3.3 Gaps in LFS coverage

The Review of Employment and Jobs Statistics identified the following main areas as not being covered by the LFS and which productivity measurement would wish to include:

- third and subsequent jobs
- communal establishments
- temporary foreign workers
- armed forces not living in private accommodation

Table 5.1 overleaf quantifies the degree of underreporting in the LFS by reproducing the results that are published by ONS (see www.statistics.gov.uk/StatBase/Product.asp?vlnk=14358). The estimates indicated (which are discussed below in more depth) highlight the significance of these gaps in coverage. Nearly half a million jobs known to be contributing to the production of UK output are not being accounted for in the LFS.

5.1.3.4 Third and subsequent jobs

The Family Resources Survey (FRS), which is run by the Department of Work and Pensions (DWP), can be used to estimate the gap for third or subsequent jobs in the LFS coverage. The FRS is a continuous survey of private households and uses the Postcode Address File (PAF) as its sampling frame. All adults who live in the selected households are eligible for inclusion in the survey, which includes specific questions related to employment. The estimates of the number of first and second jobs provided by the FRS and LFS seem to be broadly in line with one another, which gives further credence to using the FRS to estimate the number of third and subsequent jobs. **Table 5.2** illustrates some of the data that can be extracted from the FRS.

5.1.3.5 Communal establishments

Household surveys generally only extend to the adult population living in private households. Consequently there is a known under-recording of the input of labour from those living in communal establishments.

In 2000 ONS carried out a pilot survey of adults living in communal establishments, with the design of the questionnaire reflecting the LFS. This made it possible

to compare directly the estimates from this pilot survey with the estimates from the private household population taken from the LFS. **Table 5.3** shows some of the key labour market estimates produced using the Communal Establishments Pilot Survey (CEPS).

This survey, similar to the LFS and specifically for people living in communal establishments, was done in conjunction with the LFS for the autumn quarter of 2000. The combined population estimates presented in the final column give a better reflection of those who are economically active and, more importantly in terms of productivity analysis, those who contribute to producing UK output.

Table 5.1: Estimating the Gaps in LFS Coverage

Dec 2006

Gaps in Coverage	Data Source	Adjustments
Third and subsequent jobs	DWP Family Resources Survey	80,000
Communal establishments	ONS Communal Establishments Pilot Survey	80,000
Temporary foreign workers	ONS Migration Statistics, DWP National Insurance records and other administrative sources	180,000
Armed forces not living in private accommodation	Ministry of Defence	110,000
DWP = Department of Works and Pensions		

Table 5.2: Labour Market Estimates using the DWP Family Resources Survey

	LFS 1st Jobs	FRS 1st Jobs	LFS 2nd Jobs	FRS 2nd Jobs	FRS 3rd Jobs
2002	27,866,000	28,757,000	1,130,000	1,144,000	104,000
2003	28,167,000	28,761,000	1,131,000	1,107,000	100,000
2004	28,409,000	28,953,000	1,072,000	1,090,000	92,000

Table 5.3: Labour Market Estimates using the Communal Establishments Pilot Survey

Autumn 2000

	Number of people: CEPS	Number of people: LFS	Combined Estimates
In Employment	81,000	27,329,100	27,410,100
Unemployed	8,500	1,531,500	1,540,200
Inactive	510,500	15,578,800	17,089,300

5.1.3.6 Temporary foreign workers

With the expansion of the European Union in May 2004, the migration of residents of EU accession countries (A8) (Czech Republic, Estonia, Hungary, Latvia, Lithuania, Poland, Slovakia and Slovenia) to the UK received a lot of attention. Accurately estimating migration into the UK is not straightforward and the *Interdepartmental Migration Task Force Report* in 2006 commented on the various data sources' limitations.

Foreign workers who come to the UK for periods of less than a year are not covered in the LFS employment and jobs statistics. This is because:

1. The LFS sample excludes people who have been resident in their household for less than six months.

2. The population totals to which the LFS results are weighted exclude people visiting the UK for less than 12 months.

It should be noted that measures are in place to ensure that the LFS is internationally comparable and produces an accurate picture of the long-term residential working population.

ONS carries out a quarterly reconciliation of the LFS and WFJ series, and this exercise includes an estimate of the under-coverage in the LFS of temporary foreign workers, which was 180,000 for 2005/06. As there is a lack of suitable data, the estimate is inevitably approximate, using a method described in Annex F of the Review of Workforce Jobs Benchmarking. (See www.statistics.gov.uk/StatBase/Product.asp?vlnk=9765 for the latest figures)

5.1.3.7 Armed forces not living in private accommodation

As with those who reside in communal establishments, people in the armed forces not living in private accommodation are not surveyed by the LFS and therefore do not appear in the LFS employment statistics.

Administrative data from the Defence Analytical Services Agency (DASA), the statistical branch of the Ministry of Defence (MoD), is used to estimate this gap in LFS coverage. DASA is responsible for publishing all National Statistics relating to defence including employment statistics. To estimate the number of members of the armed forces who are excluded from the LFS, the difference between the WFJ and LFS estimate of those in the armed forces is added to the initial LFS estimate. Since 2000 the approximate level of under-reporting has been 115,000 jobs.

5.2 Measurement of quality adjusted labour input

Labour productivity measures have traditionally defined labour input as the sum of hours worked by employees, proprietors and unpaid workers. As a result an hour worked by a highly experienced surgeon and an hour worked by a newly hired teenager at a fast food restaurant are treated as equal amounts of labour (OECD, 2001a).

ONS has put resources into developing a measure of labour input that explicitly recognises its skill and heterogeneity and the changing composition of the labour force over time. The result is an annually produced index called quality-adjusted labour input (QALI), an improved measure of labour's input into production. The characteristics used to quality adjust labour input are educational attainment, work experience, industry and sex. Details on the are provided in **Section 5.2.3**.

ONS has chosen two ways to calculate QALI: the Tornqvist index and the Laspeyres index (see **Section 5.2.2** below for methology used). The Tornqvist is a form of index where the weight is constructed using an average of the relevant variable in the current and base period. Widely used in the construction of QALI measures (Bell, Burriel-Llombart and Jones, 2005), the Tornqvist is recommended in the Organisation for Economic Co-operation and Development (OECD) methodology (2001a), making it the preferred measure. In contrast, the Laspeyres index is constructed using only the weight in the base period and is calculated to make QALI compatible with other data sources.

5.2.1 Data

QALI is produced using LFS microdata. The LFS currently covers approximately 53,000 households every quarter, which it has done since 1992, having run biannually or annually since 1973. However, owing to breaks in the qualification variable, QALI has only been produced for the period from 1996 onwards.

5.2.2 ONS methodology

ONS uses a standard method to estimate QALI. To perform the quality adjustment, hours worked are differentiated into n types of worker (h_1 to h_n) according to their characteristics. The labour characteristics are broken down into groups:

- eight qualification levels

- six age groups

- six industries

- two sexes

Therefore hours worked are broken down into 576 (8*6*6*2) worker types. The hours of each worker type contribute to total labour input L through a function g as shown below in equation (1).

$$L = g(h_1, h_2, \ldots, h_n) \qquad (1)$$

Following the OECD (2001) methodology the growth of quality adjusted hours can be represented with a Tornqvist index, as shown below in equation (2).

$$\frac{\Delta L(t)}{L(t)} = \sum_i \left[\frac{w_i(t) + w_i(t-1)}{2} \right] \frac{\Delta h_i(t)}{h_i(t)} \qquad (2)$$

According to economic theory and under assumptions of competitive markets and constant returns to scale, labour is hired up to the point where its marginal cost (or its wage) is equal to its marginal revenue product (or what it produces). Therefore in equation (2) the growth of hours worked is effectively weighted by that worker type's marginal productivity. The weight is the average of the

wage in the current and base period and in aggregate the weights add up to one. The assumption that workers are paid their marginal product also holds even if there is not perfect competition in the labour market (this assumption is only violated under conditions of monpsony).

One reason for producing QALI is its use in multi-factor productivity (MFP) analysis (see **Chapter 7**). Since the other component necessary for such analysis, the volume index of capital services (VICS), and also National Accounts output measures, are calculated as Laspeyres indices, then QALI is also produced in this form. The formula for calculating QALI on a Laspeyres basis is provided below in equation (3).

$$\frac{L(t)}{L(t-1)} = \sum_i \left[\frac{h_i(t)}{h_i(t-1)} \right] w_i(t-1) \qquad (3)$$

Unlike the Tornqvist, when applying the Laspeyres index, growth in hours is weighted only by the wage in the base period. Since the Tornqvist uses an average of the wage in the current and base period it is a more representative index and a conceptually better measure. Therefore QALI will continue to be produced in both forms by ONS.

Table 5.4: Labour characteristics

Sex	Age groups	Educational attainment	Industry	Industry description
Male	16–19	Higher Degree	ABCE	Agriculture, hunting, forestry, fishing, mining & quarrying, utilities
Female	20–29	NVQ5 (excl. Higher degree)	D	Manufacturing
	30–39	NVQ4	F	Construction
	40–49	NVQ3	GHI	Wholesale and retail trade, hotels & restaurants, transport, storage and communications.
	50–59	NVQ2	JK	Financial intermediation, real estate, renting & business activities
	60 and over	NVQ1	LMNOPQ	Public administration & defence, education, health and social work, other social and personal services, and extra-territorial activities.
		Other qualifications		
		No Qualifications		

In this table, each category applies equally to every other category. For instance, someone in the age group 16–19 could have any level of educational attainment, work in any industry and be of either sex.

5.2.3 Labour characteristics

In ONS analysis, hours worked are differentiated into 576 types according to workers' characteristics: highest qualification attained, age, industry and sex. These characteristics have been broken down into relatively homogenous groups to try to capture quality change without stretching the underlying datasets too far. The groups are shown in **Table 5.4**.

These characteristics are chosen to represent labour quality for a number of reasons.

Age is included as a proxy for work experience. This is obviously imperfect, as it takes no account of workers who have been inactive or unemployed for any period of time. However, the assumption is that, in general, older workers will be more productive because of their greater level of work experience; this is the reason why older workers tend to receive greater compensation for their labour. Younger workers may be more dynamic, innovative, and less set in their ways (Bell, Burriel-Llombart and Jones, 2005). However, if this is true in some cases, these workers should be paid their marginal product and growth in hours will be weighted accordingly.

Sex is chosen as a characteristic because of the persistent pay differential between males and females. Although the sex of the person itself is not a driver of quality, there is a gap between the wage rates of men and women when all other characteristics, as defined in **Table 5.4**, are the same. This gap may represent hidden characteristics such as an increased tendency to take career breaks or to fulfil part-time posts that are not as well paid. If so, the importance of the sex characteristic can be attributed to age being an imperfect proxy for experience.

The alternative is that the sex characteristic is important because of discrimination in the labour market. If the pay differential reflects discrimination in the labour market, the assumption that workers are paid their marginal product is violated, resulting in hours' growth being weighted incorrectly. The quality adjustment will then carry a downward bias. These two explanations for the significance of the sex characteristic are, obviously, not mutually exclusive.

Educational attainment, measured as the highest qualification attained, is a proxy for skills. Qualifications either act as a signal to employers that workers are capable of a certain level of ability or they formally provide

specific skills to meet job requirements. This category is the prime driver of the QALI index. Eight qualification levels are used because the more levels that are included, the greater the adjustment for quality. However there is a trade-off between the amount of quality adjustment and the constraints of the sample size.

Because of the growth in the number of people undertaking higher degrees, the expectation of continued increase in such qualifications, and their association with higher wages and salaries, this group has been separated out of the NVQ5 category and included as a stand-alone qualification level.

Industry is used as a characteristic because of inherent differences in skill and productivity between industries. This also allows growth in hours to be split according to industry, making it possible to conduct MFP analysis by sector. The industry categories chosen are very broad, firstly because industry is self-reported in the LFS, which can lead to an inaccuracy of response, and secondly because of small sample sizes for some individual sectors.

5.2.4 Data issues

Approximately 30 per cent of responses in the LFS dataset are proxy responses, meaning that they are responses given by somebody on someone else's behalf. This may give rise to bias. As a check, the adjustment process was carried out on personal responses only. The relationship between adjusted and unadjusted hours remained the same and it was decided to leave proxy responses in these data because the problems excluding them would cause, in particular when grossing to population totals.

5.2.5 Consistency with National Accounts and productivity measures

For QALI to be used in productivity analysis, it must be consistent with UK National Accounts and ONS headline productivity measures. To ensure this, components of QALI are scaled to National Accounts and productivity data. See Goodridge (2006) for more details.

5.2.6 QALI Results

The results in the form of Tornqvist and Laspeyres indices are presented in Goodridge (2006), along with revisions tables. Two different datasets for each are provided, one scaled to National Accounts data and an unscaled version. The QALI measure can be compared with the unadjusted series, which is just a standard aggregation of hours represented in index form. The difference between the two is the quality adjustment, sometimes called labour composition.

The Tornqvist data are a quarterly series based on the seasonal quarters of the LFS. The Laspeyres is an annual series. Since the purpose of calculating the Laspeyres indices was to produce a measure compatible with VICS and the National Accounts, by ensuring consistency of the index form used between the numerator and the denominator, they are produced on an annual basis, based on the spring quarter of the LFS.

As a quality check **Figure 5.3** compares the whole economy Tornqvist series, with the Laspeyres series. A comparison is also made with actual hours from the LFS. A comparison is also made with actual hours from the *LFS First Release*. As can be seen, the Tornqvist series follows the same trend but the Laspeyres is at a higher level because in practice the Laspeyres can be seen as an upper bound of the Tornqvist. There also appears to be less adjustment using the Laspeyres; this is the result of the different weighting procedure used in its construction. Since the data in the *LFS First Release* is quarterly it has only been compared with the Tornqvist index. As can be seen, the two series' follow very similar trends and contain the same turning points. The data from the First Release is in calendar quarters while the Tornqvist series is in seasonal quarters, hence the slight lag.

5.3   Measurement of capital input

Defining capital and measuring its contribution to production has been a contentious issue for both economists and statisticians for many years. Early work in this area includes Jorgenson (1963), the seminal growth accounting study by Jorgenson and Griliches (1967), Hall and Jorgenson (1967) on the cost of capital, and the work of Hulten and Wykoff (1981a, 1981b) on the estimation of depreciation rates. More recently there has been a degree of international agreement about the conceptual issues concerning the stocks and flows of capital. The OECD published a manual in 2001 (OECD, 2001b) covering the measurement of capital and providing practical guidelines for estimation.

In order to calculate MFP, a measure of the quantity of capital input in the production process is needed. Capital services are the measure of capital input that is suitable for analysing and modelling productivity. This is because capital services are a direct measure of the flow of productive services from capital assets rather than a measure of the stock of those assets. In essence capital services are a measure of the actual contribution of the capital stock of assets to the production process in a given year. This is in contrast to the wealth-based estimates of capital in the National Accounts, gross and net capital stock, which are essentially a measure of the value of the capital stock of assets.

Figure 5.3: Comparison of Tornqvist, Laspeyres and Labour Force Survey First Release

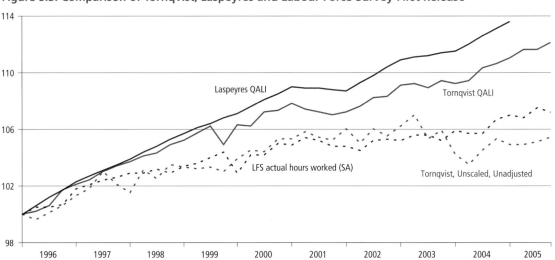

The wealth capital stock is a synonym for the net capital stock. Net capital stock is the current market valuation of a country or industry's productive capital. One purpose of the net capital stock is to measure the depreciation or loss in value of an asset as it ages. In the UK National Accounts, for instance, net capital stock is the basis for estimating capital consumption. Capital services are a direct measure of the flow of productive services from a country or industry's productive capital and so is the correct measure of capital input to use for productivity analysis. **Figure 5.4** shows why the distinction is important.

Over the late 1990s there was a divergence between the volume index of net capital stock and volume index of capital services. The reason is that computers became an increasing important part of the productive capital stock. Capital services from computers grew very rapidly over this period while the value of the productive stock of computers grew less rapidly.

As interest lies in capital services for productivity analysis and for the calculation of MFP there will be no further discussion of wealth measures of capital.

5.3.1 Practical difficulties with estimating capital services

OECD (2001a) highlights four areas where there is a specific need for further research and development of data and statistics from a productivity perspective. One of these is improving existing measures of capital input. Measurement of capital input suffers from conflicting terminology and concepts and from a lack of empirical foundation.

Specific problem areas include the empirical measurement of age-efficiency and retirement patterns of assets and also the empirical estimation of rentals. As the stock of capital in an economy or industry, or the flows of capital services, cannot be directly observed, observable investment expenditure is relied on as the basis for measuring capital input. To get from observable investment expenditure to a measure of the productive stock of capital, assumptions are required about the age-efficiency and retirement patterns of assets. These assumptions should, however, be empirically founded to ensure good quality measurement.

The price of capital services is measured as their rental price and so the estimation of rentals is an important step in producing capital services estimates. Empirically the problem is that there are not complete markets for capital services, as firms commonly purchase rather than rent capital, and so rental prices cannot be directly observed. Instead rental prices have to be imputed.

Because of the conflicting use of terminology and concepts, the rest of this section on capital services will focus on the ONS estimation method rather than provide a general overview of the various alternatives. Terminology and concepts relevant to the ONS methods will be also be discussed where appropriate. Fuller discussion of alternative methods, terminology and concepts can be found in OECD (2001a, 2001b).

Figure 5.4: Volume index of net capital stock and capital services, 1980–2005

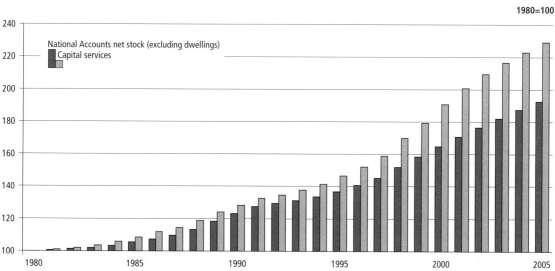

1980=100

5.3.2   ONS Methodology

Under ONS methods, the four main stages in the estimation of capital services are:

- using a Perpetual Inventory Model (PIM) to calculate a net stock series from a history of constant price investment series

- pricing the services from an asset using an estimated rental for each asset

- generating weights, using the estimated rentals and net stock series, which reflect the input of each asset into production

- combining the weights and net stock growth to give capital services estimates

A PIM is used to convert time-series data for the volume of purchases of assets (constant price investment) into a net capital stock measure. To do this, account needs to be taken of assets decaying over time and an age-efficiency profile specified. As discussed in **Box 5.3**, the assumption of a geometric PIM means that the age-efficiency profile and depreciation pattern will be identical and a slight misuse of the terminology will simplify matters when talking about depreciation.

Two commonly used depreciation functions are straight-line and geometric. Straight-line depreciation, based on a **constant annual amount** of capital depreciation over the life of the asset, is used in calculating the wealth measures of capital stock in the National Accounts. Geometric depreciation, based on a **constant annual rate** of depreciation over the life of the asset, is used for the ONS estimates of capital services. For example, if the selected depreciation rate per annum is 10 per cent, then 90 per cent of the asset will remain after the first year, 81 per cent after the second year and so on.

For ONS capital services estimates, an infinite geometric depreciation function is used to calculate net stock. This takes the following form:

$$K_{a,t}^{i} = \sum_{\tau=0}^{\infty} (1-\delta_{a,t-\tau}^{i})^{\tau} \cdot I_{a,t-\tau}^{i} \qquad (4)$$

where K is the volume of net stock for a particular asset a in industry i and t is the year under consideration. I is investment in a particular asset a in industry i and δ is the rate of depreciation for an asset purchased in a particular year.

Box 5.3: Age-efficiency, retirement patterns and depreciation

The age-efficiency profile of a capital asset is the rate at which the physical contribution to production of the capital asset declines over time, as a result of wear and tear. This is in contrast to the age-price profile, which shows the relationship between the age of a capital asset and its value. Clearly these two profiles are related but they need not be identical. For example a lorry that has lost 10 per cent of its market value after a year may not have lost 10 per cent of its capacity to transport goods.

The retirement pattern of a capital asset describes how the asset is withdrawn from use in production. This is often defined as a distribution around an expected life length mean (the average number of years that an asset lasts after purchase). The difference between the retirement pattern and the age-efficiency profile should be clear. The former, if defined as a distribution, shows the probability that the asset is still being used in production. The latter shows the contribution of the asset to the production process given that it has now been withdrawn from use in production.

Given age-efficiency profiles and retirement patterns for all capital assets, it is possible to use observable investment expenditure and the perpetual inventory method to get an estimate of the productive stock of capital as follows:

$$K_{a,t}^{P} = \sum_{\tau=0}^{T} h_{a\tau} \cdot F_{a\tau} I_{a,t-\tau}$$

Where $K_{a,t}^{P}$ is the productive stock of asset a at time t, $h_{a\tau}$ is an age-efficiency profile for asset a, $F_{a\tau}$ is a retirement function for asset a and $I_{a\tau}$ is constant price (real) investment in asset a. The gross capital stock would be estimated using the same equation but with the exclusion of the age-efficiency profile $h_{a\tau}$.

ONS capital services estimates assume a geometric age-efficiency pattern. The advantage of this assumption is that the distinction between net and productive capital stock disappears and the age-price profile and age-efficiency profiles have the same shape. This means that, although depreciation actually refers to the loss in value of an asset because of ageing, the depreciation rate gives an appropriate age-efficiency profile. The added simplification of this assumption can be seen in equation (4) below, where only a depreciation rate and constant price investment are needed to calculate net stock. The other advantage is that depreciation rates can easily be calculated from the life length means available from the National Accounts.

As can be seen in equation (4), a geometric PIM requires a time series of investment data and a time series of depreciation rates. The rates used here are calculated using the life length means assumed for each asset and each vintage in the National Accounts capital stock estimation.

The depreciation rate δ is calculated using the following equation:

$$\delta = d/\overline{T} \qquad (5)$$

where d is called the 'declining balance rate' and $\overline{T}$ is the life length mean. d will differ across asset types and the values for d are given in Table 5.5 below. When $d=2$, as it does for intangibles and computers, the result is what is referred to as the 'double declining balance' method. The life length means differ across asset, industry and time and hence so do the depreciation rates.

Table 5.5: Declining balance rates by asset type

Type of asset	Declining-balance rate
Intangibles	2
Buildings	0.9
Vehicles	1.853
Computers	2
Plant	1.65

The depreciation rate of assets can vary over vintage. This is because the life length mean of an asset can vary depending on the year of purchase. Changes across time are infrequent but, in general, life length means have reduced over time. This reduction in life length means reflects both reviews of the assumptions made by the ONS and also a shift to shorter-lived assets.

The rental price of a capital asset is the unit cost for the use of the asset for one period. The rental price is also commonly referred to as the 'user cost of capital'. Here the rental, r, for a particular asset a in industry i is modelled using the Hall-Jorgenson (1967) formula for the cost of capital in discrete time t, with an adjustment made to take account of taxes on profits and subsidies to investment.

$$r_{at}^i = T_{at}[\delta_a^i \cdot p_{at}^i + R_t\, p_{a,t-1}^i - (p_{at}^i - p_{a,t-1}^i)] \qquad (6)$$

where p is the price of an asset, δ is the rate of depreciation, and R is the rate of return. T_{at} is the tax-adjustment factor which is given by the following:

$$T_{at} = \left[\frac{1 - u_t D_{at}}{1 - u_t}\right] \qquad (7)$$

where u_t is the corporation tax rate and D_{at} is the present value of depreciation allowances as a proportion of the price of asset type a.

It can be seen from equation (6) that the rental is made up of three components. The first part reflects the fact that the asset will lose value over time (depreciation), the second is the rate of return, and the last part reflects the impact on the rental owing to a change in the purchase price of a new asset. These three components are adjusted, using equation (7) to reflect taxes on profits and the subsidies that accompany an investment.

The rate of return, R, which makes up part of the rental calculation, can be modelled endogenously or exogenously. Here, the rate of return is modelled endogenously by assuming that the rate of return exhausts the entire operating surplus in the economy. It is also assumed that the rate of return is the same across all industries and all assets. As dwellings are not modelled as part of the productive capital stock because they do not form part of the input into production, the part of operating surplus attributable to dwellings has been deducted from total UK gross operating surplus. This part of operating surplus is measured by owner-occupied imputed rents and the depreciation of the stock of dwellings.

Net stock estimates obtained using equation (4) and rentals obtained using equation (6) can be combined to generate weights for the capital services growth estimation. Capital services estimates are obtained by aggregating (over industry, asset, or whole economy) the growth in the net capital stock using the appropriate weights. These weights will reflect the relative productivity of the different asset types that make up the capital stock. If capital services are calculated for a particular industry the weight is calculated as follows:

$$w_{at}^i = \frac{r_{a,t-1}^i \cdot K_{a,t-1}^i}{\sum_a r_{a,t-1}^i \cdot K_{a,t-1}^i} \qquad (8)$$

w_{at}^i can be interpreted as the value-added attributable to the stock of each asset in a particular industry. Under an assumption of profit maximisation and competitive markets, it can be shown that these shares approximate the elasticity of output to the volume of capital services being put into the production process. Capital services for a particular industry are then calculated by constructing a chain-linked Laspeyres volume index as shown in equation (9). The use of chain-linked Laspeyres is to ensure consistency with the current UK macroeconomic aggregates.

$$Volume\ index\ of\ capital\ services_t^i = \sum_a w_{a,t-1}^i \cdot \frac{K_{at}^i}{K_{a,t-1}^i} \qquad (9)$$

Equations (8) and (9) can be generalised for any aggregate, such as whole economy or for a chosen asset. Equations (10) and (11) below are the equations for estimating capital services by asset type.

$$w_{at}^i = \frac{r_{a,t-1}^i \cdot K_{a,t-1}^i}{\sum_i r_{a,t-1}^i \cdot K_{a,t-1}^i} \qquad (10)$$

$$Volume\ index\ of\ capital\ services_{at} = \sum_i w_{a,t-1}^i \cdot \frac{K_{at}^i}{K_{a,t-1}^i} \qquad (11)$$

5.3.3 Data

Following OECD guidance (OECD, 2001a and 2001b) the core dataset used to estimate capital services is the same as that underpinning the National Accounts capital stock measures. The dataset consists of a long time series of constant price investment data, classified by SIC industries, life length means and price deflators.

Maintaining consistency with the National Accounts means that the capital services estimates presented here would be ideal for multi-factor productivity work, as this means they are consistent with the output measures (gross value added) in the UK National Accounts.

The only departure from this relates to the treatment of computers as a separate asset. The asset breakdown of the investment series in the National Account is:

- buildings
- plant and machinery
- vehicles
- intangibles

In order to treat computers as a separate asset, computer investment has to be separated from investment in plant and machinery and the associated price deflators have to be adjusted to account for this. It should be noted that, although an appropriate life length is used for computers

in the National Accounts (currently assumed to be five years) the capital stock estimates do not separately deflate computers, and so computers are not fully treated as a separate asset in the National Accounts.

As discussed in Wallis (2005), the treatment of computers as a separate asset when estimating capital services is very important. The rapid growth in computer investment in the 1990s together with the rapid falls in the relative price of computers means that capital services from computers grew very rapidly. See Wallis (2005) for further discussion on this. ONS have also carried out work on the treatment of software, another similar asset; see Chesson and Chamberlin (2006) for more details.

5.3.4 VICS Results

A full set of capital services estimates can be found on the ONS web page www.statistics.gov.uk/StatBase/Product.asp?vlnk=14205 This page contains data for whole economy capital services growth, a 57-industry breakdown of capital services growth and a six-industry breakdown consistent with the industry breakdown at which QALI is published. Data on profit shares is also available. A few of the key series are presented here.

Figure 5.5 shows the annual growth in capital services for the UK over the period 1950 to 2004. It can be seen that there is strong and sustained capital services growth up to the early 1970s. This early period suffers from one notable measurement issue: quantifying the one-off loss of capital associated with the Second World War. The official estimates of this loss are provided by Dean (1964). The 1970s saw more modest capital services growth, with growth falling in most years up until the early 1980s. This period coincides with a slowdown in the world economy, partly because of the oil shocks in 1973 and 1979. The series reaches its lowest point in 1981, with annual growth in capital services of just 1 per cent.

Post 1981, capital services growth began to increase, reaching a local peak of over 4 per cent in 1989. Capital services growth then fell rapidly in the early 1990s, as a result of the recession in the UK. In the late 1990s and in more recent years, capital services have shown very strong growth, peaking in 1998 at over 7 per cent. As will be seen later, this strong capital services growth is driven by high levels of investment in computers and the associated growth in capital services from this asset. Average growth for the period 1950 to 2004 was just over 3 per cent, while

Figure 5.5: Annual growth in net capital stock and capital services, 1950–2005

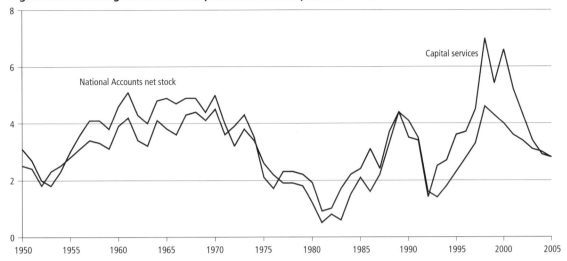

growth in the last 10 years averaged close to 5 per cent.

Also shown in **Figure 5.5**, is the annual growth in the wealth measures of net stock from the National Accounts. The National Accounts series is the growth in total net stock excluding dwellings. The close fit of the two series is to be expected as they are both based on the same raw data set, consisting of long time series of capital formation data, deflators and life length means (assumed life lengths of assets). The differences in the two series are because of the separate deflation of computers, the use of geometric rather than arithmetic PIM and the weighting of net asset growth by profit shares rather than in asset value terms as in the National Accounts. Both series peak in 1998, but the National Accounts net stock peaks at a growth rate of just over 5 per cent compared to capital services at over 7 per cent. Average growth over the whole period 1950 to 2004 is the same for both series at just over 3 per cent.

The larger divergence in the series, starting in the late 1990s, is because of the separate deflation of computers in the capital services estimates, a method not currently used for estimating the National Accounts capital stock, and also the fact that capital services accounts for the contribution of computers better that a capital stock estimate does. The period after 1990 was one of fast growing investment in computers while their price fell rapidly. This combination makes the share of computers in the whole economy capital services estimates grow over time and makes capital services grow more rapidly.

Figure 5.6 overleaf shows growth in capital services for computers over the period 1987 to 2004. Capital services from computers grew rapidly over the whole period, with an average growth rate of over 21 per cent. Annual growth is lowest in 1991, but at nearly 8 per cent, it is still well above growth in capital services from other assets for this period. The time trend of capital services growth for computers also differs dramatically from other assets. Other asset types saw a fall in capital services growth in the early 1990s, associated with the recession in the UK. There was no fall in capital services growth in the early 1990s for computers and growth in capital services actually shows a sustained increase in growth from 1991 to 2000. It should be noted that the growth in capital services from computers will be reflecting both the increased quality of computer power, as well as changes in the level of investment. For some of the years in the period 1991 to 2000, investment declined year-on-year, but capital services still increased owing to increased quality of computer power.

Figure 5.6: Annual growth in capital services – computers, 1987–2005

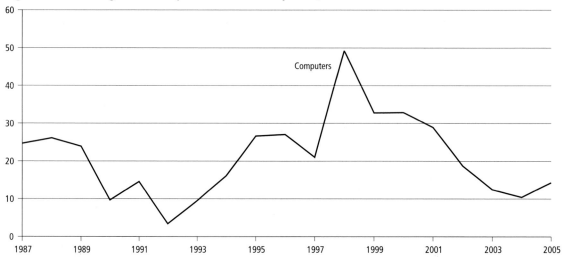

Peak capital services growth in computers occurs in 1998, with an annual growth rate of around 45 per cent. This peak is because of high levels of investment in computers, associated with the year 2000 effect, when firms invested in the latest computer technologies to avert the 'millennium bug'. The other contributing factor is the growth in the so-called dot-com firms and the increased use of the Internet by firms, which meant that computers became a more common feature in everyday business. This highlights the importance of treating computers separately when estimating capital services. A similar asset is software; ONS will be moving to a different treatment of software in the National Accounts in 2007. Further details are provided in **Chapter 13** and in Chesson and Chamberlin (2006). It will be important that once these new software estimates are incorporated into the National Accounts they are also included in updated capital services estimates. These new estimates will also allow software to be treated as a separate asset.

Figure 5.7: Annual growth in whole economy capital services and market sector capital services, 1950–2005

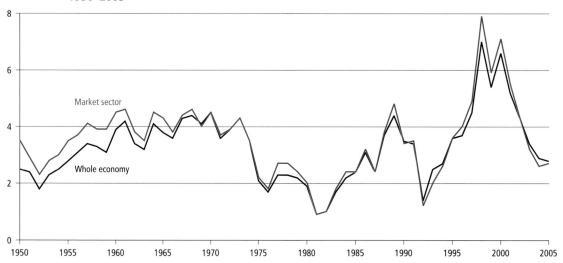

An additional capital services series, first published in Wallis (2007), is shown in **Figure 5.7**. This shows whole economy capital services growth against market sector capital services. The market sector here is defined in a way that is consistent with the definition of the market sector in **Section 7.2** and so the capital services estimates could be used in conjunction with market sector output estimates. As can be seen from **Figure 5.7**, as the market sector accounts for a large proportion of total capital input in the economy, the growth rate of market sector capital services moves very closely to that of whole economy capital services. However, it can be seen that market sector capital services growth has generally been slightly higher over the period 1950 to 2005.

5.4 Future developments

ONS will continue to produce labour productivity measures and publish these in the quarterly *Productivity First Release*. There is also work in progress to identify and move to more consistent data sources to ensure a better industry breakdown; further information can be found in **Chapter 13**.

Additionally, there are plans to generally improve labour market statistics, following the National Statistics Quality Review of Employment and Jobs Statistics (2006). A key project in this area is the development of routine linkage of the IDBR with LFS records, using the address and postcode of respondents' workplace addresses. The aim of this is to increase the accuracy, consistency and coherence of estimates of employment and jobs statistics from household and business surveys. This is turn would improve both labour and multi-factor productivity measures.

ONS will also continue to produce QALI and VICS measures annually, looking to review the experimental status of both series in the near future. From this year, these measures will be used on an annual basis to produce MFP estimates; there are more details of this new index in **Chapter 7**.

5.5   References

Bell V, Burriel-Llombart P and Jones J (2005) 'A quality-adjusted labour input series for the United Kingdom (1975-2002)', *Bank of England Working Paper* No. 280.

Bowman J, Gatward R and Lound C (2002) 'A Pilot Survey of People Living In Communal Establishments', *Labour Market Trends* 110, Edition 3, pp 141–149, available at: www.statistics.gov.uk/cci/article.asp?ID=221

Dean G (1964) 'The Stock of Fixed Capital in the United Kingdom in 1961', *Journal of the Royal Statistical Society* Series A (General) 127, pp. 327–358.

Draft International Conference of Labour Statisticians (ICLS) (2006) Resolution on Working Time Measurements, available at: www.insee.fr/En/nom_def_met/colloques/citygroup/2006_meeting.htm

Goodridge P (2006) 'Experimental quality-adjusted labour input measure – 1996 to 2005', *Economic Trends* 637, pp. 46–56, available at: www.statistics.gov.uk/ccs/article.asp?id=1693

Hall R E and Jorgenson D W (1967) 'Tax Policy and Investment Behaviour', *American Economic Review* 57, pp. 391–414.

Holmwood R, Lau E, Richardson C and Wallis G (2005) 'An experimental quality-adjusted labour input measure', *Economic Trends* 624, pp. 30–41, available at: www.statistics.gov.uk/CCI/article.asp?ID=1298

Hulten C R and Wykoff F C (1981a) 'The estimate of economic depreciation using vintage asset prices', *Journal of Econometrics* 57, pp. 367–396.

Hulten C R and Wykoff F C (1981b) 'The measurement of economic depreciation', in Hulten, C. R. (ed.), *Depreciation, inflation and the taxation of income from capital,* The Urban Institute Press: Washington.

Jorgenson D W (1963) 'Capital Theory and Investment Behaviour', *American Economic Review* 53, pp. 247–259.

Jorgenson D W and Griliches Z (1967) 'The explanation of productivity change', *Review of Economic Studies* 34, pp. 249–283.

Lau E (2002) 'Skills and Productivity: Developing New Measures'. Article presented at the Royal Economic Society Annual Conference, March 2002.

Lau E and Vaze P (2002) *Accounting growth: capital, skills and output*, available at www.statistics.gov.uk/CCI/Nscl.asp?ID=8311

OECD (2001a) *Measuring Productivity: OECD Manual,* Organisation for Economic Co-operation and Development: Paris.

OECD (2001b) *Measuring Capital: OECD Manual,* Organisation for Economic Co-operation and Development: Paris.

Review of Employment and Jobs Statistics, available at: www.statistics.gov.uk/about/data/methodology/quality/reviews/labour.asp

Solow R (1957) 'Technical change and the Aggregate Production Function', *Review of Economics and Statistics* 39, pp. 312–320.

Vaze P (2003) 'Estimates of the volume of capital services', *Economic Trends* 600, pp. 58–66, available at: www.statistics.gov.uk/cci/article.asp?ID=599

Walling A (2006) 'Comparisons of Statistics on Jobs', *Labour Market Trends* 114, pp. 373–388, available at: www.statistics.gov.uk/cci/article.asp?ID=1648

Wallis G (2005) 'Estimates of the Volume of Capital Services', *Economic Trends* 624, pp. 42–51, available at: www.statistics.gov.uk/CCI/article.asp?ID=1297

Wallis G (2006a) 'ICT Deflation awnd Productivity Measurement', *Economic Trends* 637, pp. 40–45, available at: www.statistics.gov.uk/cci/article.asp?id=1695

Wallis G (2007) 'Volume of Capital Services: Estimates for 1950 to 2005', Forthcoming in *Economic & Labour Market Review.*

Chapter 6

Quality Adjustment

In order to reflect changes in real values of inputs and outputs, measures of productivity should take quality changes in both into account. This is usually achieved by ensuring that the price indices used for deflation are adjusted for these quality changes. At the most basic level, volume measures are regarded as a combination of quantity and quality.

This chapter discusses the principles of quality adjustment, the practical issues encountered in quality adjustment within the market sector side, and the limits these impose on productivity measures. It also considers how these principles can be applied when considering productivity in government services.

The main focus here is on quality adjustments to output measures, but the principles apply equally to inputs.

Refining Productivity Measurement through Quality Adjustment

The need to take account of quality change has long been recognised in the measurement of price inflation, and in economic inputs and outputs in the National Accounts. If quality change is not captured then inflation rates and estimates of economic growth may be under- or over-estimated.

Adjusting for quality change is extremely challenging, however, both conceptually and practically. Having said that, various methods have been developed, and are widely employed, to adjust price indices for quality change. Adjustment, though, is much more common for goods than services.

These adjustments feed through to real output (and input) measures in the National Accounts where the adjusted price indices are used as deflators. Where output (input) volumes are calculated not by deflation but by directly observing quantities, taking account of quality change is much more difficult. This is highlighted in the case of government services where it can be extremely challenging both to identify the characteristics affecting overall quality and to measure them.

In the same way that quality change is fundamental to the measurement of output (input) volumes, it is an important consideration in productivity measurement. Hence the frequent concern that productivity increases might be achieved at the expense of quality. The level of customer service provided in out-of-town shopping centres is often cited as an example.

This chapter explains the principles of quality adjustment and the extent to which adjustments are made on the market sector side. It goes on to describe the work being undertaken in ONS to develop methods for quality adjusting the volume measures of government services.

6.1   Quality: concepts and definitions

Productivity is calculated as the volume of output per unit of input. In the National Accounts, volume is regarded as having two dimensions: quantity and quality, where quantity is the number of units (of a product) and quality is the description of the characteristics of each unit. So if the growth in volumes both produced and consumed is to be measured correctly, then both changes in quantity and quality must be taken into account. If quality change is not accounted for, then some volume change (growth) will be missed.

The difference between the terms 'quantity' and 'volume' is explained in the 1993 System of National Accounts (SNA93), Section 16.12, using the example of cars:

> It is not legitimate to add together quantities that are not identical with each other even though they may be measured in the same kind of physical units... Adding together quite different models of 'automobiles' is no more meaningful than adding together tons of different kinds of 'foods' – e.g. adding tons of rice to tons of apples or beef.

The point is made that physical units cannot be added together where the unit is specified at a high level such that the products within the specification are, in fact, quite variable in type, or quality. This becomes particularly dangerous where the mix between the different types changes over time. The effects of changes in composition of the aggregate and changes in quality are illustrated in **Box 6.1**.

Deriving a definition of quality is not straightforward, but a good starting point is to look at the characteristics of a product. The *Eurostat Handbook* on price and volume measures in National Accounts (2001) states:

> The quality of a product is defined by its (physical and non-physical) characteristics. In principle, whenever a characteristic of a product changes, the product is thought to be of a different quality. These changes in characteristics are to be recorded as changes in volume [of the output] and not as changes in price.

SNA93, Section 16.105 – 129 discusses quality in terms of characteristics, where characteristics may be:

- physical (tangible)
- connected with performance (reliability, ease of use, safety)
- connected with conditions of sale or delivery
- the result of timing of availability (ice cream in summer vs. winter), or location of availability

Box 6.1: Example of changes in output over time

The following example sets out the case of an economy with two types of cars as output: Mini and Porsche.

The basic data for two consecutive years are as follows:

	Year 1			Year 2			Growth (no. of cars only)
	Number of cars	Price (£)	Total (£)	Number of cars	Price (£)	Total (£)	
Mini	100	10,000	1,000,000	110	12,000	1,320,000	+10%
Porsche	50	30,000	1,500,000	80	31,000	2,480,000	+60%
Total	150			190			+26.7%.

Method 1 – Looking just at the change in the total number of cars sold, the growth rate of output is said to be 26.7 per cent (the increase from 150 cars sold to 190 cars sold).

$$\frac{190-150}{150} \times 100 = 26.7\%$$

However, this wrongly assumes that there is no difference in value between the two cars. Instead the case is that the Porsche is valued at three times the Mini in Year 1 by consumers, if prices are taken as an indication of that product's quality.

Method 2 – If the growth rates of the two different cars are weighted by their relative values in Year 1, and it is assumed that the price changes only reflect inflation rather than any quality improvement, then the total growth rate would change like this:

1. price change is assumed to be inflation

2. calculate the base year value weights (also called the price relative) by finding the proportion of the total value of sales for each car

3. produce a weighted measure of total output, based on these base year value weights, for both Year 1 and Year 2

4. this results in an increased growth rate of 31.4 per cent

These calculations are shown below.

Calculating the base year value weights:

Mini:

$$\frac{(100 \times 10,000)}{(100 \times 10,000)+(50 \times 30,000)} = 0.4$$

Porsche:

$$\frac{(50 \times 30,000)}{(100 \times 10,000)+(50 \times 30,000)} = 0.6$$

Calculating the weighted output

Year 1:

$$(100 \times 0.4)+(50 \times 0.6) = 70$$

Year 2:

$$(110 \times 0.4)+(80 \times 0.6) = 92$$

Calculating the growth rate:

$$\frac{92-70}{70} \times 100 = 31.4\%$$

The increased growth rate of 31.4 per cent takes account of the changes in the composition of the total number of cars sold: the relative share of the more expensive Porsche compared to the less expensive Mini has increased.

Method 3 – If it is now assumed that the price change from Year 1 to Year 2 represents a quality improvement (for example a situation where there is no inflation) the growth rate of output adjusted for the change in quality will be as follows:

1. price change is assumed to be quality change

2. adjust output for quality by dividing the sales value of each car in Year 2 by the corresponding base year value

3. produce a weighted measure of total output, based on the base year value weights, for Year 2

4. this results in an increased growth rate of 46.3 per cent

The calculations for the base year value weights are the same as above. The quality adjustment calculation is shown below.

Quality adjustment:

Mini:

$$\frac{(110 \times 12,000)}{10,000} = 132$$

Porsche:

$$\frac{(80 \times 31,000)}{30,000)} = 82.7$$

Calculating the weighted output

Year 1:

$$(100 \times 0.4)+(50 \times 0.6) = 70$$

Year 2:

$$(132 \times 0.4)+(82.7 \times 0.6) = 102.4$$

Calculating the growth rate:

$$\frac{102.4-70}{70} \times 100 = 46.3\%$$

Comparing this output growth rate of 46.3 per cent with the two previous ones, it is obvious that quality change can impact significantly on the growth rate of output.

The typical examples of products where quality change is important are:

- PCs and software
- telecommunications
- cars, high tech goods
- medical services, pharmaceuticals
- banking and insurance services

So, for goods, changes in characteristics are in most cases constituted in physical differences (for instance the size of a packet of sugar, the safety and comfort features of a car or the processing capacity of a PC). These are easier to measure than the non-physical characteristics possessed by services.

So, quality change refers to any change in the characteristics (physical and non-physical) of a unit. Change typically happens where an old model is withdrawn from the market and replaced with a new model with an 'improved' specification

It should be noted, however, that although quality may be **defined** in terms of characteristics, the **measurement** of quality change is primarily discussed in terms of consumers' preferences for characteristics as revealed through market and price mechanisms in a utility- or profit-maximising environment. The latter is discussed extensively in both the Consumer Prices Index (CPI) and *PPI Manuals.*

Conceptually, the need to capture quality change follows from the economic intuition that consumers derive a higher utility from products of a higher quality (though the SNA is rather cautious with regard to the economic theoretic approach). In a market with perfect competition, these differences in utilities would be revealed in the market prices. This implies that a higher price is associated with a higher quality. Although in practice, most markets do not exhibit perfect competition, the assumption that quality differences existing at the same point in time are revealed in the market prices is still powerful.

6.2   Capturing quality change in National Accounts volume measures

As stated earlier, volume is regarded as having the dimensions of quantity and quality. Therefore for growth in volumes to be measured correctly, then changes to both these dimensions must be taken into account. This means that if quality change is missed, then some volume change (growth) will equally be missed.

6.2.1 Measuring volumes in National Accounts

For National Accounts, volumes must be aggregated and therefore expressed in a common metric, and since this metric cannot be tonnes, litres or another physical measure the metric used is economic value in the prices of a price-base period. Therefore volumes are said to be expressed in the 'constant prices' of a certain period or in 'real terms'. So, any adjustments for quality change must also be, or must translate into, a value in the same constant price terms.

National Accounts volumes in constant price terms are estimated either by:

1. Extrapolation or quantity revaluation – where the number of units in the current period is multiplied by the unit price in the base period. This is arithmetically equivalent to deriving an index of quantity for each product, and aggregating product indices using base-price weights

2. Deflation – nominal values in the current period are deflated to constant prices using price indices such as Consumer Price Indices (CPIs), Producer Price Indices (PPIs), Services Producer Price Indices (SPPIs – previously called the Corporate Services Price Index or CSPI) – Import Price Indices (IPIs) Export Price Indices (EPIs) and earnings indices

Method 1 is, in theory, the more straightforward method, but can rarely be used in practice. This is because **Method 1** is regarded as only suitable for products for which quantities can be counted over time with no change in the characteristics (and therefore the quality) of the units. Such products are said to remain homogenous over time. This is the case for some agricultural and energy products, but most other products are too heterogeneous for this method and their volumes must be derived through deflation (**Method 2**). This is why, in National Accounts literature, the capture of quality change is largely addressed through the quality adjustment of the price indices used as deflators.

Quality change also affects volume measurement where there is a change in the mix of different models within an aggregate, but the weights for the sub-indices are not updated accordingly. This happens, for example, where old and new models are available side by side, and a volume sub-index is compiled for each, but their weights are not updated to account for the fact that the new model is acquiring market share as consumers substitute it for the old model.

In fact, this latter case of groups of products is conceptually the same as the change in characteristics of a single product. In both cases the problem is caused by a breakdown of homogeneity, either of products or aggregates.

6.2.2 Bundles of characteristics

Whether volumes are estimated through direct quantity measurement (**Method 1**), or through deflation (**Method 2**), the ultimate aim is always to compare like with like: homogeneity. For a heterogeneous product (one with several model-types), this homogeneity is approached by the use of very detailed specifications.

The drive for homogeneity, through more and more detailed descriptions of characteristics, leads towards the idea of products being 'bundles (or baskets) of characteristics'. Products with evolving model-types (heterogeneous) can be viewed as bundles of (homogeneous) characteristics, where the ultimate aim would be to measure the quantities of each homogeneous characteristic, and weight together these characteristics' sub-indices (this is the basis of the hedonic approach see **Section 6.2.3.2**).

It could be said that seeing heterogeneous products as bundles of homogeneous characteristics is the equivalent of moving towards the principles of **Method 1**, meaning an approach in terms of weighting together indices of homogeneous characteristics. So the boundary between quantity and quality depends entirely on the definition of 'product'. The *PPI Manual* (7.3) suggests 'It follows that products are the most detailed entities on which prices may be compared from period to period'.

6.2.3 How to adjust?

In principle, there are two different ways in which output (input) can be adjusted for quality change:

1. adjust the price indices that are used as deflators, or
2. find quality indicators and use these to adjust volume measures directly.

Price indices are compiled by comparing prices between different time periods, and decisions have to be made as to whether an observed price change is a pure price change (for example inflation) or is the result of a change in the quality of the product. In addition, it is not uncommon for the quality of a product to change but the observed price to remain the same between two periods, in which case the price should be adjusted.

The CPI and *PPI Manuals* and *Eurostat Handbook* devote much space to quality adjustment methods and what follows here is intended to supplement not summarise. The methods known as options costing, hedonic regression, and X specs are discussed, and **Box 6.2** gives examples of some ot the more challenging quality adjustment issues faced by the ONS on the market side.

Box 6.2: Examples of quality adjustment challenges in the market sector

Goods with frequent model changes, in particular ICT industry – Because of continuous product innovations, old models get frequently replaced by new versions that are generally regarded as of higher quality but are offered for a lower price. The assumption that relative prices reflect relative quality differences breaks down regularly for these products. To account for the quality changes, the hedonic pricing method has been developed (see **Section 6.2.3.3**).

Market services – Taking rail services as an example (see Richardson (2005) for a detailed application of quality adjustment to rail fares), the time of day of the travel can be thought of as a quality characteristic. If the output of rail services were categorised into, say, peak and off-peak travel, a change in the mix of those two categories would constitute quality change and would be captured through an appropriate differentiation of rail services into sub-categories peak and off-peak.

For other services such as management consulting, it is much less clear how quality changes in the output could be captured. It starts with the question of how the output of a consulting service could best be defined (amount of advice given? hours of consulting provided?), let alone what constitutes a 'better' consulting service (increased company profits for client? increased hourly rate for hiring a consultant?).

Public services – The main difficulty of services such as public healthcare or education is that at the point delivery, these services are provided for free. In other words, no prices exist for these services. Hence the above argument – that in a perfect market relative prices indicate differences in quality – cannot be applied. Other means of identifying and measuring quality change in these services must be found (see **Section 6.3** below).

6.2.3.1 Option costing

If the difference between two products consists of one extra option (such as parking sensors in a car), this extra option could be valued by its price as if it were purchased separately. To illustrate this, take a car model that costs £15,000 in year one and £18,000 in year two, but in year two it includes parking sensors as standard. The price of parking sensors, if purchased separately, is £1,000 in year two. From this information, a pure price change of £2,000 for the basic model can be imputed. The £1,000 will be recognised as quality change in the output.

The disadvantage of this method is that the price of the option, if purchased on its own, very often will be higher than the price of the old model of the product plus the option. It is also only applicable for cases in which the option is separable and an individual market price is available for the option.

6.2.3.2 Hedonic price adjustment

Hedonic regression is based on the principle that market mechanisms allow consumer preferences to be revealed through price (under certain market assumptions):

> a hedonic regression is a regression equation that relates the prices of items … to the quantities of characteristics… where the items are defined in terms of varying amounts of their characteristics (*PPI Manual*, 21.12).

The hedonic approach is built upon the principle that:

> the depiction of an item as a basket of characteristics, each characteristic having its own implicit (shadow) price, requires in turn the specification of a market for such characteristics, since prices result from the working of markets (*PPI Manual*, 21.12).

When a new model specification is introduced to the market, it tends to represent an improvement on an existing product. When the differences between two versions of one product become manifold and are no longer as straightforward to isolate, that leads to the application of hedonic pricing. The price differential between the old and the new version reflects both the pure price effect and a quality improvement. Using hedonic pricing, it is possible to separate these two effects so that only the price effect is being captured.

To apply hedonic pricing, products are defined as bundles of characteristics, which is in line with how Eurostat defines the quality of a product. A hedonic regression relates the measurable price of a good to its measurable characteristics. The price of the new model can then be predicted given its characteristics. The difference between this predicted price and the actual price then represents the pure price change. This is illustrated in **Box 6.3.**

Box 6.3: Example of hedonic price adjustment

A hedonic regression aims to decompose the price of a product into its observable characteristics.

In the hypothetical example below, the price of a PC is examined over two time periods. The rise in price of £200 is caused by two factors: general inflation (pure price change) and improvements in quality in the form of increased processing speed.

The price of the PC is regressed on each of three observable characteristics (in practice more than three would be used). The estimated coefficient shows the change in price if there is a one-

unit increase in these components. If the processing speed of the PC increases by 1 MHz the price of the PC will increase by £3.50. In the example above, there has been an increase of 100 MHz in Model A which would increase the price of Model A by £350 based on the hedonic regression. This means that of the £200 observed increase in price, £350 was because of a quality improvement. This means that the price effect was actually negative (-£150).

Therefore the PC in period t is actually cheaper than in the previous period, once adjustments are made for quality.

	Model A Period t-1	Model A (ii) Period t	Estimated (i) Coefficient	Quality Adjusted Model A (ii) Period t
Price	£1000	£1200	-	£850
Processor Speed	2000 MHz	2100 MHz	3.5	£350
Hard Disk Size	80 GB	80 GB	2.5	£0
Memory	512 MB	512 MB	1.0	£0

6.2.3.3 X specs

X specs is a method used for the construction of price indices for services, in particular for the SPPI). X specs denote additional information collected from service providers about the expected price of services. For a service they delivered in the current period, they are asked to estimate for which price they would have provided the identical service in the preceding period. Because this information is only collected for relatively few services (approximately 90 out of 4,500 items), its overall effect on the index is very small.

While this method helps to compare identical services over time, it is based on opinion and hence could be seen as less robust than other methods. It is also based on the viewpoint of the service providers', as opposed to that of the consumers, which makes it less useful for deflators for final consumption services.

6.2.3.4 Direct volume measurement

As an alternative to deflation, volumes can be measured directly to arrive at output in constant prices. Examples of this include motor vehicles, some energy products, alcohol, air travel, property rentals and TV licenses.

Quality is captured by differentiating according to quality characteristics, so that compositional changes in the aggregate automatically capture quality change. For products that are not sufficiently homogeneous, the breakdown into lower level activities for the application of quality adjustment is based on GVA-weighted activity. This is done for some activities in the areas of extraction of crude petroleum and natural gas and related activities, national post activities or manufacture of motor vehicles.

6.2.4   Conclusion

Measurement of quality change is not a precise science. Although a plausible theory has been constructed for the market sector based on consumer and producer behaviour, it depends on assumptions which do not hold in practice for all goods and services. The theory is also not always supported by data availability, and is therefore not able to be fully implemented in many cases. This is, consequently, an area in which future research will take place.

6.3   Quality adjustment of public sector productivity

The issue of quality adjustment in public services is parallel and analogous to the market sector. The task

for public services is, then, not to clarify the conceptual framework, but rather to operationalise the need to incorporate quality variations in the output measures for complex services such as health and education.

Taking the example of education, the demography of the UK means that using pupil numbers alone will give only a very low or constant growth in education output over the past decade. This implies that in reality the actual output of the public education system may not have significantly improved during this period. In all possibility, pupils are receiving better care, more individual teacher attention, are being taught syllabuses in more depth and are graduating with more skill sets than ever before. If these changes in quality are accounted for, as they should be, there is no reason why the volume of education output should not be steadily increasing even if demographic factors keep student numbers constant. Therefore the volume measure of public service output should be capturing how the quality of the service provided has changed over the years.

Measuring quality of public services is, however, a difficult and complex task complicated by three general problems.

1. properly capturing quality changes in complex services such as healthcare or social services is more difficult than tangible goods with clearly defined physical quality characteristics (the issue is similar to that of some services in the market sector)

2. the major difference from market output is the lack of a market and hence market prices. Non-market services are provided free of charge at the point of consumption. Hence, there are no prices to reflect differences in quality

3. some public services are entirely or partly collective in nature, meaning they are non-exclusive services provided to society as a whole as opposed to individuals (for example, defence, police, and courts of law). This raises the question how an increase in the volume of these services can be reasonably measured

For measuring quality changes in non-market output, the *Eurostat Handbook* advocates defining the outputs in as much detail as possible to facilitate homogeneity of output categories. This technique of differentiation enables capture of the quality change arising from a shift between different homogenous categories of services within the overall public service. In addition to measuring quality change arising from change in composition of aggregate output, the following approaches are put forward in the *Eurostat Handbook*.

- to measure the quality of output using a direct volume method (by using direct quality indicators, for example, GCSE attainment to adjust education output). Because of the lack of market prices, the production costs are used to determine the relative value of each service

- to measure the quality by measuring the quality of the inputs. The input based quality adjustment is based on the assumption that the quality change of the inputs leads automatically to a quality change of the output. Collective services are still measured according to the traditional <output = inputs> convention, implying productivity for these services is unchanging over time

- to measure quality using the outcomes. The reasoning used is that change in outcome is the most telling factor of the quality of service delivered. However in practice it is difficult to separate the changes in outcomes directly attributable to public services output from changes attributable to other exogenous factors

The international guidelines offered by these very general options are not wholly satisfactory and questions remain as to how they can be applied in practice. The *Final Report of the Atkinson Review* published in January 2005 concentrated on developing this work further and suggested more detailed methods to capture quality change in public service output. The *Atkinson Review* not only covers the measurement of quality but approaches the whole methodological issue of measuring public sector output and productivity in a principled fashion. The principles, and particular methods and practical application proposed in the *Atkinson Review*, are explained in more detail in **Chapter 9**.

The *Atkinson Report* proposes three important ways in which the variation in the quality of output might be approached:

1. differentiation of services into homogeneous categories

2. defining the volume measure in reference to the degree of success of the activity concerned

3. basing the estimate of output volume on an activity indicator but then marking that indicator up or down according to the attributable contribution of the activity to a desired outcome

As mentioned earlier (in **Section 6.2.3**) the first of these has traditionally been used in the National Accounts; often in differentiation of services. Increased use of the differentiation of services will automatically pick up changes in quality associated by a shift in the mix of services from low to higher quality at the aggregate level of output. Use of differentiation has considerably improved the measures of NHS output where the number of healthcare treatment categories was extended from 16 to around 2,000 categories at present.

Differentiation, however, may not be enough on its own within public services for several broad reasons:

- generally, differentiation will be carried out by cost of activity whereas it is really more important to capture the attributable contribution to the outcome

- in practice, it is unlikely to be possible to differentiate so as to obtain wholly homogeneous groups

- the weightings also should ideally be value weights reflecting the relative values to consumers, for example to describe the proportional contribution of the service categories to the outcomes. But it is likely to be cost weightings that are readily available

- all the different quality dimensions cannot be considered through differentiation alone

The second approach, based on incorporating the 'degree of success', is based on the idea of 'simple repackaging'. A clear non-public service example to illustrate this concept is petrol. If one kind of petrol gives 10 per cent more miles to the gallon than does the same quantity of another kind, then it should be regarded as of 10 per cent higher quality. Using another public service example – social security administration – since the aim is to process benefits correctly, then benefits processed with 90 per cent accuracy might be regarded as of nine-eighths of the quality of operations associated with a target level of 80 per cent accuracy.

In the case of the health service, the use of 'degree of success' in quality adjustment means, for example, that a failed hip replacement operation is not equated as having created the same volume output as a successful hip replacement operation. It is intuitive why quality of output should be adjusted for effectiveness of service rendered and not to record output at the same level for a service that was not effective as one that was. Or even worse, if quality adjustment does not incorporate degree of success, in the example of the failed hip replacement this may record a higher output because more corrective treatments may be required subsequently.

The third method to capture quality is the directive from Atkinson's **Principle B**:

> The output of the government sector should in principle be measured in a way that is adjusted for quality, taking account of the attributable incremental contribution of the service to the outcome.

To do this would be to define the output straightforwardly as the directly identifiable contribution to the outcome. However, the main obstacle to this approach is that outcomes are often influenced by a wide range of factors, and not just by the specific service under consideration. As already indicated, the main outcome of the NHS is better health status of UK citizens, and will depend upon a range of influences such as diet, exercise habits, the extent of smoking and so on, as well as the output of the health services. In this sense the most important criteria for this approach is being confident that the outcome in question 'is largely attributable' to the public service in question. The success of this method would therefore depend on:

- whether outcome information exists to allow such an inference to be made with regard to quality

- whether it is possible to make a clear inference from the outcomes data as to what change in quality may have occurred

- whether it is possible to separate out from the overall effect on the outcome factors the effect of the public service in question

To date, there is only one such explicit quality adjustment of public service output, namely education, used in the National Accounts (which existed before the Atkinson Review). It is an annual adjustment of +0.25 per cent to account for rising GCSE levels and educational attainment. However experimental quality adjustments have been used for productivity analyses in the public service productivity articles for some services. **Box 6.4** gives examples for health and education for which research is most advanced to date.

Another important issue to be considered in measuring the quality of public service output is the different quality dimensions that arise, and how these can be weighted together. For complex services such as healthcare or the criminal justice system, quality is unlikely to be one dimensional. For example, in the case of NHS output, the quality of the medical treatment delivered to the patient will depend on the effectiveness of the treatment, the quality of the patient's (subjective) experience

---

Box 6.4: Examples of quality-adjustment in health and education

Health – The main research on quality indicators for healthcare output was conducted by the University of York and the National Institute of Economic and Social Research (NIESR) and the Department of Health (DH). The primary quality indicators for health outcomes used by York/NIESR covered survival rates and health effects for a limited number of NHS treatments (both adjusted for life expectancy) and waiting times. Further quality indicators research by the DH included outcomes from primary medical care, longer term survival rates from myocardial infarction, and patient experience obtained from the National Patient Experience Survey Programme (see the NHS example in **Chapter 9**).

Education – The Department for Education and Skills (DfES) researched improved quality indicators for educational attainment, based on GCSE grades and progress made between the four Key Stages. The disadvantage of using GCSE grades for which data are most readily available is that they only capture one cohort of students at the end of their compulsory education of eleven years. The use of data on Key Stages progress overcomes this problem by measuring the progress of all pupils between the beginning and the end of the four Key Stages, but has the disadvantage of having to rely on a number of untested assumptions.

---

while undergoing treatment, and the speed of access to treatment.

When there are multiple dimensions of quality, care must be taken not to take progress (or deterioration) in any one aspect as necessarily typical of the other areas. Indeed, in some respects, there may be a presumption against any such universal correlation. If there has been a quality improvement, it might well reflect special attention being accorded to that aspect of the service, perhaps as a result of earlier concerns. If so, there would be no presumption of a similar improvement in other domains. Indeed, if resources had been diverted from such areas to deal with the quality issues of concern, the correlation may even be negative.

Pertinent to these issues is how to combine all the different quality domains, assuming all of them can be measured. One possibility is that all the quality domains will not have equal weights. It may be assumed, for example, that patients in an NHS hospital will prefer to survive in a dirty bed rather than die in a clean bed. The question of who should 'value' the relative weights necessary to aggregate these different qualities requires further research. So far, satisfactory answers to these issues have not been found.

Quality adjustment is more challenging in the case of public services because of the degree of subjectivity involved in determining quality domains and quality weights. For these reasons, great caution must be exercised before accepting quality adjustment procedures. In the final report, Atkinson counselled ONS that 'a relatively high threshold should be set ... before adjustments are introduced into the National Accounts' (Atkinson Review, 6.32). Important elements for a high threshold would include:

- quality adjustments where required in measuring output are carried out with maximum transparency

- methods adopted should be robust and widely accepted through a consultation process with experts and practitioners in the field

- quality adjustment should include the relevant set of all quality dimensions so as to avoid unrepresentative bias. Bias arises when one or two domains are used to adjust for quality while the quality change in other domains is ignored

- quality dimensions and the proposed weights of these dimensions should be robust and based on research and international collaborative evidence

- where statistical and professional judgement is called for, a more stringent criteria of significant probability as opposed to balance of probabilities need to be adhered to

- new measurement methods should be published first experimentally by some means such as within a productivity article

Quality adjustment is also a factor when constructing the weights used for aggregating public services output – see **Box 6.5** for more details.

6.4   Conclusion

Although it is often said that only a few quality adjustments are made to output data, this is because many quality adjustments are not made explicitly but are made implicitly through the quality adjustment of deflators. That is not to say that there is not a lot left to do. In certain areas, for instance in some market output in the ICT industry, some market services such as consulting, or in the whole of public services, there is ongoing research about improving the measures for quality change.

The work on quality adjustments has so far been characterised by individual and insular solutions suiting the particular problem at hand. What has been missing so far in this work is an overarching principled approach to quality adjustments. Such a framework is needed to avoid ad hoc solutions that are convenient for the particular problem at hand but inconsistent with other individual solutions. This is why ONS is currently developing a general guide for the treatment of quality adjustments in economic statistics. In addition, the UK Centre for the Measurement of Government Activity (UKCeMGA) has recently published a strategy paper outlining a quality measurement framework for measuring the output of the non-market sector.

References for this chapter appear on page 82.

Box 6.5: Value weights for public service output

The SNA(93) guidance on the weighting mechanism for goods and services is to be 'weighted by their economic importance as measured by their values in one or other, or both, periods'. In the market sector relative prices are used to weight the output for aggregation. Relative prices provide weights according to economic weight as it incorporates the relative cost of production as well as relative benefit to the consumer.

In the non-market case, however, there are no prices available and the most common method is to use unit costs to weight the different outputs together. The use of cost weights signifies that output is weighted using producer valuation instead of valuation by recipients or society.

Using unit costs to weight output means that switching to higher cost services from lower cost services will lead to higher output growth. In most instances it could be that higher cost services are of higher quality and generate more value to consumers. However in instances where technological improvements enable services to be produced to a higher quality expending fewer resources, the use of unit costs will provide odd results in the volume index. In fact, where the unit cost of a service is significantly lower than the marginal benefit to the consumer, using cost weights instead of value weights could create a managerial incentive to provide less effective and more expensive services. This is comparable with technological effects in the market sector – such as producing a price index for computers.

In those instances where the unit cost deviates from the marginal value of a service, the use of value weights can provide a more accurate volume measure of public service output. The argument for using value weights is promoted in the *Atkinson Review* and is also validated in the SNA(93): 'In principle volume

indices may always be compiled directly by calculating a weighted average of the quantity relatives for the various goods and services produced as outputs using the values of these goods and services as weights'. Further support on the concept of using value weights can also be found in research carried out by the National Institute of Economic and Social Research (NIESR) and the University of York (York, 2005).

If value weights are constructed properly, they can help to capture changes in quality in addition to working as an aggregating mechanism. Value weights in this way can operate to factor in the attributable contribution to outcomes of public services. For example, if an NHS prevention activity for obesity has a large impact in reducing levels of obesity in the population compared to stomach stapling operations, then the prevention activity should have a higher value weight relative to the stomach stapling operation, holding everything else constant. There are, however, a number of practical problems that still need to be addressed before value weights can be adopted.

Firstly, in the absence of a market mechanism it can be very difficult to determine what is the 'value' of a public service to consumers and society. There would need to be rigorous research done in this area to produce a set of values for all the different quality dimensions of each public service. Results from such research would also need to determine who is best placed to determine reliable and appropriate values: providers, users, experts or perhaps the general public.

The work to determine value weights is made easy in such cases where there are parallel markets for the provision of the same or similar services. Even in these cases, however, it is likely that shadow prices from the market sector have to be adjusted further for reasons of distortion created

through monopolistic or monopsonistic market structures (where government is the main provider or purchaser, respectively, of the particular service).

Revealed preference techniques can also be used in surveys to recipients of services and the general public to determine the value associated with services. 'Willingness to pay' or 'willingness to accept' are the most common methods in determining the implicit valuations of the various aspects of public services.

The second critical issue raised against the use of value weights is based on mathematical grounds within the context of a National Accounts framework. If value weights are not obtained for all separate non-market output and market output, this would imply a mix of cost and value weights. Adopting the two different weighting systems within the National Accounts can also cause the very important derived GDP deflators to become meaningless. At the moment it is not well understood how a total index can be obtained for value weights, and how it can be disaggregated amongst the diverse goods and services delivered in the public sector. These are stumbling blocks for the current use of value weights.

6.5 References

Atkinson A B (2005) *Atkinson Review: Final Report. Measurement of Government Output and Productivity for the National Accounts*, Palgrave Macmillan: Basingstoke, available at: www.statistics.gov.uk/about/data/methodology/specific/publicSector/atkinson/final_report.asp

Eurostat (2001) *Handbook on price and volume measures in national accounts,* Office for Official Publications of the European Communities, available at: http://epp.eurostat.cec.eu.int/cache/ITY_OFFPUB/KS-41-01-543/EN/KS-41-01-543-EN.PDF

International Labour Organization (2004), *Consumer Price Index Manual: Theory and Practice* (2004), ILO: Geneva, available at: www.ilo.org/public/english/bureau/stat/guides/cpi/index.htm#manual

International Monetary Fund (2004) *Producer Price Index Manual: Theory and Practice*, IMF: Washington, available at: www.imf.org/external/np/sta/tegppi/index.htm

Office for National Statistics (1998) *National Accounts Concepts, Sources and Methods*, TSO: London, available at: www.statistics.gov.uk/statbase/Product.asp?vlnk=1144

Richardson C (2005) 'Using the Value of Time for Quality Adjustment – Testing the concept for Rail fares', *Economic Trends* 621, pp 63–69, available at: www.statistics.gov.uk/cci/article.asp?ID=1204

UKCeMGA (2006), *Public Service Productivity: Health*, Office for National Statistics: London.

United Nations Statistics Division, 1993, System of National Accounts (SNA93), available at: http://unstats.un.org/unsd/sna1993/toctop.asp

York, NIESR Study (December 2005) *Developing new approaches to measuring NHS outputs and productivity: Non-technical Summary of the Final Report*, University of York and National Institute for Economic and Social Research: York.

Chapter 7

Productivity: Whole Economy and Multi-Factor

The headline ONS measures of labour productivity are for the whole economy and manufacturing labour. These were established as the main measures in 2004 following a review of productivity methodology. Starting in 2007, ONS also began publishing experimental multi-factor productivity estimates.

The quality of productivity estimates depends on a number of factors. These include definitions, coverage and coherence of the input and output, as well as consistent measurement. Once these potential sources of error are accounted for, users are left with 'genuine' estimates of productivity differences over time, or between economic units, which can be related to economic effects. These are what policy makers aim to influence.

The discussion in the first part of this chapter presents historic UK productivity trends on a whole economy basis. It focuses on the ONS labour productivity series and relates the trends seen to the shift from manufacturing to services, the major structural shift in the composition of the economy over the period.

This chapter goes on to define the multi-factor productivity (MFP) concept. It describes the methodology and data required to produce MFP estimates, and ends by presenting and discussing recent results.

Measures of Productivity for the whole economy

Productivity estimates using aggregate data are to some extent influenced by underlying measurement assumptions. The degree has been greatly reduced in recent years, but remains an issue in particular for deflation of certain service sector activities. Related issues are the measurement of government output, where the use of input measures have been particularly prevalent, productivity within the service sector and the development of market sector measures.

Government is a special case that has been subject to a great deal of attention; this is dealt with in **Chapter 9**. Likewise detailed sector and industry estimates are covered within **Chapter 8**. Instead, the focus below is on the whole economy, for which ONS produces specific labour and multi-factor productivity (MFP) series.

7.1   Whole economy labour productivity

Whole economy labour productivity is of interest both nationally and internationally. By covering all sectors and industries in the UK, it provides an overall picture of productivity for the complete economy. While useful in terms of providing an overview, whole economy measures need to be broken down to understand them better.

Headline productivity measures are measures of labour productivity based on output per worker. There are other types of productivity; there is more detail about these

alternatives in **Chapter 1** and a comparison with per hour worked in **Box 7.1**.

Figure 7.1 shows the ONS annual growth rate for gross value added (GVA) per worker along with a five-year moving average. This series is rather volatile, although it becomes less so over the most recent years. The peak years are 1973, 1976, 1982, 1986 and 1993 while the deepest troughs are 1974, 1980, 1984 and 1989.

Over the period shown the average annual productivity is 1.8 per cent, beyond that it is quite difficult to discern any changes in the trend rates over time. To understand further these movements in productivity growth, the figures need to be decomposed into the components.

Figure 7.2 shows growth of output per worker alongside the growth of output, measured as GVA in chained-volume terms (as defined in **Chapter 4**), and employment using the jobs series created for productivity measurement (as defined in **Chapter 5**). At the start of the 1970s, productivity followed output quite closely. Since then, there has usually been a lag between output growth and employment growth. Peaks and troughs of productivity are related to the underlying economic cycle, reflected in both gross domestic product (GDP) and employment data.

The relationship is complicated by the lagged relationship between output and employment, with employment tending to follow changes in output growth with a lag, seemingly of a year on this annual time series. For example, the high productivity growth in 1973 is shown to

Figure 7.1: Annual labour productivity growth

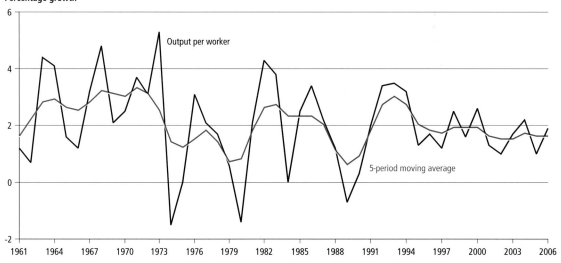

Figure 7.2: Decomposition of labour productivity growth
Percentage annual growth

follow largely from the very high GDP growth. In contrast, in 1992 the high productivity growth follows from a decrease in employment.

In certain periods, notably 1980 to 1988, the relationship between output and employment is so close that it is likely to indicate a relationship between the underlying data sources, as much as a relation between the macroeconomic variables. As will be discussed in **Chapter 8**, output measures for the service sector previously made use of employment proxies, with ad hoc adjustments for productivity.

Box 7.1: Output per hour worked

ONS also publishes a productivity measure of output per hour. This series can be compared to the headline per worker series on a percentage annual growth basis.

In the earlier periods of the comparison, output per hour worked tended to have a lower growth rate than the output per worker measure. Over the last ten years, output per hour worked has increased faster than output per worker. This reversal reflects the increase in part-time working being more accurately reflected in the per hour measure.

In this way, output per hour worked is theoretically a better measure of

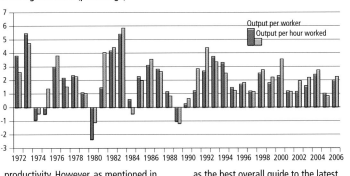

Figure 7A: Output per worker compared to per hour worked
Annual growth rate (percentage)

productivity. However, as mentioned in **Chapter 5**, because short-term changes in hours are difficult to measure accurately, the per worker series is still regarded as the best overall guide to the latest movements in productivity.

7.1.1   User requirements

The productivity measures produced by ONS are determined by the data series available, international guidelines and recommendations. A key use of productivity estimates is by HM Treasury (HMT) as part of their derivation of estimates of trend growth. For information about other users, please see **Chapter 2**.

HMT's methodology for estimating trend productivity is set out briefly in table B2 in the Budget document and is explained further in HMT's 2006 paper *Trend Growth: new evidence and prospects*. The technique is summarised in **Box 7.2**.

More recently there has been increased interest from the Bank of England (BoE) and HMT in measures of market sector activity, and associated measures of productivity (see Herbert and Pike, 2005). These techniques are discussed in **Chapter 8**.

7.1.2   Historical data

The above comparisons are based on the full time series of official productivity estimates. Longer-term comparisons are more difficult because official National Accounts output data are generally only available from 1948 and the Labour Force Survey (LFS) only began in 1973. However, a long-term series has been constructed as described in **Box 7.2**.

Figure 7.3 is difficult to interpret other than noting the years with the highest productivity growth rates (1901, 1915, 1921, 1940 and 1959) and those with the lowest (1919, 1920, 1926, 1939 and 1945). Most of these peaks and troughs seem to be associated with abrupt but lagged movements in output and employment during times of war.

Table 7.1 gives the figures for productivity growth alongside GDP and employment growth as annual average compound rates across the decade. The figures show employment changes having a smaller order of magnitude, and productivity growth generally mirroring GDP growth. Employment changes in the 1910s and 1930s were more dominant, though during periods covering the First World War and the Great Depression these are clearly rather

---

Box 7.2: HM Treasury's trend productivity measure

In measuring trend productivity growth, HMT uses non-oil gross value added as its trend output growth measure. This is because while the oil and gas sector significantly affects output, it has little impact on the sustainable level of employment and so non-North Sea output is largely unaffected by North Sea output. In other words, fluctuations in oil and gas output do not signal change in the amount of slack in the economy (such as the output gap).

In addition HMT adjusts for the lag between employment/hours worked and output. Employment is assumed to lag output by around three quarters, so that on-trend points for employment come three quarters after on-trend points for output, an assumption that can be supported by econometric evidence. Hours are easier to adjust than employment, and the decomposition assumes that hours lag output by just one quarter, though this lag is harder to support by econometric evidence. Hours worked and the employment rate are measured on a working-age basis. On this basis HMT finds productivity growth over the most recently completed half cycle (1997H1 to 2001Q3) equal to 2.60 per cent per annum.

Box 7.3: Estimating historical labour productivity growth

Figure 7.3 shows annual labour productivity growth throughout the 20th century. This historical series was constructed as follows.

GDP data was previously published in the ONS article *100 Years of GDP 1900–1999*, meaning that data before 1948 primarily comes from *The Economist* publication, *One Hundred Years of Economic Statistics* by Thelma Liesner, published co-operatively by *The Economist* and ONS in 1989. From 1948, ONS National Statistics are used. Employment data are also from *One Hundred Years of Economic Statistics* for the period up to 1983 and then the LFS data are used beyond that. This means that there is a potential inconsistency because the former is based on Census of Employment data whereas the latter is based on the number of people in employment. However, this does not detract from the overall message seen in these data and the two series do appear reasonably compatible.

Productivity estimates for this graph use GDP data at constant 1995 market prices rather than GVA because this is the data series available across the time period. Employment data are the number of people in employment. While using these measures means that the productivity estimate is significantly cruder than the official headline series, it does provide a more substantial period for analysis.

Figure 7.3: Labour productivity growth in the 20th century
Percentage annual growth

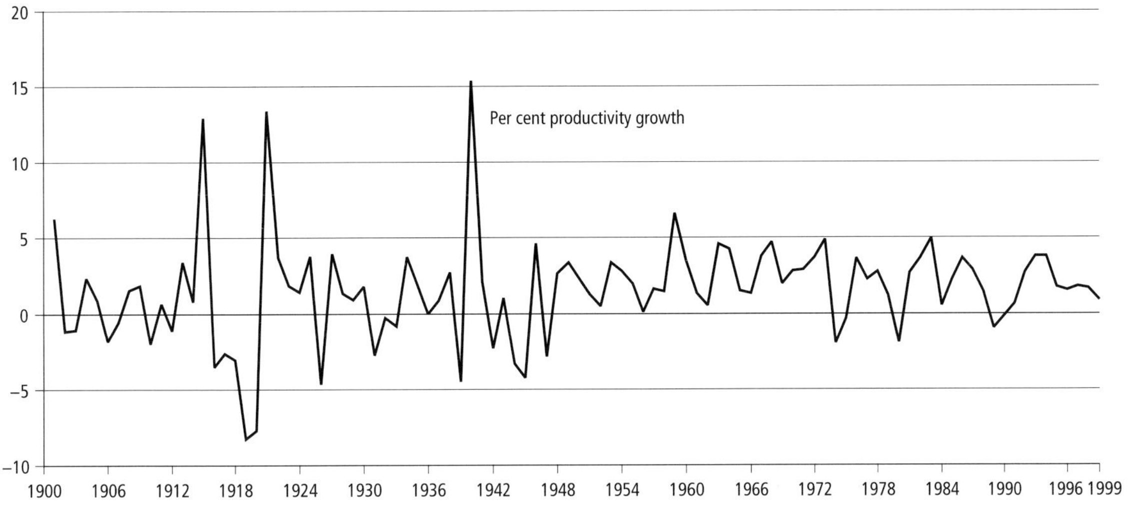

exceptional. **Figure 7.4** shows this same productivity growth over each decade of the twentieth century in graph form.

Productivity growth was far stronger in the second half of the twentieth century than the first. The third quarter of the century is also seen as a little ahead of the fourth; this extra growth appears to follow from the stronger output growth. The next section discusses whether the shift from manufacturing to services may offer explanations for this slowdown.

Table 7.1: Ten-year averages, United Kingdom
(Percentage annual growth)

Year range	Productivity	GDP	Employment
1901– 1910	0.6	1.3	0.7
1911–1920	-0.9	0.3	1.1
1921–1930	2.8	1.5	-1.0
1931–1940	1.6	3.5	2.0
1941–1950	0.3	0.4	0.1
1951–1960	2.3	2.7	0.4
1961–1970	2.7	2.9	0.2
1971–1980	1.8	2.0	0.2
1981–1990	2.0	2.7	0.7
1991–2000	2.1	2.3	0.2

7.1.3   Contributions to the whole economy from the manufacturing and services sectors

Figure 7.5 overleaf shows that manufacturing output peaked in 1973, and has since grown to only a modest degree, with a number of periods of falling growth (1979–1982, 1990–1992 and 1999–2001).

Over the period for which data are available, the service sector generally shows more subdued productivity growth while there is very high productivity growth in the manufacturing sector (**Figure 7.6** overleaf).

The latter follows from the sharp falls in manufacturing employment that have been recorded over the past three decades (see **Table 7.3** overleaf). Relatively fast output growth, but not a correspondingly fast pace of productivity change, has accompanied the move to the service sector.

In economic terms, the divergence in these measures is likely to follow from the more capital intensive nature

Table 7.2: Productivity and output for each quarter of the 20th century

	Productivity	Output
00–25	0.8	0.9
26–50	0.8	1.7
51–75	2.4	2.7
76–00	2.0	2.3

Figure 7.4: Ten-year averages of GDP, employment and labour productivity growth

Percentage annual growth

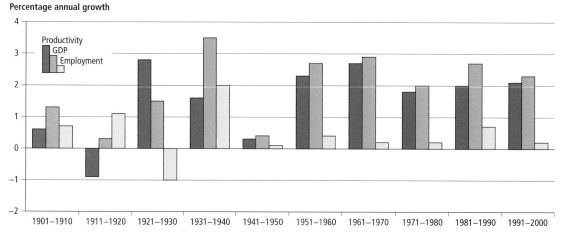

Figure 7.5: Manufacturing and services output

Indices   **1948=100**

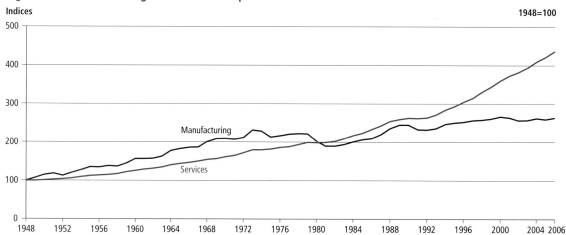

Figure 7.6: Productivity growth by sector

Percentage annual growth

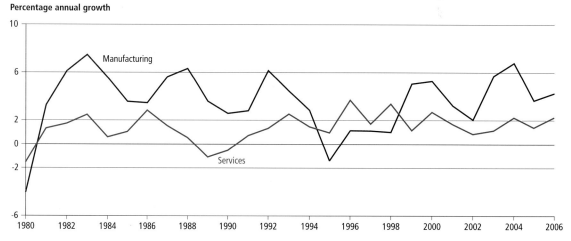

Table 7.3: Decomposition of productivity growth by average percentage per annum

	Productivity			Output			Employment		
	Total	Manu-facturing	Services	Total	Manu-facturing	Services	Total	Manu-facturing	Services
1980s	1.9	4.3	1	2.6	1.9	2.8	0.7	-3.1	1.4
1990s	2.2	2.9	1.9	2.4	0.9	3.2	0.1	-1.9	1.3
2000s	1.6	3.8	1.5	2.4	-0.5	3.2	0.9	-4.6	1.8

of manufacturing activity. This means that gains in productivity can be achieved by the increased expenditure on capital goods. At this point the multi-factor productivity analysis is required, and is set out below. Other factors that may be influencing recent productivity trends are discussed in **Box 7.4** overleaf.

There is further information on the measurement of the service sector in general in **Chapter 8**.

7.2   Multi-factor productivity

MFP analysis, sometimes called total-factor productivity (TFP) analysis or growth accounting, can be used to further analyse productivity of the whole economy and, data allowing, some industry breakdowns. It apportions growth in output to growth in the factor inputs of capital and labour, and growth in a residual representing disembodied technical change. Therefore, if the growth rate of output is greater than the growth rate of the combined factor inputs, capital and labour, then the residual can be interpreted as an approximation of growth in disembodied technical change, that is, advances in technology not embodied in capital. Examples of such a change are increased knowledge through research and development (R&D) or improvements in organisational structure or management. In general it captures any improvement in output that is not captured in the data on the factor inputs.

Embodied technical change comes in the form of advances in the quality of capital or other inputs and so is captured when calculating the contribution of the inputs. An example of this is the rapid improvement in the quality of Information and Communication Technology (ICT) over the last 20 years.

Other possible inputs, usually defined as intermediate inputs, that could be included in MFP analysis are purchases of energy, materials and services. These are used

in the EU KLEMS project, details of which are given in **Chapter 12**.

Although a fundamental area of any analysis on productivity or economic performance, part of the current interest in MFP lies in the growth in use of ICT. Use of ICT, and its spillover effects, has frequently been proposed as an explanation for the acceleration in the productivity performance of the US in the late 1990s. Observers of this phenomenon wish to know whether the UK has experienced any such surge in productivity growth as a result of increased use of ICT. As well as hardware – physical ICT capital – there has been considerable growth in investment in software, both purchased and own-account (developed in-house by the firm).

Software is an intangible asset, that is, an asset that does not have a physical, material existence. It is one of the few intangible assets included in National Accounts investment figures, although in the future it will be joined by R&D investment. Other intangible assets are not included in estimates of capital, mainly because of their nature and the difficulty in measuring them, including brand equity, firm-specific human capital, organisational capital and non-scientific R&D. Since investment in these categories is not measured, their contribution will also be present in the MFP residual. However attempts are now being made to measure such investments and investigate their productivity effects. For further details see **Chapter 13**.

MFP analysis is not only a useful productivity measure but also can be used as a diagnostic check on the consistency of National Accounts input and output data and help to identify measurement issues. For instance, a decline in MFP growth within a growing sector would be plausible and would suggest there are issues with the underlying data. This is particularly relevant for certain service sector industries, such as financial intermediation and business

---

Box 7.4: Offshoring: another factor influencing productivity and productivity measurement

Offshoring is generally defined as the relocation of business processes from one country to another. This is usually assumed to include any business process such as production, manufacturing, or services. The best known area for offshoring is business support services, for which there are now dedicated outsourced firms who take up this work, such as call centres.

There is debate, however, over whether or not the definition of offshoring should include both materials and services and also whether it should include direct foreign investment by firms. Bhagwati, Panagariya and Srinivasan (2004) proposed a tight definition of services offshoring as 'purchase of services abroad with the supplier and buyer remaining in their respective locations' and this is the one generally used by ONS when conducting studies on offshoring.

The economic logic behind offshoring services is to reduce costs. If a firm can provide specific skills more cheaply than other firms, then that company is at an advantage. Taking that to the international stage, the idea is that countries should freely trade the services that cost the comparative least for them to produce and provide. This is often best achieved by going to a country with cheaper labour costs. There is also the possibility of specialisation.

A company may purchase services from elsewhere because its own area of specialisation does not cover such things.

Offshoring, from the productivity viewpoint, is regarded as a good thing. Theory suggests that by moving away from areas where it is less skilled or less competitive, a company can become more productive. By considering the international range of providers, companies considering offshoring have access to a larger variety of services than those employing only domestic services; they can either choose the same services at a lower cost or services of a better quality.

However, offshoring is also looked upon with suspicion from the viewpoint of the workers whose jobs are in the areas where offshoring occurs. In particular, there have been fears that skilled UK workers would lose their jobs to others in developing countries because they were much cheaper to hire. However, a number of studies investigating these types of issues and concerns have shown that this does not currently appear to be the case and that offshoring to date has been from developed countries to other developed countries (Criscuolo, 2006).

It is worth remembering that offshoring has occurred relatively recently in

history owing to advances made in ICT technology and travel. Additionally, many developing countries have fast growing economies that are expected to catch up with those of the developed world. Therefore the current picture may change as more companies turn to offshoring (in 2002/03 approximately 8–10 per cent of UK firms offshored services (Criscuolo and Leaver, 2005)), and equally as developing countries develop.

Offshoring is about purchasing services from elsewhere. However, just as business processes can come from abroad, so can the workforce and the UK has workers who commute in from abroad. This is not as high a proportion of foreign workers as for some other countries, Luxembourg being a key example, however there are those who commute over the English Channel or the Irish border.

Also, the resident UK workforce has changed substantially over the last two decades with the fall of the Berlin Wall and the enlargement of the European Union. Migrant workers have substantially added to it. The UK workforce, and the measurement of these flows, is regarded as a key issue for macroeconomic statistics, with implications for productivity.

---

services, where output, and quality change associated with output, are notoriously difficult to measure. In the UK, where these sectors are growing faster than the economy as a whole, this is of particular importance.

Another area of interest, particularly in relation to government policy, is the contribution of skills to productivity growth. Skills are listed as one of the five key drivers of productivity by the Department of Trade and Industry (DTI) and it is part of government policy to improve the skill level of the UK workforce and therefore help reduce the productivity gap with the US and other industrialised nations (see **Chapter 3** for more details of the drivers).

The results in this handbook estimate the contribution of skills by producing two sets of MFP results based on quality-adjusted and standard hours worked, and also by estimating the contribution of labour composition to labour productivity growth.

7.2.1 Multi-factor productivity methodology
MFP can be derived from the growth accounting framework as shown in **Chapter 3**. Below is the more usual presentation of the formula.

7.2.1.1 Multi-factor productivity theory

A standard production function is shown below in equation (1). It states that output (Y) is a function of capital (K) and labour (L), as well as the exogenous factor of technical change (A).

$$Y(t)=A(t)\mathrm{F}(K(t),L(t)) \qquad (1)$$

This can be used to derive the following equation stating that growth in output is explained by the share-weighted growth in the factor inputs plus growth in a residual. This is the MFP term or the 'Solow residual' (Solow, 1957), which is defined in **Chapter 3**. The weights, α_K and, α_L are the income shares of capital and labour and sum to one under the assumption of constant returns to scale.

$$\frac{\Delta Y(t)}{Y(t)}=\alpha_K\frac{\Delta K(t)}{K(t)}+\alpha_L\frac{\Delta L(t)}{L(t)}+A(t) \qquad (2)$$

In practice this involves calculating the income that accrues to labour – compensation of employees plus imputed compensation for the self-employed – as a proportion of total income. The income share for capital is simply one minus the share for labour.

More specifically MFP growth is calculated using a rearrangement of the following equation, which uses natural logarithms:

$$\Delta Y(t)=[1-\bar{s}_L(t)]\Delta\ln K(t)+\bar{s}_L(t)\Delta\ln L(t)+\Delta\ln A(t) \qquad (3)$$

where s_L is the average of labour's income share in the current and previous period.

$$\bar{s}_L(t)=[s_L(t)+s_L(t-1)]/2 \qquad (4)$$

As mentioned above, ideally the labour input measure would be adjusted for quality to capture fully the contribution of this factor, meaning that part of its contribution is not attributed to MFP growth. However, in practice some improvements in the quality of the factor inputs will still be present in the MFP term. Factors other than technical change will also be included in the residual such as economies of scale, omitted inputs, adjustment costs, cyclical effects, inefficiencies and measurement error.

The same technique can be used to decompose labour productivity growth into the contributions of physical capital deepening, labour composition (skills) and MFP growth, as shown below in equation (5):

$$\Delta\ln\left[\frac{Y(t)}{H(t)}\right]=\left[1-\bar{s}_L(t)\right]\Delta\ln\left[\frac{K(t)}{H(t)}\right]+\bar{s}_L(t)\left[\Delta\ln L(t)-\Delta\ln H(t)\right]+\Delta\ln A(t) \qquad (5)$$

where $L(t)$ and $H(t)$ denote quality-adjusted and unadjusted hours respectively. The use of unadjusted hours assumes labour to be homogenous regardless of characteristics, while adjusted hours use workers' characteristics to estimate the change in labour quality. The quality-adjustment of labour input is described in detail in **Chapter 5**.

Therefore equation (5) decomposes growth in labour productivity into the contributions of capital deepening (the capital share multiplied by growth of physical capital per hour worked), growth in labour composition and MFP growth.

An alternative methodology for calculating MFP growth is to use an econometric approach. The principle, however, remains the same. The growth rates of the factor inputs are calculated and regressed on the growth rate of output. The income shares of the factor inputs are the resulting coefficients and the MFP term is the residual.

The advantage of this approach is that firm level data can be used, allowing for more detailed and specific analysis within narrow sectors or by firm characteristics. Researchers at ONS have produced a number of such pieces of work using business microdata held in the Business Data Linking (BDL) Laboratory, most notably the work done on producing firm level ICT capital stocks and calculating their associated productivity effects. Further detail on the BDL laboratory and microdata is provided in **Chapter 10**.

7.2.1.2 Multi-factor productivity data

The minimum data required for conventional MFP analysis are the following (either at whole economy or sector level):

- a constant price measure of output – preferably GVA if data on intermediate inputs are not available or to be used

- a measure of labour input – preferably adjusted for labour quality

- a measure of labour's income share

- current price total income – this can either be current price GVA or the sum of factor income measures from National Accounts

- a measure of capital input – preferably the flow of services stemming from the capital stock

As part of the ONS productivity strategy ONS has developed the inputs required for MFP analysis. These are a quality-adjusted labour input (QALI) measure and the volume index of capital services (VICS), details of which are provided in **Chapter 5**. Because of the limitations of the QALI data, MFP analysis using these measures as inputs can only be calculated for the whole economy and six broad sectors. These improved measures of the factor inputs mean that MFP growth can be estimated with a good degree of accuracy. The relevant output data and income shares can be found in the National Accounts (constant price GVA and current price income measures).

Compensation for the self-employed is not used for calculating MFP measures because it is 'mixed income', that is income that accrues to both capital and labour. However, it can be derived by either using data from the LFS taking the average hourly wage for employees and multiplying by total self-employed hours for each relevant sector, or by simply applying the split for the employed to self-employed 'mixed income'.

For the results in this chapter the total income measure used is the sum of compensation of employees, gross operating surplus and mixed income rather than current price GVA, which also includes the basic price adjustment for taxes/subsidies. Regarding the income shares, obviously compensation of employees and gross operating surplus provide the shares for the employed sector. For the self-employed we have applied the same split as for the employed to mixed income – we have made the assumption that capital and labour generate the same proportion of income in the self-employed sector as in the employed sector.

The alternative was to use the LFS to impute a wage for the self-employed. However examination of the data suggested such an estimate would mean that virtually all of mixed income would be allocated to labour, meaning zero return to capital. Therefore it seemed preferable to use the same split as for the employed. However, results were produced using both methods and the overall impact is minimal.

Any MFP results produced are obviously going to depend highly on the output data series used. In other words, the less confidence there is in these output data, the more doubt will be cast on the results. As mentioned above, this is particularly relevant to parts of the service sector such as financial intermediation and business services, and also the public sector. As these sectors make up a large part

of the UK economy, this is especially unfortunate. The output measure used for this analysis is a chain volume measure (CVM) of GVA compatible with *Blue Book 2006*. However it has not been subject to National Accounts adjustments for coherence and balancing. Rentals have also been removed from nominal income and constant price output.

Measurement of output in the public sector is improving, however, as a result of the Atkinson Review and the work of the UK Centre for the Measurement of Government Activity (UKCeMGA) at ONS. It should also improve in the financial sector in the near future with the introduction of a new methodology for financial intermediation services indirectly measured (FISIM), due to be introduced. This, in turn, will improve the quality of any MFP results produced.

Finally, this chapter has only discussed using data for the factor inputs, capital and labour, to produce MFP analysis. As mentioned previously, intermediate inputs, such as energy, materials and services, can also be included using the same methodology, except that the GVA output measure would need to be replaced with total output.

7.2.1.3 Multi-factor productivity results

Table 7.4 shows the decomposition of output growth into the contributions of the factor inputs and MFP growth in two forms, using quality-adjusted and unadjusted hours respectively, while **Box 7.5** provides a detailed description of exactly what is contained in each broad sector.

As can be seen below MFP using unadjusted hours is estimated to have grown by 0.8 per cent a year between 1997 and 2005. Looking at individual sectors the strongest growth has occurred in manufacturing (D), while there has also been growth in financial intermediation and business services (JK) and the combined sector of the distributive trades and transport (GHI). MFP growth in the other sectors was negative over the period studied. For construction this was expected and is consistent with other studies over similar periods. The result for LMNOPQ, which is mainly comprised of public services, probably partially reflects the measurement of output in this sector in National Accounts, which is still largely based on measures of inputs. For measures of public sector output based on outcomes that contain adjustments for quality readers should consult work produced by UKCeMGA, some details of which are given in **Chapter 9**.

Table 7.4: Decomposition of output growth, average percentage growth per annum, 1997–2005

SIC Sectors	Output growth	Capital input	Labour input (unadjusted)	MFP growth (unadjusted L)	Labour input (adjusted)	MFP growth (adjusted L)
			Contributions from			
ABCE	-0.4	-0.2	0.0	-0.2	-0.3	0.0
D	0.3	0.3	-2.4	2.3	-1.8	1.8
F	2.2	0.6	2.7	-1.1	2.5	-0.9
GHI	4.2	1.7	1.1	1.4	1.2	1.3
JK	6.1	2.0	2.6	1.6	2.8	1.3
LMNOPQ	1.8	0.8	1.3	-0.3	1.7	-0.8
Whole economy	2.9	1.1	1.0	0.8	1.1	0.7

When the adjustment is made for labour quality MFP growth tends to reduce in most sectors suggesting an improvement in labour composition or skills over the period studied. However this is not the case for all sectors and the reverse is actually true in agriculture, mining and utilities (ABCE) and construction (F), reflecting a decline in the quality of labour in these sectors. Interestingly this means the result for ABCE actually changes from negative to positive when quality-adjusted hours are used.

Table 7.5 overleaf presents a similar analysis on the decomposition of growth in labour productivity.

This table shows that the contribution of labour composition for the whole economy was 0.1 percentage points a year, just 6.3 per cent of labour productivity growth, with capital deepening and MFP making much larger contributions. However labour composition did

make a larger contribution in manufacturing (D), making up 16.3 per cent of growth in labour productivity.

Table 7.6 overleaf shows the growth in labour composition, by sector, from 1997 to 2005.

For the whole economy, labour composition grew on average at 0.1 per cent a year with the highest growth occurring in manufacturing (D) and public and other services (LMNOPQ). However few conclusions can be drawn on the change in labour composition because of the short time period studied. The labour measure is based on hours worked which is a far more cyclical measure than workers or jobs, with firms responding to changing demand conditions by increasing or reducing hours in the short-term rather than hiring or dismissing workers. Therefore if such changes affect different worker types differently there will be a change in labour composition. In general it

---

Box 7.5: Industry descriptions

Industry	Industry Description
ABCE	Agriculture, hunting, forestry, fishing, mining and quarrying, utilities
D	Manufacturing
F	Construction
GHI	Wholesale and retail trade, hotels & restaurants, transport storage and communications.
JK	Financial intermediation, real estate, renting & business activities
LMNOPQ	Public administration & defence, education, health and social work, other social and personal services, and extra-territorial activities.

Table 7.5: Decomposition of labour productivity growth, average percentage growth per annum, 1997–2005

SIC (2003) Sectors	Labour Productivity Growth	Contributions from		
		Capital deepening	Labour composition	MFP growth
ABCE	-0.5	-0.2	-0.3	0.0
D	3.4	1.1	0.6	1.8
F	-0.8	0.3	-0.3	-0.9
GHI	2.7	1.3	0.1	1.3
JK	2.9	1.3	0.2	1.3
LMNOPQ	0.2	0.5	0.4	-0.8
Whole economy	1.6	0.8	0.1	0.7

Table 7.6: Growth in labour composition, per cent per annum, 1997–2005

	1997	1998	1999	2000	2001	2002	2003	2004	2005	Average
ABCE	0.3	-0.8	0.4	-1.0	-0.8	-2.6	2.7	-4.2	-2.7	-1.0
D	0.5	0.3	1.4	1.3	0.7	0.8	0.7	0.3	0.6	0.7
F	2.2	0.2	0.7	-1.3	0.9	-0.6	-3.8	0.4	-1.2	-0.3
GHI	-0.9	0.1	0.5	0.4	0.5	-0.5	0.3	-0.5	0.9	0.1
JK	2.3	0.1	0.1	-0.7	0.1	0.7	-0.2	0.6	-0.2	0.3
LMNOPQ	-0.2	1.3	0.4	0.9	-0.4	0.8	0.3	1.0	0.8	0.5
Whole economy	0.2	0.4	0.4	0.2	-0.1	-0.1	-0.1	0.1	0.3	0.1

would be expected that labour composition will rise during a 'slump' when the less skilled and experienced workers are the first to be laid off, and fall during a 'boom' when less productive workers are drawn back into the labour market because of increased demand. Therefore the seemingly slow growth in labour composition since 1997 may reflect the strength of the UK economy over this period.

As a final piece of analysis, the period studied has been split into two separate parts: pre- and post-2000, the main reason being the difference in capital investment. Pre-2000, firms made larger, possibly unnecessarily large, investments in ICT in attempts to avert the 'millennium bug'. A decomposition of output growth for the two periods is presented in **Table 7.7** and **7.8**.

The results show that the contribution of capital in the latter period was lower, although so was growth in output. In terms of percentages, the contribution of capital to growth in output was 41.9 per cent in 1997 to 2000 compared to 36.5 per cent in 2001 to 2005. Results for the other sectors tell a similar story. The difference is particularly stark in manufacturing where, in the latter period, the contribution of capital was actually zero, although output did decline over the period. The same is true of construction where the contribution of capital fell from 55.4 per cent of output growth to 21.4 per cent between the two periods.

Looking specifically at MFP growth, the latter period shows a significant decline in agriculture, mining and utilities but strong improvement in manufacturing and construction.

Table 7.7: Decomposition of output growth, average per cent per annum, 1997–2000

SIC (2003) Sectors	Output growth	Contributions from				
		Capital input	Labour input (unadjusted)	MFP growth (unadjusted L)	Labour input (adjusted)	MFP growth (adjusted L)
ABCE	1.6	0.1	-0.2	1.8	-0.3	1.8
D	1.4	0.8	-1.2	1.9	-0.6	1.2
F	1.1	0.6	1.7	-1.3	2.1	-1.7
GHI	5.5	2.4	1.5	1.6	1.5	1.6
JK	7.8	2.6	3.2	2.0	3.5	1.7
LMNOPQ	1.4	0.8	0.7	-0.1	1.2	-0.6
Whole economy	3.6	1.5	1.0	1.0	1.3	0.8

Table 7.8: Decomposition of output growth, average per cent per annum, 2001–2005

SIC (2003) Sectors	Output growth	Contributions from				
		Capital input	Labour input (unadjusted)	MFP growth (unadjusted L)	Labour input (adjusted)	MFP growth (adjusted L)
ABCE	-2.0	-0.3	0.2	-1.9	-0.3	-1.4
D	-0.6	0.0	-3.3	2.7	-2.8	2.2
F	3.2	0.7	3.5	-1.0	2.8	-0.3
GHI	3.2	1.2	0.8	1.2	0.9	1.1
JK	4.8	1.5	2.1	1.2	2.2	1.0
LMNOPQ	2.1	0.9	1.8	-0.5	2.2	-0.9
Whole economy	2.3	0.9	0.9	0.6	0.9	0.6

Tables **Tables 7.9** and **7.10** overleaf decompose labour productivity growth for each period.

The results show that the decline in labour productivity growth between the two periods is mainly owing to a fall in labour composition, again reflecting the view that with employment at historically high levels, less productive workers are being drawn into the workforce because of favourable demand conditions, although this does vary between sectors. The contributions of physical capital deepening and MFP growth are broadly similar between the two periods, although again there is some variation in individual industries.

7.3 Looking forward

The short time period studied is not ideal for analysis of this sort because growth of MFP is volatile in the short run and the estimates will improve as the series is lengthened. Unfortunately it is not possible to extend the series further back because of breaks in the qualification variable on which QALI is partially based. However, as production of this series is continued, there will be more scope for analysis.

In terms of the results, the UK is still not experiencing a surge in productivity growth possibly driven by increased investment in ICT as seen in other countries, most notably the US. This suggests that ICT in the UK may not be employed as effectively, possibly as a result of the relatively low skill base of the UK labour force or less effective organisational structure and management. Therefore policy may be needed to assist the five drivers of productivity, particularly skills and investment.

Table 7.9: Decomposition of labour productivity growth, average per cent per annum, 1997–2000

SIC (2003) Sectors	Contributions from			
	Labour Productivity Growth	Capital deepening	Labour composition	MFP growth
ABCE	2.2	0.4	-0.1	1.8
D	3.1	1.2	0.7	1.2
F	-0.9	0.4	0.4	-1.6
GHI	3.4	1.8	0.0	1.6
JK	3.8	1.7	0.3	1.7
LMNOPQ	0.5	0.6	0.5	-0.6
Whole economy	2.1	1.1	0.2	0.8

Table 7.10: Decomposition of labour productivity growth, average per cent per annum, 2001–2005

SIC (2003) Sectors	Contributions from			
	Labour Productivity Growth	Capital deepening	Labour composition	MFP growth
ABCE	-2.6	-0.8	-0.4	-1.4
D	3.6	1.0	0.5	2.2
F	-0.7	0.3	-0.8	-0.3
GHI	2.2	1.0	0.1	1.1
JK	2.2	1.0	0.2	1.0
LMNOPQ	-0.1	0.5	0.4	-0.9
Whole economy	1.2	0.6	0.0	0.6

7.4   References

Bhagwati J, Panagariya A and Srinivasan T N (2004) 'The muddles over outsourcing', *Journal of Economic Perspectives* 18 No. 4, pp 93–114, available at: www.columbia.edu/~jb38/Muddles%20Over%20Outsourcing.pdf

Criscuolo C (2006) *Does offshoring matter for productivity?*, London School of Economics: London.

Criscuolo, C and Leaver M (2005) *Offshore Outsourcing and Productivity*. Paper presented at the OECD and ONS workshop, 'Globalisation of Production: Impacts on Employment, Productivity and Economic Growth', Paris, 15–16 November 2005.

HM Treasury (2005) 2005 *Pre-Budget Report*, TSO: London, available at: www.hm-treasury.gov.uk/pre_budget_report/prebud_pbr05/report/prebud_pbr05_repindex.cfm

HM Treasury (2005) *Evidence on the UK economic cycle*, TSO: London, available at: www.hm-treasury.gov.uk./media/2E6/A5/economic_cycles190705.pdf

HM Treasury (2006) *Trend Growth: New evidence and Prospects*, TSO: London, available at: www.hm-treasury.gov.uk/pre_budget_report/prebud_pbr06/assoc_docs/prebud_pbr06_adtrendgrowth.cfm

Lau E (2002): 'Skills and Productivity: Developing New Measures'. Article presented at the Royal Economic Society Annual Conference, March 2002, available at: www.statistics.gov.uk/events/new_economy_measurement/downloads/NEMW(03)_EL_Skills_and_Productivity.pdf

Lau E and Vaze P (2002) *Accounting growth: capital, skills and output*, Office for National Statistics: London, available at: www.statistics.gov.uk/CCI/Nscl.asp?ID=8311

Solow R (1957) 'Technical change and the Aggregate Production Function', *Review of Economics and Statistics* 39, pp 312–320.

Herbert R and Pike R (2005), 'Market Sector Gross Value Added – A new experimental National Accounts aggregate', *Economic Trends* 623, pp 15–19, available at: www.statistics.gov.uk/cci/article.asp?ID=1171

Liesner T (1989) *One Hundred Years of Economic Statistics*, The Economist Publications Ltd: London.

Lindsay C (2003) 'A century of labour market change: 1900 to 2000', *Labour Market Trends* 111 (3), pp 133–44, available at: www.statistics.gov.uk/cci/article.asp?ID=653

Office for National Statistics (2000) '100 Years of GDP 1900–1999', in *The UK National Accounts (Blue Book)* 2000, TSO: London, pp 32–34.

Chapter 8

Productivity: Market Sector, Services and Industries

The increasing use of productivity growth assessments for monetary and fiscal policy has led to demands for more information on the competitive sectors of the economy. In 2005, ONS developed experimental measures of market sector output, and from March 2007, began publishing experimental estimates of market sector productivity.

The growing importance of the service sector across the last 30 years has also been a wide-reaching economic development. The complexities in measuring a service dominated economy rather than a manufacturing one have proved challenging. Therefore identifying the main issues and their efforts has been a central concern.

The first section in this chapter details these market sector measures and provides results for recent years. It also comments on how market sector and public services fit together. The chapter continues by considering the measurement of the service sector, in particular, it focuses on those issues affecting measurement of output.

The chapter concludes with a section on productivity by industry, showing details of what is available and explaining important issues for users of these data.

Measuring Productivity of Subsections of the Economy

Productivity measures in the UK are produced for different areas of the economy such as the market sector but also for manufacturing and services (see **Chapter 4** for more details of how these are defined). These measures are distinct from each other (although the market sector overlaps both manufacturing and services), reflecting different characteristics associated with the industries they contain. The market sector should be treated differently to the non-market sector. Details of productivity measures for parts of the latter – specifically public services – are given in **Chapter 9**.

When analysing trends within the economy it is useful to look at these more detailed figures.

8.1   Market sector gross value added productivity measures

Measurement of the market sector is becoming increasingly important to policy makers. In response to user demand, ONS began publication of two experimental market sector productivity measures in March 2007, namely market sector gross value added (GVA) per worker and market sector GVA per hour (Marks 2007). Both series utilise the experimental market sector GVA series and employment data to calculate labour productivity measures for the market sector.

In recent years the Bank of England (BoE) has placed an increased emphasis on market sector data. In particular they argue that, as the consumer prices index (CPI) and other price indicators are based almost exclusively on prices from the private sector, the level of CPI inflation will reflect the balance of demand and supply pressures in the market sector of the economy. As a result, the BoE now analyse movements in market sector output and productivity in their *Inflation Report.*

In the 2005 *Budget Report*, HM Treasury (HMT) discussed the use of market sector productivity to estimate the output gap and trend output.

> The output gap should measure fluctuations in activity arising from the business cycle, and as such it should be determined by factors affecting the behaviour of only the private or market sector of the economy.

Market sector productivity figures are also helpful in making international comparisons of productivity, especially with the United States as it does not publish a whole economy measure of productivity. Instead, the US publishes an output per hour series for the business and non-farm business sectors. A market sector output per hour productivity measure for the UK enables more meaningful productivity comparisons to be made between the two countries.

8.1.1   Market sector gross value added per worker

Market sector GVA per worker is a quarterly series calculated using the experimental market sector GVA series and an index of market sector workers, where SA denotes a seasonally adjusted estimate. The index of market sector workers uses data from the Labour Force Survey (LFS) and Public Sector Employment (PSE) figures.

$$\text{SA Market sector GVA per worker} = \frac{\text{SA market sector GVA}}{\text{SA Index of market sector workers}}$$

The index of market sector workers is defined as follows:

$$\text{Market sector workers} = \text{LFS workers - public sector workers} + \text{public corporation workers}$$

Market sector GVA per worker growth rates can be calculated in the form of quarter on quarter and quarter on the same quarter a year earlier. In practice, the quarterly growth rate is volatile; this is partly because of lags between output and employment. These lags exist as it takes time for employers to change their employment levels in response to changes in output. In particular, employers would need to determine whether a change in output is permanent or temporary before making employment decisions. The annual rate is probably a better guide to movements in market sector productivity, although this is still affected by cyclical lags. **Figure 8.1** shows, for market sector GVA per worker, the quarter on quarter, and quarter on the same quarter a year earlier growth rates. As would be expected movements in the growth rates of market sector GVA per worker correspond with events in the UK economy as a whole.

Figure 8.1: Market sector GVA per worker

Percentage change

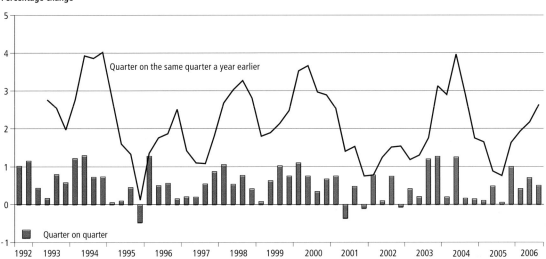

Figure 8.2: Comparing whole economy and market sector productivity per worker

Percentage change, quarter on the same quarter a year earlier

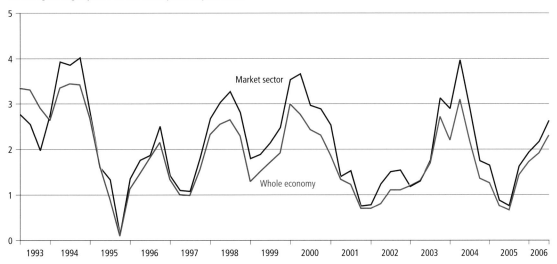

The publication of market sector productivity measures allows the comparison of market sector and whole economy productivity. As can be seen in **Figure 8.2**, between Q2 and Q4 1993 the recession had a greater impact on market sector productivity than whole economy productivity. From Q1 1994 onwards the market sector growth rates are at least as high as those for the whole economy; during some periods, for example Q1 1998 to Q2 2001, the growth rate for the market sector is considerably higher.

8.1.2 Market sector GVA per hour

The market sector GVA per hour series is a ratio of market sector output to the total hours worked in the market sector. As with the per worker series, the output of the market sector uses the market sector GVA series. The total actual weekly hours worked in the market sector series is derived using several data sources: LFS microdata, public sector employment data and headline LFS data. **Figure 8.3** overleaf illustrates the construction of the market sector GVA per hour series.

Figure 8.3: Construction of market sector (MS) GVA per hour

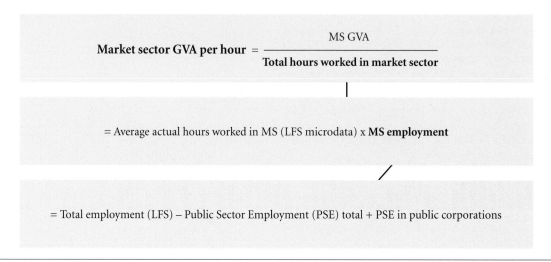

Figure 8.4: Market sector GVA per hour

Pecentage change

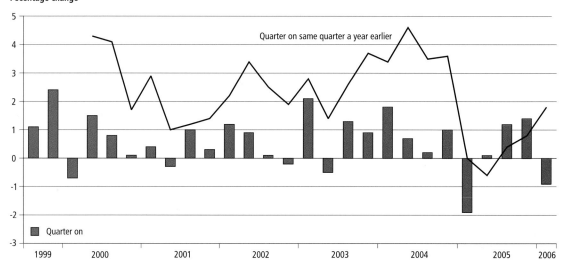

Figure 8.4 shows the market sector GVA per hour series in the form of quarter on quarter, and quarter on the same quarter a year earlier growth rates. It follows a similar pattern to that of market sector GVA per worker (**Figure 8.1**), but is more volatile. The extra volatility is because hours worked can change more rapidly in response to a change in economic conditions (by increasing or decreasing the hours of overtime worked), whereas extra labour is not employed if the conditions are not expected to continue.

In conclusion, the market sector productivity measures illustrated in this section broadly follow the economic cycle. In general, the growth rate for market sector productivity per worker tends to be higher than the rate of growth for the whole economy. However, both the market sector and whole economy measures follow the same general trends. This is unsurprising as the market sector makes up a significant proportion of the whole economy measure.

Box 8.1: Dividing Whole Economy into Market and Non-Market Sector

It is obviously possible to construct an implied measure for the non-market sector using the counterparts to market sector output and employment. However, this does not take into account the recent approach agreed when producing productivity measures for the public services.

Work on improving the measurement of government output and productivity is being undertaken by the UK Centre for the Measurement of Government Activity (UKCeMGA) within ONS, in response to the Atkinson Review. This is detailed further in **Chapter 9**. ONS currently measures about two-thirds of government output by directly estimating the change in the volume of service provided. For instance, health output is partly measured by counting the number of treatments carried out by the NHS, and education output partly by counting the number of pupils who attend school.

The examination of how to incorporate quality change into existing output measures is one of UKCeMGA's key priorities. Education is the only government function for which output in the National Accounts is measured including quality change. ONS's October 2005 Public Service Productivity: Education article demonstrated, however, that the existing approach needed updating. ONS's October 2004 Public Service Productivity: health article included estimates of NHS output which did not take account of quality change, but the health article was able to draw on quality measures designed by the University of York, the National Institute of Economic and Social Research and the Department of Health.

The remaining one-third of government output is assumed to grow at the same rate as the real value of the inputs used to produce it. This is used mainly for services such as defence, which are consumed collectively, and for which the benefits are difficult to quantify. In areas where input measures are used the implied assumption is of no change in productivity.

Over time this work will lead to a fuller analysis of government productivity from a bottom-up perspective. Therefore any attempt to measure productivity for the non-market sector by subtracting the market sector from the whole economy will not take into account this improved approach.

ONS has plans to produce market sector productivity and public services productivity as its headline measures in the future. Such a move will occur after these data series have been quality assured. These future plans are noted in **Chapter 13**.

8.2   Service sector productivity

Measuring output and productivity growth in many services is not straightforward. What exactly does a lawyer or an economist produce? How can the rapidly changing pricing schemes of telecommunications providers be compared over time? – Organisation for Economic Co-operation and Development (*OECD*) *Compendium of Productivity Indicators (2006)*

To address these issues raised by OECD, aggregate statistics can be decomposed to examine different aspects of the determinants of productivity. This section is motivated by the need to be able to examine productivity from an industrial perspective.

8.2.1   Data availability

From a statistical perspective, at the time of publication such analysis is severely restricted by the limited availability of disaggregated industrial detail. From an economic perspective, the analyses are based on simple assessments of productivity; fuller analysis requires the use of multi-factor productivity techniques, which are discussed in **Chapter 7**.

The *Productivity First Release* includes headline whole economy measures and aggregate manufacturing data, also disaggregated into 11 industries (such as 'rubber and plastics'). In addition to these, two service sector measures are available as experimental statistics, an aggregate measure and a measure for 'distribution, catering and hotels'. The reasoning behind this limited availability is set out is Daffin, Reed and Vaze (2002). More service sector productivity data will be available in the future (see **Chapter 13**).

8.2.2   Measurement of the service sector

Nonetheless, as is widely understood, UK economic growth now greatly depends on the service sector. This has led to concerns because of long-recognised difficulties with measuring service sector activity. Some of these concerns are relevant to productivity measurement, in particular the historical use of measures of employment as proxies for output, which used to be commonplace for the public sector. The use of such measures is, however, now greatly reduced. Service sector activity is also increasingly based on surveys of turnover deflated by Services Producer Prices Indices (SPPIs) and direct measures of government output. The ONS headline monthly measure of service activity, the Index of Services, became a National Statistic in March 2007.

Nevertheless there are measurement issues which mean that service sector productivity is more difficult than in the manufacturing sector, and it is worth revisiting some of them here.

8.2.3   The definition of a service

The early economists such as Smith (1776) equated service production with unproductive labour. Smith famously describes examples of unproductive labour in services as including 'menial servants…, the Sovereign…, buffoons, musicians and opera singers' (Quoted in Hill, 1999). A second possible definition is to equate service production with 'intangible' goods. This definition, however, is not useful in the face of technical progress. In Smith's time the output of a musician could be regarded as intangible, but with recording technology it can now be preserved, reproduced with property rights assigned to it and sold.

A third definition, suggested by Pavitt (1984), and rather influential in the technology literature, is to describe services as primarily 'supplier-dominated' (see **Box 8.2**). Under this definition, services have little scope for multi-factor productivity growth since improvements in the technology of manufactured goods would be the dominant factor in improving productivity in services.

Box 8.2: The supplier-dominated approach

Consider air transport services. There is no questioning the astonishing rise in the ability of airlines to fly more passengers faster and over longer ranges in the last 75 years. However, under the supplier-dominated view, this should properly be ascribed to productivity growth in the aircraft **manufacturing** industry rather than anything that the air transport service industry has done.

This approach has some taxonomic appeal but is subject to a number of problems which mostly revolve around the pre-supposition that services are incapable of intrinsic productivity growth. First, the approach began to be undermined when a number of services arose, such as business services and R&D consultancy (largely because of contracting out by manufacturing firms), that did look like possible candidates for rapid intrinsic technical progress. Second, the perceived use of IT and business organisation and consequent rise in labour and multi-factor productivity in fields such as banking suggests that defining services in terms of their scope for technical progress is unlikely to be helpful. Third, closer examination of the airline industry suggests that not all efficiency is driven by capital equipment such as aircraft: consider the different organisational methods of low cost airlines (ticketless boarding for example).

Another approach is to define services and manufacturing in terms of the fundamental economic activities of production (including distribution) and consumption and think of output as having the dimensions of quantity, space and time. This is a view advanced by Betancourt and Gautschi (2002) and Melvin (2002). Consumers value the quantity of output but also its location in terms of space and time (see **Box 8.3**).

In some cases, of course, consumption and production cannot be separated in time or space: haircuts, medical operations and teaching for example. Therefore Melvin (2002) defines services that overcome the time or space separation between consumers and producers as 'intermediation services'. These include transport, retailing and some financial services. He defines 'contact services' as those that arise when production and consumption cannot be separated, such as education, medical and financial advice.

Box 8.3: The quantity, space and time approach

For example as regards space, consumers of wheat do not want to have to live near a farm and hence the transportation industry has grown up as a result of the willingness to pay for this separation. Similarly as regards time, consumers wish to smooth consumption and producers to borrow money against future projects and so the financial services industry, which holds savers' money safely and screens borrowers, has developed.

This definition helps clarify thinking about the output of the service sector. The key point is simple: in intermediation the output is not the good itself but the bundle of intermediation services offered. Therefore output of a shoe manufacturer is shoes. The output of the shoe transporter who moves the shoes from the manufacturer to the retailer is the bundle of transport services, **not** the shoes themselves. Likewise the output of the shoe retailer who sells the shoes to the final consumers is the bundle of retail services (ambience, convenience etc.), **not** the shoes themselves. Similarly, in contact services, the output of the management consultant or doctor is the advice, not, as is sometimes measured, the number of management consultants or doctors, or the number of clients.

In both these cases, as Hill (1976 and 1999) argues, services are a change in the condition of a person or good carried out by the service provider with the agreement of the consumer of the service. For this reason, the outputs produced are not separate entities that exist independently of the producers or consumers. Service outputs must impinge in some way on the condition or status of the consuming units and are not separable from them. A repair, a haircut or advice cannot be stored and is not separable from the consumer of the repair or the haircut. Therefore no ownership rights can be established over it and it cannot be traded independently of production or consumption the way that a good can be. The production of neither exists independently of the consumption.

In many cases therefore, an important aspect of a service is the 'jointness' of production and consumption – that goods can be produced meaningfully without consumers (think of a firm producing a car) whereas services require jointness (a haircut, or repairing a car). Note that this depends somewhat on the definition of the transaction: while many service goods are jointly consumed and produced, the intermediation role of services is often to enable separation of at least some aspects of production, distribution and consumption over time (see **Box 8.4**).

What are the implications for the measurement of output? The first step is measuring the value of a service. Measuring the value of a bundle of services, like advice, retailing services or transport, would appear to be to

intangible to measure. However, if the basis of a service is the change in condition of a consuming unit then consumers should be willing to pay for this. Therefore the reason that the retail price of an item is above its wholesale price presumably reflects the value that the consumer places on obtaining the good in an environment that provides assurance of supply, ambiance and is more convenient than going to the factory door. In a well functioning market, then, the value of such an item should reflect the value consumers place on that service.

This in turn suggests a way to measure the value of a service: the value of the bundle of services provided by a shoe retailer is revealed not by the sales of the shoes, but the gap between the sales to final consumers of the shoes and the costs of buying the shoes in from the manufacturer. Therefore a general approach in measuring the value of a service, given that many services are intermediation activities, is to measure the margin involved in providing that service: the value of the final sales of the goods less the cost of buying them in. This has an obvious resonance in retailing (in transport services the margin is just the charge for transporting since no ownership changes hands).

8.2.3.1 Official measurement techniques

The most developed production systems for the measurement of service sector activity are those aimed at estimation of service sector output. These systems provide an estimate of the contribution of the service sector to GDP each quarter as well as a monthly indicator of growth. The measurement systems have a lot in common with those for measuring manufacturing output. The basic approach assumes that, in the short period, changes in deflated sales or turnover are a good indicator of changes in real value added. Timely measures of GDP from the output/production perspective are therefore based on estimates of turnover. The basic information for this approach is collected through monthly, quarterly and annual industrial surveys of turnover and prices for industry.

Box 8.4: Joint services

For example, consider a restaurant meal (which would seem to be the archetypal example of jointness), but one for which the customer makes a reservation a day in advance. This separates at least some aspects of distribution from consumption and production. While one can reserve the restaurant meal in advance, the production of the meal still requires the joint presence of the restaurateur (producer) and the consumer. Likewise making the reservation also requires the joint presence of the producer and consumer but this is a different good to serving the meal. It is a good that producers and consumers are quite willing to transact (it reduces uncertainty on both sides) but it means that restaurants are offering two goods, namely the meal and the reservation for the meal (and, indeed, some restaurants only offer one service: the meal).

One of the interesting implications of jointness is that service providers can get consumers to do some of the work in providing a service. A high-street travel agent and internet travel agent both provide travel services, but in the latter case the consumer does much of the work.

Many aspects of service sector activity are measured by direct measures of output and some examples are given below:

■ rail and air transport use passenger per kilometre and freight tonnes per kilometre

■ mail communications use letters delivered, parcels delivered and other postal services.

■ pension funding uses the number of pension policies and members, in effect broken down by type of policy

■ armed forces is based on total numbers of armed forces

While there is a good deal of common ground in the approach to the measurement of both the manufacturing and service sectors, there are significant differences in terms of complexity. Although the manufacturing sector produces a wide range of products, measurement is aided by the tangibility of outputs. For nearly all industries, outputs could, if desired, be relatively straightforwardly counted or measured, because metaphorically they can be seen coming off production lines. With service sector outputs, matters are not so straightforward (see Tily, (2006) for more details).

In general terms, the diversity of activity within services is the key challenge. Units of output cannot be so easily defined and are not common from service to service or even within a specific service. Consider, for example, the diversity of services provided by estate agents, Internet service providers and life assurance companies. Moreover, and perhaps this is the critical problem, many services, in particular business-to-business services, tend to be tailored to each client's needs. This gives them a uniqueness that makes them difficult to categorise as output units and consequently difficult to price. Many services also have generally low set-up costs (that is, barriers to market entry are very low), are able to change rapidly (no production lines to dismantle), product innovation is continuous and can generally be very difficult to keep track of over time. The services where outputs can be tightly defined and turnover and prices relatively simply measured, for example haircuts or cinema tickets, are perhaps rarer.

Box 8.5: Finance

The importance of the finance sector to the UK economy has grown alongside the increased importance of the service sector. There are two main categories:

Financial intermediation – including investment and high street or retail banks and building societies. Here output measures are based on a number of proxy indicators such as employment, loans granted or deposits held. Where relevant, deflation tends to be based on consumer price indices.

Insurance and pension funds – non-life insurance indicators are based on measures of premiums minus claims (supplied by the Association of British Insurers). Life assurance is based on consumer expenditure on these products and prices are adjusted with consumers' expenditure deflators. The financial services adjustment (FSA) reflects the special treatment of the earnings banks make from interest earned on loans net of interest paid on deposits (known as financial intermediation services indirectly measured or FISIM). EU legislation demands that countries make an estimate of these earnings (which are included in financial intermediation), but all such earnings are assumed to be intermediate consumption by other businesses. The FSA is introduced to reflect this intermediate consumption and basically offsets the growth in financial intermediation. Countries are now obliged to assess the amount of FISIM that constitutes final demand and to allocate it to the relevant sectors (mainly the household sector) and, in addition, to allocate the intermediate demand to individual industries.

The UK government is working with the BoE to derive the necessary figures. Early provisional estimates of the impact of the changed treatment on current price figures were sent to the European Commission on 31 March 2006. These figures were included in the routine release for the Government Debt and Deficit under the Maastricht Treaty on the same day. In 2007 ONS will produce an assessment of the volume impact, see Tily and Jenkinson (2006) for further information on FISIM.

There are then a number of specific services for which there are specific methodological challenges:

■ the retail sector where the contribution to GDP is the margin between revenues and costs and removal of price effects is not straightforward

■ the services of the financial sector present a great challenge for both cash and volume measures, with distinct issues for the measurement of insurance and pensions, as well as complexities related to the earnings banks make through lending activities (see **Box 8.5**)

- government output has traditionally been regarded as difficult to measure in volume terms. However, the UK has made advances in a coherent approach to output measurement, with recent improvements under the impetus of the Atkinson Review and UKCeMGA that was established to take forward the recommendations of the review (see **Section 9.1.4**)

- for real estate the largest measure is expenditure on rents including an imputed value for owner-occupiers (to ensure compatibility with other countries where the size of the rental sector differs)

- other difficult areas are research and development, artistic originals, and rental and general real estate activities

In terms of productivity measurement, a key outstanding issue is the use of productivity assumptions in deflators. For certain industries, particularly business services, deflation is based on the average earnings index with an adjustment for productivity. These techniques tend to be used where services are tailored to individual clients, and the best that can be done is to measure input prices, namely wages. But growth in wages should reflect both changes in productivity and changes in prices, hence the need for an adjustment. It is of note that this deflation technique is used fairly extensively in the industries most closely associated with the high growth in the present data. **Appendix Table 8A** at the end of this chapter sets out a comprehensive categorisation of the measurement of each aspect of service sector activity by Standard Industrial Classification (SIC (2003)) division.

A related problem is quality adjustment of volume measures, as discussed in **Chapter 6**. At present adjustment is not as prevalent as it, perhaps, should be.

The above issues all impact on the measurement of output in the short term. In the longer term GDP data are aligned with fuller annual survey data, through an Input-Output Supply and Use framework (see **Chapter 3**).

The output data described above are not, however, fully incorporated into this framework, and instead are brought into line with benchmarked estimates through a number of adjustments to industry level aggregates. While the technique for making these adjustments has recently been improved (see Marks, 2006), the process is still not ideal and the volume measures particularly by industry do not fully reflect all the data available. Furthermore the measures remain underpinned by the use of deflated

output/turnover as a proxy for value added. Strictly, a more complete method should be based on value added, deflating output and intermediate consumption separately. Techniques will, however, be optimised with the introduction of statistical modernisation.

8.3 Productivity by industry

While the *ONS Productivity First Release* concentrates primarily on whole economy, manufacturing and service sector figures, some industry data are also available.

8.3.1 User requirements

The productivity measures produced by ONS are determined by the availability and quality of data, and by international guidelines and recommendations. A key use of productivity estimates is by HMT as part of their derivation of estimates of trend growth at the macro level. Department of Trade & Industry (DTI) also has interests in productivity estimates at the detailed micro industry level. For information about other users, please see **Chapter 2**.

HMT's methodology for estimating this productivity is set out in table B2 in the Budget document and is explained further in HMT's 2002 paper *Trend Growth: Recent Developments and Prospects*. The technique is summarised in **Box 7.2**.

As part of a wider study into business services, the DTI has recently published estimates of productivity at the detailed industry level for business services (see DTI, 2007). A discussion of this approachand these estimates is given in **Box 8.6**.

8.3.2 ONS industry level productivity

As noted earlier, the ONS currently publishes productivity indices disaggregated by industry according to the SIC (2003) classification, for the production industries (SIC (2003) sections: C – E) and an experimental series for services (G – P). A productivity index for manufacturing (Section D) is also published together with disaggregations for manufacturing into 11 industry categories. Currently, the only disaggregation for services is an experimental series for Distribution, Hotels and Catering (G – H).

While output and input data are available for more detailed industry categories, quality assessments of input and output estimates and their deflators limit the detail published in National Statistics productivity releases to the current scope. A further quality issue when considering detailed disaggregation is that within a particular SIC

(2003) grouping, the size of component industries vary in terms of output and employment; hence the quality of productivity estimates would vary significantly for different SIC (2003) codes at a common detailed 2, 3 or 4 digit level.

8.3.3   Using ONS sources

An estimate of productivity at a detailed industry level could be made using available GVA output data and corresponding jobs data, giving output per job, although there are quality concerns about series at detailed levels. At the whole economy level, the jobs series used for productivity measurement is scaled to the LFS but this is not recommended beyond a broad production and services industry split, as this scaling is considered inaccurate if applied below an aggregate level. This is because industry classification in the LFS is self-defined and known to be of lower quality than from Inter-Departmental Business Register (IDBR) based WFJ data (see **Chapter 5** for more details). For the same reason, it is considered better to disaggregate using output per job rather than output per hour, since hours worked are also sourced from the LFS.

Experimental productivity levels and growth can be estimated at detailed 2 digit SIC (2003) industry levels within manufacturing, other production and the services industries using the constant price GVA output indices and employee jobs, although it is known that some of the results at 2 digit level will not be of sufficient quality. This, however, has little meaning for non-market industries within sections L–M and it is recommended that such estimates are limited to the market sector. At a more detailed 3 or 4 digit SIC (2003) level, productivity can be estimated from available ABI/2 GVA data and ABI/1 employment data, although these will be subject to more volatility and uncertainty.

All of the estimates discussed in this section need to be considered in the context of uncertainties in data quality because of small sample sizes and the suspect reliability of input and output measures and their deflators. Even with these limitations, however, the estimates give a useful insight into the productivity levels and growth for detailed industries defined at the 2 and 3 digit SIC 2003.

In view of the quality concerns for the detailed input and output measures, it is recommended that, in any future work that develops the available range of productivity statistics, only annual rather than quarterly estimates of productivity are derived for lower industry levels.

Box 8.6: Industry productivity measures produced by the Department of Trade & Industry using ONS data

Output per job can be estimated for most 2 digit SIC 2003 divisions using available constant price GVA output indices and employee jobs data, as shown in **Figure 8A** (see DTI, 2007), although not all estimates at a 2 digit level are of sufficient quality. The 2003 constant price indices have been converted to constant price values using the published current prices in the National Accounts 2003 Input-Output and Supply and Use tables. Constant price output indices are available for all 2 digit SIC (2003) divisions from 1986, with data being available prior to this in manufacturing and for some service industries. Corresponding employee jobs data are available from 1978.

Comparing productivity levels has limitations since individual 2 digit SIC (2003) industries may not be homogeneous in terms of skills and labour intensive activities. For instance, of the two industries shown in **Figure 8A**, SIC 72 is a knowledge-based industry and is more homogeneous than SIC (74) which has a mixture of knowledge-based industries such as legal and accountancy services and labour intensive industries such as security and industrial cleaning.

Figure 8A also gives a comparison of productivity estimates for SIC (72) and (74) showing the effect of including self-employment, which can be estimated from the LFS from 1992. Including self-employment decreases the level of the productivity estimates but has little effect on their growth.

Setting aside quality concerns, estimating productivity at a more detailed 3 digit group or 4 digit class SIC (2003) level (see **Box 5.2** for more details of SIC (2003)) could be undertaken using ABI/2 data for GVA and ABI/1 data for employees (although this excludes the self-employed). These ABI productivity estimates are shown in **Figure 8A** and show more volatility, but over a longer time-scale they and the two NA series show reasonably consistent growth. Changes between the three estimates do not affect the ranking of the productivity

levels for the two SIC (2003) industries.

There may, however, be considerable variability in both the productivity levels and growth for different detailed industries within SIC (74). **Figure 8B** shows ABI based productivity estimates for each detailed 3 digit SIC (2003) group within SIC (74) Other Business Activities. Some of the industries' volatility between years may be partly because of sampling variability. Because of these quality uncertainties a linear trend-line has been shown and this provides an aid in visualising the estimated growth over time.

If quality concerns are set aside, the levels and growth shown in **Figure 8B** can be used to estimate rankings over time. It is recommended that growth between

individual years is not used as key estimators owing to uncertainties and data volatility at this level in some instances. Estimates from trend-lines will depend on the choice of curve fitted but probably distil more information of value than would be gained directly from the actual raw data. For example, the estimate for 74.4 in 1998 is considerably lower than for subsequent years and the trend-line helps to smooth out this variability. As expected, productivity levels are lowest for the three labour intensive industries – 74.5, 74.6 and 74.7. Miscellaneous business activities 74.8 is not a homogeneous group and, within it, are 7 further sub-divisions defined by separate 4 digit SIC (2003) codes, which show even greater volatility and productivity estimates at this level of detail are likely to be correspondingly less meaningful.

Figure 8A: Comparison of Productivity estimates, SIC (72) and (74)

GVA per job £ thousand

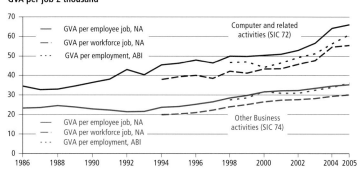

Source: GVA constant price output indices, 2003 prices, Workforce jobs series and ABI data, ONS

Figure 8B: Productivity Estimates for detailed Industries (74) Other Business Activities (74.1 – 74.4)

GVA per employment per thousand

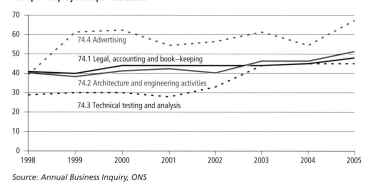

Source: Annual Business Inquiry, ONS

8.4   References

Betancourt R and Gautschi D (1993) The Outputs of Retail Activities: Concepts, Measurement and Evidence From U.S. Census Data, *Review of Economics and Statistics* 75 (2), pp 294–301.

Betancourt R and Gautschi D (2001) *Product Innovation in Services: A Framework for Analysis*, University of Maryland: College Park, available at: www.bsos.umd.edu/econ/betancourt/distribution/scvrjai.s01.pdf

Crespi G, Criscuolo C, Haskel J and Hawkes D (2006) Measuring and Understanding Productivity in UK Market Services, Oxford *Review of Economic Policy, Oxford University Press*, 22(4) Winter, pp 560–572.

Daffin C, Reed G and Vaze P (2002) Labour productivity measures for the non-production industries, *Economic Trends* 579, pp 41–56, available at: www.statistics.gov.uk/cci/article.asp?id=144

Department of Trade & Industry (2007) *Business Services and Globalisation*, DTI Economics paper No. 19, available at: www.dti.gov.uk/files/file37006.pdf

Griffith R and Harmgart H (2005) *Retail Productivity*, IFS Working Paper No. WPo0/07, Institute for Fiscal Studies: London.

Haskel J and Sadun R (2007) Regulation and UK Retailing Productivity: Evidence from Microdata, to be published in 2007.

Hill T (1976) *On goods and services, The Review of Income and Wealth*, pp 315–338, Blackwell Publishing: Oxford.

Hill T (1999) Tangibles, Intangibles and Services: A New Taxonomy for the Classification of Output, *Canadian Journal of Economics* 32 (2), Special Issue on Service Sector Productivity and the Productivity Paradox (April 1999), pp 426–446, available at www.csls.ca/journals/sisspp.asp

HM Treasury (2002) *Trend Growth: Recent Developments and Prospects*, TSO: London, available at: www.hm-treasury.gov.uk/media/D6678/ACF521.pdf

HM Treasury (2005) *2005 Budget Report*, TSO: London, available at: www.hm-treasury.gov.uk/budget/budget_05/bud_bud05_index.cfm

Marks C (2006) Analysis of revisions to the early estimates of Gross Domestic Product (GDP) Presenting a new approach to monitoring revisions to UK economic growth, *Economic Trends* 632, pp 25–31 available at: www.statistics.gov.uk/cci/article.asp?ID=1604

Marks C (2007) Market Sector GVA productivity measures, *Economic and Labour Market Review*, 1 (3), pp 47–53 available at: www.statistics.gov.uk/cci/article.asp?id=1742

McGuickan R.H, Spiegelman M, and van Ark B (2005) The Retail Revolution. Can Europe Match U.S. Productivity Performance? Perspectives on a Global Economy, Reseach Report R-1358-05-RR, The Conference Board: New York.

Melvin, J (1990) Time and Space in Economic Analysis, *Canadian Journal of Economics* 23 (November), pp 725–747.

Pavitt K (1984) 'Sectoral Patterns of Technical Change: Towards a Taxonomy and a Theory', *Research Policy* 13, pp 343–373.

Sadun, R., (2006) *Does Planning Regulation Distort Firm Reallocation?*, London School of Economics: London.

Smith A (1776) *The Wealth of Nations, Books I-III*, with an Introduction by A Skinner (1969) Penguin Books: London.

Tily G and Jenkinson G (2006) *Recording payments for banking services in the UK National Accounts: A progress report*, Office for National Statistics: London, available at: www.statistics.gov.uk/articles/nojournal/FISIM_progress_report.pdf

Triplett JE and Bosworth B (2004) *Productivity in the U.S. Services Sector: New Sources of Economic Growth*, Brookings: Washington.

UK Centre for the Measurement of Government Activity (2006) 'Public Service Productivity: Education', *Economic Trends* 626 (January), pp 13–47, available at: www.statistics.gov.uk/cci/article.asp?ID=1345

Appendix Table 8A: Measurement of Service Sector Activity by SIC (2003)

	Division	% of GVA	% of division containing MIDSS	% of division containing direct volume and other	% deflated by SPPIs
	Distribution, hotels and catering; repairs				
50	Motor trades	2.1	100	0	8
51	Wholesale	4.4	100	0	0
52	Retail	5.7	0	100	0
55	Hotels and restaurants	3.1	99	1	35
	Transport storage and communication				
60	Land transport	2.2	77	23	57
61	Water transport	0.3	0	100	57
62	Air transport	0.6	0	100	0
63	Supporting and auxiliary transport activities	1.8	82	18	45
64	Post and telecommunications	3.0	81	19	81
	Business services and finance				
65	Financial intermediation	5.2	0	100	0
6x	Financial services adjustment	-4.6	0	100	0
66	Insurance and pension funding	1.7	0	100	0
67	Activities auxiliary to financial intermediation	1.1	0	100	0

other deflators used in division	Direct volume measures and other
Retail prices indices (RPI)	
Producer prices indices (PPI), Import Price Index (IPI)	
RPI	Volume of retail sales (smuggling – interpolated from annual estimates of deflated Gross value added based on HMRC data)
RPI	(Smuggling – interpolated from annual estimates of deflated Gross value added based on HMRC data)
RPI	Number of passengers travelling and amount of freight transported
Household expenditure (HE) deflators	Household expenditure on taxis
RPI	International passenger revenue, number of road goods vehicles travelling to mainland Europe, tanker and dry cargo receipts, interpolated from annual series for non-seasgoing waterway traffic, interpolated from annual series for interport coastal and one-port shipping
No deflation (volume series)	Index of airline services
RPI,	Index of airport services
DTI Labour & Supervision in Civil Engineering Index.	
RPI	Number of letters, parcels and services
RPI excluding mortgage interest payments and indirect taxes (RPIY)	Deflated bank fees, commission income, loans, deposits, National Savings and Investments indices
Average Earnings Index (productivity adjustment)	
US$ middle closing spot rate at end period.	
Index derived from 'Money Management' magazine's UK unit trusts performance indicator.	Total funds held in unit trusts and investment trust
RPIY	UK banks deflated outstanding loans, deposits, credit company loans, total outstanding interest in National Savings
US$ middle closing spot rate at end period.	
Index derived from 'Money Management' magazine's UK unit trusts performance indicator.	Total funds held in unit trusts and total funds held in investment trusts
	Number of life insurance polices/members, number of pension policies/members, and exposure years for UK motor insurance
GDP (E) implied deflator	Provisions adjusted for claims
Some volume data, some deflated at source, FTSE All Shares Actuaries Index, GDP (E) implied deflator	British government securities, stock exchange transactions, derivatives transactions, total unit trust fund, total investment trust fund, total financial assets, number of life insurance polices/members, number of pension policies/members, exposure years for UK motor insurance and provisions adjusted for claims

Appendix Table 8A: Measurement of Service Sector Activity by SIC 2003

	Division	% of GVA	% of division containing MIDSS	% of division containing direct volume and other	% deflated by SPPIs
70	Real estate activities	10.4	0	100	21
71	Renting of machinery and equipment	1.1	68	32	22
72	Computer and related activities	2.9	100	0	0
73	Research and development	0.4	100	0	0
74	Other business activities	9.6	99	1	27
Government and other services					
75	Public administration and defence	5.2	0	100	0
79	Letting of own dwellings	7.9	0	100	0
80	Education	5.9	9	91	9
85	Health and social work	7.2	0	100	0
90	Sewage and refuse disposal	0.7	84	16	84
91	Membership organisations	0.6	0	100	0
92	Recreational, cultural and sporting activities	2.9	27	73	0
93	Other service activities	0.6	100	0	12
95	Private households with employed persons	0.5	0	100	0

MIDSS – Monthly Inquiry into Distributive and Service Sectors.

RPIX – RPI Excluding Mortgage Interest Payments.

RPIY – RPI Excluding Mortgage Interest Payments and Direct Taxes.

SPPI – Services Producer Price Index (formally the Corporate Services Price Index - CSPI).

other deflators used in division	Direct volume measures and other
Some deflated at source, RPI	Interpolated from no. of property transactions
Investment Property Databank Rental Value Index.	IPD net income received
Some deflated at source, PPIs,	Household expenditure on self-drive car hire
HE deflator.	
Average earnings index (AEI) adjusted for changes in productivity.	
RPIY	
AEI adjusted for changes in productivity.	
RPIY	
AEI adjusted for changes in productivity.	Employees in central offices
RPIY	
Grade drift deflator	No. of civil servants, no of staff employed, total strength of armed forces, number of police and civilians employed, index of output for fire service, justice services and social security
Deflated at source	Household expenditure on rent, imputed rent of owner occupied dwellings
Output per head productivity adjustment.	Index of output, private sector employees, private school pupil numbers.
RPI,	
Output per head productivity adjustment.	Index of government health services, private sector employees, employees in social work activities index of output for probation, index of output for Local Authority Personal Social Services
Grade drift deflator	LA employees in sewage and refuse disposal
Output per head productivity adjustment.	TU employees, employees in membership organisations
Some deflated at source, RPI, RPIY	LA employees in recreation, culture and sporting activities, household expenditure on betting, gambling and on national lottery
Average Earnings Index.	
HE deflator.	
Grade drift deflator	
RPI	
Deflated at source	Household expenditure on domestic service

Chapter 9

Public Service Productivity

Public service output covers both central and local government output, and in most developed economies accounts for a significant share of total GDP. In the UK, the public sector is just over a fifth of total GDP in expenditure terms. An accurate and realistic representation of the contribution made by the public sector to overall GDP and productivity is therefore very important, simply because of its size.

A reinforcing reason for better measurement of public service output, inputs and productivity is public accountability. Public expenditure is financed largely by taxation and taxpayers have an interest in how the government uses the proceeds from their tax payments. Similarly, users have a right to information about the quantity and quality of the services they are being offered. The performance of public services is therefore of interest to tax payers, to those who use the services and to those who provide the services, as well as for the government to assess the success of its performance agenda.

This chapter sets out guidelines for measuring public service productivity: the measurement of non-market government output and of government expenditure on the inputs used to produce the output. Similar to the market sector, public service productivity is defined as the ratio of outputs to inputs. Productivity growth is the change in this ratio over time. All public service productivity measurement is multi-factor productivity measurement. It should be noted that while significant progress has been made in measuring public service productivity, it is still a developing area and ONS will be consulting with experts and practitioners at various stages of this development.

Measuring Productivity of Public Services: the Challenges and Developments in Methodology

Analysis of public service productivity, like any other productivity calculation, requires accurate measurements of input and output. Obtaining these for the public sector, however, is much less straightforward than in other sectors. For this reason, this chapter first explains how ONS measures public sector output and inputs, from both central and local government, and then discusses productivity issues for the sector.

9.1 Measuring public service output

Prior to 1998, the traditional approach to measuring public service output had always been to set them equal in value to the expenditure used to produce them. In effect, this was the simple solution to the main problem that non-market output – unlike market output – does not have prices that would typically be used to give weight of importance in a growth measurement index. Using this <output = input> approach, therefore, meant that productivity growth had been assumed to be constant over time.

However, recommendations in the UN System of National Accounts 1993 (SNA93) proposed moving away from this convention of <output = input> and, consequently, ONS changed its approach. In doing so, the UK made faster progress with the post-SNA93 agenda than did most other national statistical institutes.

By 1998, ONS had moved to a system of direct indicators, with two-thirds of spending on public services measured using new direct output measures. The limited international experience of direct measurement in public services meant, however, that ONS had few sources to draw help from and had to resolve various issues in a piecemeal fashion. Furthermore, available data sources meant that compromise was sometimes necessary to create direct indicators that helped the measurement of output over time.

The new direct measures implemented to measure public services are cost-weighted activity measures. Examples of direct output measures currently used to measure volume output of public services include:

■ health volume output measured by cost weighted activity index of NHS activities and Family Health Services (number of GP consultations, prescriptions, sight tests, dental treatments etc).

■ education volume output measured by pupil attendance adjusted for quality by a fixed factor of 0.25 per cent

■ administration of Social Security volume output measured by the number of benefit claims for the 24 largest benefits

■ volume output of fire services measured by number of fires, number of incidences attended (special services) and fire prevention (which is indirectly measured using the input method)

The pioneering nature of the work meant that by 2003, it was appropriate to take stock of the methodology and direction. This meant checking whether the new estimates of output and productivity were capable of bearing the weight that was being put upon them. For these reasons, the UK National Statistician at that time, Len Cook, decided to commission Sir Tony Atkinson in December 2003 to carry out an independent review of how public service output and productivity should be measured.

The Atkinson Review published two reports, an interim report in July 2003 to allow experts across the world to have some input into the review, and the final report in January 2005. The final *Atkinson Report* strongly endorsed the basic direction that ONS methods had taken since 1998 in moving towards direct measures of output. The report went on to outline a strong principled approach to measuring public service output and productivity, and also made many recommendations for measuring specific public services.

This section provides detail of how public service output is measured. **Box 9.1** gives a summary of the methods currently included in the National Accounts for comparison with the way forward. Examples for the health service are used to illustrate how the Atkinson principles have been applied to date.

Box 9.1: Current treatment of public services outputs in the National Accounts

In light of the recommendations in the SNA93, European Systems of Account 1995 (ESA95) and the Eurostat Price and Volume Manual from 1998, the UK National Accounts broke away from the traditional approach of measuring government output. Rather than setting it equal to the expenditure used to produce it, ONS instead introduced direct methods for certain components, in particular health and education. The Atkinson review followed and further changes were made.

At the present time, General Government Final Consumption Expenditure (GGFCE) is calculated using direct measures for some classifications of functions of government (COFOG) categories and for others it uses basically deflated inputs. GGFCE is a component of the expenditure measure of GDP and equates to approximately 20 per cent of the total value.

Approximately 63 per cent of GGFCE is calculated using some form of direct measurement and these categories include:

- health
- education
- social protection (adult social services, children's social services and social security administration)
- courts
- fire service
- prisons
- probation

The remaining output of government including military defence and central and local government administration is calculated differently.

Pay for military defence and central government administration is calculated using numbers of employees, which makes it a volume method; for local government administration pay is deflated using a pay index. Military defence, central government and local government procurement expenditure is deflated using mainly producer price indices.

9.1.1 Public service output: the volume of goods and services provided by government

Government output can be categorised as individual or collective services.

Individual services are those provided by the government and consumed by households individually, such as school education and health care treatments. (Some of these services can also be collective in nature, however, for example, general education and health advice to the population as a whole.)

Collective services, on the other hand, are those provided to society as a whole, such as defence and law and order, where individual households cannot be excluded from the benefits of those services. (Although again, some law and order activities could be classified as individual services, for example, criminal justice interventions for individuals.)

Public service output, whether individual or collective in nature, should be estimated as a volume measure, similar to that for market output in the National Accounts. A volume measure is comprised of two separately observable characteristics:

- the **quantity** of a good or service
- the **quality** of a good or service

Determining the volume of output as defined above is complicated in the case of government output, because public services are non-market outputs. As stated in **Chapter 6**, unlike market sector output, government output is not traded in the market, but is provided either free of charge at the point of delivery, or at a nominal price which is not intended to cover the cost of production. The lack of a market environment where the price mechanism operates to match demand and supply of output creates problems in measuring the volume, quality and value attached by consumers to public sector services.

The absence of prices for non-market output, however, should not imply that consumers do not value government services or that such services do not add to consumers' and society's welfare. This is clearly not the case. However it does mean that measurement of public service output and productivity is complicated by the lack of a rich information set provided by market prices. In the absence of market prices, broadly speaking there are therefore only two options by which to measure government output in constant volume terms:

- the indirect volume method: deflating inputs (the <outputs=inputs> method)
- the direct volume method: counting the outputs

9.1.2 Direct methods used to measure public service output

To begin with, it is useful to clarify what is meant by inputs, activities, output and outcomes, particularly as these terms are used throughout this chapter.

The simple definitions for these terms follow:

- inputs are simply the resources such as labour, goods and services and capital used to produce activities, output and outcomes

- activities describe the processes of producing public services

- outputs are the goods or services produced by the government. In the case of public service, services are the main output. A service can be defined as the physical or mental change brought to a good or a person by the activity of the pubic service provider

- outcomes are the ultimate goals or objectives sought by government and individuals in consuming the public services

Table 9.1 provides sector specific examples for inputs, activities, outputs and outcomes

It is worth expanding on the important relationship between these concepts. Activities involve the process of producing the public sector service and measures what the government is doing with the inputs for which it spends money. For example, activities in the health sector include heart and lung operations, physiotherapy sessions, and other interventions. Activities in the education sector include lessons taken by teachers while in the case of the police force they include the number of patrols carried out. Activities can therefore be a very close measure to output, but nevertheless are not output.

Outcomes are the goals sought by government and individuals. For example, improvements in exam results can be regarded as an outcome of education services (in the sense that pupils have gained knowledge and human capital) and a healthier population is an outcome of health services. However outcomes will also be influenced

Table 9.1: Examples for inputs, activities, outputs and outcomes

Public service	Inputs	Activities	Outputs	Outcomes
Health	■ Labour and skill of doctors and nurses ■ Prescription drugs and other medical supplies ■ Hospitals, clinics and other buildings	■ Operations carried out ■ Drugs administered ■ Advice given	Health care: a change in physical capability or additional health knowledge – proxied by health treatments	■ Better quality of life (more social interaction, mental well-being, etc) ■ Longer life ■ Enhanced employment prospects
Education	■ Labour and teaching skill of teachers and support staff ■ Teaching aids, gas and water ■ Buildings and computers	■ Lessons taught ■ Homework marked ■ Guidance given	Additional knowledge and skills imparted – proxied by full time equivalent number of students effectively attending lessons	■ Better job/earning prospects ■ Improved citizenship ■ Enhanced life skills ■ Enhanced health and nutrition knowledge
Social Care	■ Labour of staff processing claims, welfare officers ■ Stationary and meals ■ Buildings and equipment	■ Accommodation provided ■ Cleaning and catering services ■ Equipment provided ■ Advice given and assessments made	Social care – a change in physical or mental state – proxied by care-weeks	■ Better quality of life (more social interaction, safer, mental wellbeing)

by external factors that have nothing to do with the government service provided. For example, improvements in exam results may be influenced by greater use of the Internet, better public libraries or more support from parents, all of which fall outside the remit of the government. This means, therefore, that it is important to estimate how government outputs actually influence what are largely social outcomes.

The Eurostat Handbook (*Handbook on Price and Volume Measures in National Accounts, 2001*) offers four conceptual approaches by which the volume of public services can be measured:

1. **input method:** measure output by units of input, so growth in output will always be equal to growth in inputs

2. **activity method:** measure output by activities which assumes that the output depends mainly on the activities performed by staff (for example the output of the NHS can be measured by the different health treatment activities)

3. **output method:** measure output directly by counting what services the consumer receives, as opposed to services offered (for instance, pupils attending school lessons rather than using school lessons offered)

4. **outcome method:** the eventual results of public service output. The main difficulty here is establishing the link between the public service output and the outcome (for example health care treatment and life expectancy)

The input method is the 'indirect method' of measuring output. Prior to 1998 the indirect method had been the traditional approach used in the National Accounts. It is known as the so-called <output = inputs> convention, where it is assumed that the output of public service is equal to whatever was spent by government and public authorities. The convention had been adopted because of the complexity of measuring output directly.

It is, however, easy to demonstrate that the indirect method of using <output = input> to measure the volume of output can be erroneous. For example, this method leads to the conclusion that doubling government expenditure or doubling the inputs would lead to a doubling of public services. This is unlikely to be the case when money is being used inefficiently or, for example, if money is spent on a new process or technology that can lead to more than doubling of output.

International guidelines favour the adoption of direct output methods as the most preferred approach to measuring the volume of government output. This is the recommendation of the SNA93, the *Eurostat Handbook,* and most recently the Atkinson Review (see later sections for details from the review). The guidance from the *Eurostat Handbook* has now been reinforced by a European Commission decision in 2002 that has the force of law. It requires all member states to have moved to direct measurement of output for individual services by the time of the accounts covering 2006. The only exception is Denmark, which has secured derogation until 2012.

The *Eurostat Handbook* classifies the different methods of public sector output according to what is termed A, B and C methods, where:

- A methods are the most appropriate
- B methods are methods that can be used where it is not possible to apply an A method and
- C methods are methods that should not be used.

Table 9.2 provides further clarification on these methods.

Input and activity methods are not considered to be ideal approaches in measuring output. Employing the input approach for measuring individual public services is classified as a C method (meaning a method that is not valid) in the *Eurostat Handbook*. For collective public services the use of an input method is still acceptable and is classified as a B method.

This is because it is very difficult to determine the volume output of collective services consumed in the economy as a result of the nature of non-excludability. Collective services are provided for the benefit of the population at large rather than to individuals separately and no one person can be separated out to receive the service or excluded from receiving the service. (Consider, for instance, police patrols and fire prevention awareness campaigns.) For an input method to be considered a B method in the Eurostat classification, the requirement is that indicators for each input category should be used instead of just a single input measure.

The main reason why the activity method is not favoured is because activities do not directly cover what is happening to the public service. The use of activities best measures how the public sector is using their inputs. This can be illustrated using an example for the heath service. If the output of the NHS is measured by activity

Table 9.2: *Eurostat Handbook* recommendations for government output

Type of service	A/B/C Method
Individual services (such as Education, Health, Social Security, Recreation and Cultural Services).	**A methods** – output indicator approach where the indicators satisfy the following criteria: a) they should cover all services provided b) they should be weighted by the cost of each type of output in the base year c) they should be detailed as possible and d) they should be quality adjusted **B methods** – output indicator approach where the criteria are not fully satisfied: for example the level of detail could be improved or the measure does not take into account changes in quality. **C methods** – if input, activity or outcome is used (unless outcome can be interpreted as quality-adjusted output) or if coverage of output method is not representative.
Collective services (such as General Public Administration, Defence, Police, and Research and Development)	Broadly the same for individual services but: **B methods** – input methods are B methods, as are the use of volume indicators of activity. If input methods are used they should estimate the volume of each indicator separately, taking quality changes of inputs into account. Applying productivity or quality adjustments to the sum of the volume of inputs in not recommended **C methods** – the use of a single input volume indicator is not a B method

Source: The Atkinson Review 2005

then a decline in the number of operations would strictly imply a reduction in output. However if it is the case that it is improvements in other health treatments that has enabled a reduction in the number of operations (such as from new and more effective drugs), from the consumer's perspective this is an improvement in output rather than a decline in output as suggested by the activity measure.

Because of this likely divergence between the trend in activity and output, if the activity indicators used are not sufficiently detailed or represent output inadequately, the activity method is classified as a C method in the Eurostat Handbook for measuring individual public services. But in the case for collective services it is classified as a B method.

For these reasons, as already stated, a direct output measurement approach is the internationally acceptable method for measuring the volume of output. As indicated in **Table 9.2**, for the direct method to be valid, it has to

have full coverage of services and must be measured in sufficient detail that is differentiated according to the distinct services provided within a service area.

In practice, 'full cover' really means that sufficiently high coverage is needed such that anything less than 100 per cent coverage can be relied upon to represent the whole. The starting point for measuring output, therefore, is to identify robust volume output indicators and then to establish the volume index for the base year. The base year volume index can be used in two ways: to determine the growth in output volume by comparing it against the following year's volume index and also to measure productivity by comparing it against a volume input index.

To calculate the total output of a particular functional area of the government, for instance health, the volume output of various NHS services has to be measured at a disaggregated level and then added up. Adding up quantities in volume terms would require complete homogeneity of services or products, which is not possible even within functional areas, let alone across different functional areas.

For example, the quantity of heart operations and physiotherapy sessions in the NHS cannot be added together for the simple reason that they are not like for like. For this reason – heterogeneity of outputs – a weighting mechanism is required to aggregate the different output quantities together. The market sector also faces the same issue in aggregation, for example measuring the output of the automobile industry requires a weighting mechanism to aggregate the volume of all the various models of cars together (see **Box 6.1** for an example of this).

> **Weighting mechanisms** – The purpose of a weighting mechanism is to convert the different output quantities into the same value units (which can then be aggregated) in a way that accounts for the economic importance of the good or service. In the market sector the prices of the goods or services are used to weight the volume of the non-homogeneous commodities together. In the non-market case, prices are not available and the method recommended by the Eurostat Handbook is to use the unit costs to weight the outputs together. Use of unit costs leads to producer valuation of public services as opposed to valuation by recipients or society.

In addition to measuring the quantity changes of output over time, the volume index must be adjusted to take changes in the quality of output into account. Quality measurement is an important component of public service volume output measurement and is covered in detail for both the public and market sector in **Chapter 6**.

9.1.3 Direct measures of public service output: the Atkinson Review's approach

The most important general conclusions of the Atkinson Review can be summarised as:

1. public accountability required that appropriate measures of output and productivity of public services are made available

2. it was neither possible nor desirable to revert to an <output = inputs> convention

3. that future work needed to be underpinned and strengthened by an explicit set of principles which forms a methodological framework

On the first point, as already mentioned, there is much interest among citizens who want to know the performance of the public sector in delivering services, just as there is interest in the performance of private firms who set prices for the goods and services produced and purchased in the market sector.

On the second point, the public sector is too important to be treated just by means of a stylised measurement convention, any more than it would be appropriate, say, to treat the output of the manufacturing sector by means of a pure convention. It is sometimes argued that, given the vast complexities of measuring public service output, sticking to the <output = input> convention can ensure comparability of figures between different countries. Nothing, however, could be further from the truth. The <output = input> measure of activity will correspond or not to reality in different degrees in different countries and to different extents over time within the same country, depending on whether productivity is actually flat or whether it is departing from that.

The other favoured argument to continue with the convention relies on the difficulties in obtaining accurate indicators. The reason presented being that if there is not 100 per cent certainty of the accuracy of direct measurement, then it is better to avoid altogether the risk that productivity measures are inaccurate. Such an argument, however, is an easy way out and moreover ignores the point that sticking to the convention is not actually being neutral, but is imposing a strong judgement of zero productivity in the public services, which is unlikely to be true.

On the third point, the Atkinson Review revealed many issues and problems with the current approach. In an attempt to find direct indicators of output in a particular service, sometimes any reasonably related information source may have been accepted. It is important therefore to avoid the inevitable temptation to proceed on an opportunistic basis and to guard against inconsistencies in the general methodology. The disciplined approach advocated in the Atkinson Review is essential to ensure the reliability as well as credibility of the output and productivity measures.

To this end, the Atkinson Review looked in more detail into the specific measurement issues in the key areas of public spending: health, education, social protection and public order and safety. The final report put forward nine principles about the general way in which the methodology might be best be taken forward and some 54 detailed recommendations on the specific service areas listed above.

The nine principles key to the methodology proposed in the Atkinson Review in measuring public service output and productivity are set out in full in **Box 9.2**. **Principles A** to **E** directly address the measurement of output.

Box 9.2: The Nine Principles of the Atkinson Review

Principle A: The measurement of government non-market output should, as far as possible, follow a procedure parallel to that adopted in the National Accounts for market output.

Principle B: The output of the government sector should in principle be measured in a way that is adjusted for quality, taking account of the attributable incremental contribution of the service to the outcome.

Principle C: Account should be taken of the complementarity between public and private output, allowing for the increased real value of public services in an economy with rising real GDP.

Principle D: Formal criteria should be set in place for the extension of direct output measurement to new functions of government. Specifically, the conditions for introducing a new directly measured output indicator should be that (i) it covers adequately the full range of services for that functional area, (ii) it makes appropriate allowance for quality change, (iii) the effects of its introduction have been tested service by service, (iv) the context in which it will be published has been fully assessed, in particular the implied productivity estimate, and (v) there should be provision for regular statistical review.

Principle E: Measures should cover the whole of the United Kingdom; where systems for public service delivery and/or data collection differ across the different countries of the United Kingdom, it is necessary to reflect this variation in the choice of indicators.

Principle F: The measurement of inputs should be as comprehensive as possible, and in particular should include capital services; labour inputs should be compiled using both direct and indirect methods, compared and reconciled.

Principle G: Criteria should be established for the quality of pay and price deflators to be applied to the input spending series; they should be sufficiently disaggregated to take account of changes in the mix of inputs; and should reflect full and actual costs.

Principle H: Independent corroborative evidence should be sought on government productivity, as part of a process of 'triangulation', recognising the limitations in reducing productivity to a single number.

Principle I: Explicit reference should be made to the margins of error surrounding National Accounts estimates.

In considering the methodological framework suggested by Atkinson, **Principle A** is the cornerstone upon which everything is based. It is the key guidance confirming that the measurement of public service output should comprise a method that captures the 'value added' of the public services to the economy, as is the case for private service output.

The Atkinson Review also made an important contribution to the very definition of output in the case of public services. Using **Principle B** outlined in **Box 9.3**, a more precise definition of output has been put forward as: the incremental contribution that the public service provider makes towards the desired outcome/s. This is a new development in output measurement, where output volume is explicitly linked with the outcome through quality adjustments, giving a more accurate definition of what public services provide to the individual and society in general. In short, it is recognised that unless public service output does actually contribute to outcomes, then no output would be recorded (for example there would be little point in public money being dedicated to health treatments that do not have any impact on health).

In summary, using the principles and recommendations from the Atkinson Review, the broad methodological framework proposed for measuring government output and productivity is based on the following key steps:

- measure public service output using a direct volume approach

- adjust the volume measures of output for quality change

- measure public service inputs using direct or indirect methods

- ensure that appropriate input deflators that are specific to the public service are used in the indirect method

- use corroborative evidence to verify the plausibility of final productivity estimates

9.1.4 Measuring the volume of public service outputs

The important question is how to ensure that the direct volume measure used is a valid one and not based opportunistically on whatever data are available. For example, the direct volume measure for education output introduced in 1998 was based on measuring the number of pupils. This was not, however, really a valid measure of education output. A more relevant measure is the actual number of pupils taught where the volume measure of output is based on pupil numbers and pupil attendance rates.

Expanding on this example, it is still questionable whether the one volume measure described really does justice in measuring the volume of output delivered by the education system. It can be argued that the education system, aside from academic skills, also provides a broader range of services including child-care, emotional support and counselling, sports, art, music, drama, communication skills and other benefits, which also should be accounted for by separate volume measures.

The guidance provided by the *Atkinson Report* on improving volume measures is to:

- widen the coverage of output volume indicators for each function

- increase the level of detail at which output indicators are measured

- adopt more reliable data sources

- revise the weighting process

- replace activity indicators with output measures that reflect changes in quality or outcome attributable to a unit of output

- introduce or revise an overall quality adjustment

- improve timeliness and in-year indicators and

- improve geographical/UK coverage by making full use of measures from Scotland, Wales and Northern Ireland

An important consideration in measuring the volume of output is the intractable link between output and outcomes. As already mentioned, this close relationship is neatly summed up by considering that if there is no outcome (no value) then there is no output. It also implies that outcomes are often influenced by a wide range of factors, not just the specific service under consideration.

For example, the main outcome of the NHS is to produce better health status, but this will depend upon a range of influences such as diet, exercise habits, the extent of smoking and so on. NHS output would have little value if it did not at least contribute to these outcomes. But it would be a mistake to attribute all of the change in health status to NHS output. The methodological approach suggested to include the effect of output on outcomes is through a quality adjustment of the conventional volume output

measure. This is explained in more detail in **Chapter 6**.

When it comes to collective public services, while the *Eurostat Handbook* recognises 'the difficulty in defining the output of collective services', it still requires volume of output to be measured using a direct approach to qualify as an A grade method. Because of the difficulties present in identifying direct measures of output, for the time being the options seem to be limited to the following approaches.

The current ONS approach: assume that the collective service volume of output grows at the same rate as the individual services of the same function. For example, output based on public health campaigns will be assumed to grow at the same rate as NHS output.

The combined output and input approach: use a direct volume output method for individual service components, and use the input method for the collective service components. For this approach to quality as a B grade method, it must be that the volume of each indicator is estimated separately, accounting for any quality changes.

The activity approach: this alternative is considered as a B grade method in Eurostat, and for activities like fire prevention, can be a valid method.

9.1.5 Measuring the quality of the volume of public service output

As already outlined, the measure of output in the National Accounts context is one framed in volume terms. Also, what is meant by a volume measure for any good or service consists of two components: quantity and quality. A high quality service is clearly worth more than a low value service, and vice versa. How public services are adjusted for changes in quality over time has already been outlined and discussed in **Chapter 6**.

9.1.6 Consider complementarity between the public and private services

The Atkinson Review highlighted a paradox which arises in measuring public service output if changing private sector conditions are ignored. This concept is outlined in **Principle C** as:

> Account should be taken of the complementarity between public and private output, allowing for the increased real value of public services in an economy with rising real GDP.

The proposal is that the added value of a public service will inevitably be affected by the context in which the service is provided. In particular, the value of the public service to consumers is likely to depend upon the value the private sector is generating in parallel. An example is the case of fire services. Through its activity the fire services can protect a given number of properties to a particular standard. In considering the actual value added by the fire services to the economy, the conditions of the private sector receiving the fire service is also an important factor. This is because when the value of properties and of their contents rise over time, the value generated by the services of fire protection also increases accordingly. In the limit, if the properties and their contents had no value, then the value of the fire services' protection would also be zero.

Similarly, it is also the case that the value of health and education services provided to consumers by the public sector will depend on rising income levels. The extended life years, sickness absences avoided and qualifications obtained would all have higher money values as the economy grows. Atkinson suggests that:

> If we see the output of Education in terms of the acquisition of skills and qualifications, then their value increases with rising real earnings. If a university adds, say, 20 per cent to earnings, then today's degree adds 20 per cent of a larger number (even adjusted for inflation) than the degrees of a generation ago.

Principle C outlined above should be seen as a symmetric two-way relationship. The dependency of private sector output and productivity upon public sector factors is, perhaps, more familiar. The output and productivity of a particular manufacturing company will depend in part upon the productive capacity of its workforce, the stock and quality of capital equipment and the management's ability to combine the factors of production effectively. But, as in the examples below, the output and productivity outcome are also liable to be affected by government.

- Improved infrastructure may well have an impact. If the government invests to improve the road system such that the company can transport essential components in a more timely way, productivity may rise. Other infrastructure improvements may act in the same direction

- Improvements to the commercial legal system or to competition and regulatory practices may also be associated with enhanced private sector productivity

When measuring the volume of public service output, it still has to be determined how **Principle C** could be applied. The channels of influence between private sector and the public service output will differ in each case, and will depend on the particular circumstances. For example, in the case of fire services, it is through the rise in the value of property, and in the case of education it is through the rise in real earnings for educated workers. The indicator and specific measures that could be used will be from the result of research into the particular service area. Attention should also be given to the possibility of double counting increased value when it may have already been captured in the outputs of one sector.

Preliminary work carried out to measure complementarity suggests that the principle can have significant net impact on output growth. However, the measurement technique that could be used to apply **Principle C** still requires a lot of development. The UK Centre for the Measurement of Government Activity (UKCeMGA) has recently undertaken further consultation on this issue with a panel of economic experts. The panel concluded that an adjustment based on complementarity should not be used to measure output for National Accounts purposes unless such an adjustment already fits with existing conventions (for example, the volume of goods protected by public services may rise in line with real earnings growth). A wider welfare measure of GDP, however, would be appropriate for productivity articles as long as the methodology used is robust and clearly explained, and adjustments are tailored to meet the needs of specific public services.

This issue is covered in more detail in the UKCeMGA strategy paper, *Measuring output of Public Services – Towards a Quality Measurement Framework*, published in July 2007 and summarised in **Box 13.1**.

To conclude, much progress has been made in how public service output is measured since direct measurement was first introduced in 1998. The measures used have moved closer to actual output generated by the respective functional areas, and a greater degree of differentiation has been allowed for better measure of quality changes. Where required, as described in the above examples, specific adjustment to quality of output is also being undertaken. But this is a developing area and more work still needs to be done to improve the measurement of the volume of public service output.

Box 9.3: Example: Measurement of the output of the National Health Service

The NHS is the largest of all public services (excluding social security payments, which are treated as transfers) accounting for approximately 30 per cent of final government consumption. In terms of GDP, NHS accounts for around 7 per cent of total gross domestic product. The provision of health services in the UK is devolved with important differences in the organisation of services in the different UK countries (England, Wales, Scotland and Northern Ireland). Health services are provided free of charge at the point of delivery except for when patients are liable to pay (such as prescription and dental charges). The primary aim of the NHS is to improve and maintain the health of the population. The outcomes of health include, for example, increases in life expectancy, decreases in infant mortality and increases in health more generally.

However these outcomes are also influenced by other external factors, for example those owing to changes in diet and environmental factors, which are outside the control of the NHS. The main areas of NHS service include:

■ hospital inpatient and outpatient activity

■ community health care

■ ambulance service

■ NHS direct

■ walk-in centres

■ independent contractors such as GPs, dentists, pharmacists and opticians

Measuring the volume of NHS output

– following the Atkinson Review conclusions, the output of health services is defined as the contribution they make to improved health outcomes, excluding improvements caused by other factors outside NHS control. This includes the quantities of health care received by patients that has been adjusted for changes in quality of the services delivered. As per earlier guidelines,

the output of the NHS is measured using direct volume measures and is activity based. The various NHS treatment activities covered are weighted by the relative costs of producing them to provide a measure of health output growth. The unit costs of treatments are obtained from a Reference Cost database. As the volume of activities change over time, the volume is automatically adjusted according to the relative weight given to it. The cost weighted index is based on a Laspeyres index. The index series is then adjusted for changes in quality using data on the impact of NHS output on health outcomes.

The output methodology since June 2004 has been broadened in geographic coverage to include Northern Ireland as well as England. Currently 81 per cent of the value of NHS activity in England is captured and for Northern Ireland the corresponding figure is 79 per cent. In the case of England, the change in NHS output is measured using many different data sources:

■ the Department of Health (DH) National Schedule of Reference Costs

■ the General Household Survey

■ information from NHS Direct

■ walk-in centres

■ NHS Direct Online

■ the Prescription Pricing Authority

■ general dental services

■ general ophthalmic services

■ emergency ambulance journeys

Measuring the quality of NHS Output
Quality adjustment by Differentiation

– prior to June 2004, health service output was measured using activity series based on 16 different categories of inpatient and day cases. These very broad treatment categories did not adequately address the vast difference in quality of treatment or the complexity of the different procedures. The consequence for output measurement was that the output generated by a

simple procedure, such as one to correct an in-growing toenail and the output of a complex procedure, like a heart and lung transplant surgery, were treated with equal weight. As a first step, greater differentiation of the activity categories has now been employed, with the activities having been refined into around 2,000 categories classified according to Health Care Resource Groups (HRGs). These also have similarly refined unit cost weights.

As already described, the technique of differentiation is powerful and well suited to capturing the quality changes arising from variations in the mix of NHS output categories. The method of differentiation in measuring NHS output is responsible for an increase of approximately 10 percentage points in the estimated output of healthcare over the period 1995 to 2004. Based on the above described methodology, without using any other quality adjustments apart from the differentiation technique, NHS output as used in National Accounts is estimated to have increased by an average of 3.2 per cent per year during the period 1995 to 2004.

Quality adjustment through attributable contribution to outcomes – new experimental work has been used to adjust NHS output using the third method for quality adjustment recommended by the Atkinson Review: the proposition that NHS output should be defined as the contribution it makes to health outcomes. Two reports published in 2005 by the University of York and National Institute for Economic and Social Research (York/NIESR) ('Developing new approaches to measuring NHS output and productivity') and the DH ('Accounting for Quality Change') have contributed greatly in developing quality adjustment indicators. The indicators that have been used to adjust NHS output include those from the York/NIESR study: survival rates, health effects, adjustments for life expectancy and waiting times.

Indicators from the DH study are also included: patient experience, use of more effective drugs to treat coronary heart disease, longer term survival rates for Myocardial Infarction, and some limited but improved general practitioner outcomes.

Accounting for quality using value weights – statins are drugs used for the treatment of coronary heart disease and this form of treatment is much cheaper than alternatives, which can involve surgical intervention and hospitalisation. The DH study reports that the marginal value of statins for patients is considerably higher than the £27 unit cost of the drug. In this situation, where statins are a higher quality treatment delivered at a cheaper price, the use of cost weights to measure output would result in underestimation of output following a switch to treatment by statins. Consequently, to adjust for the improvement in quality of NHS output arising from the use of statins, the DH study has experimented with the use of value weights.

The weights are calculated on the basis of marginal benefits in life years (where each life year has been valued at £30,000). Using this method increases NHS output growth by an annual average of 0.81 percentage points during the period 1999 to 2004. However, it should be noted that the use of value weights to measure output growth still requires much development. The example in this section should only be used for illustrative purposes. More detail on how the measurement of quality of NHS output is being taken forward (and for the next section on complementarity) is covered by the UKCeMGA strategy paper.

Accounting for complementarity between the public and private sectors – the proposition of the Atkinson Review **Principle C** is that the effect on output arising from the interconnections between private and public sector need to be accounted for. In the case of the health service, apart from the direct effect of NHS measures as described in the above sections, interactions with the private sector can arise as a result of several factors.

- NHS services contribute to healthier populations which support a more productive workforce

- With technological progress, the same workforce with a given health status can be more productive. If the complementarity principle is used, then NHS output would be measured

along with its contribution to improved outcomes for individuals and society including the consequence of being healthy in an economy with an advancing technological frontier

- In addition to its effect on productivity, NHS services, by improving general health, enable elderly people or those more generally outside the workforce to better enjoy their leisure time for much longer

Table 9A: Estimated impact on NHS output growth using various methods of quality adjustment

England	Percentage points **Average impact on growth per year**
York/NIESR effects	+0.17
DH proposals:	
Value for statins	+0.81
Improved blood pressure control[1]	+0.05
Heart attack survival	+0.01
Patient experience	+0.07
Annual increase in value of health	+1.5
Total DH effect[2]	+2.51
Overall quality adjustment	**+2.68**

1. Results from the two most recent years have been averaged over five years.

2. The total is greater than the sum of individual adjustments because of cumulative effects.

Figure 9A: NHS output growth without quality adjustment, 1995 –2004, and with quality adjustment, 1999–2004

Index 1999=100

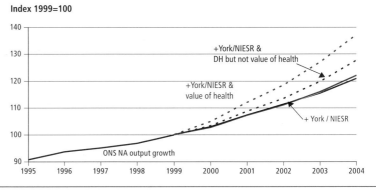

The general argument here is that as society, supported by technological advances, gets wealthier then the value of NHS services increase. This is because at any given health status, technological improvements cause the productive potential of the work force to increase over time. The ability of society in general to enjoy leisure also increases by a greater extent because of additional resources becoming available. Poor health and sickness absences in the labour market will therefore become more costly to individuals and to society in general over time.

In order to measure the complementarity effect of NHS services as described above, the Atkinson Review recommended that NHS output could be adjusted in line with the trend in rising real earnings or income. The real earnings/income trend will reflect the technological advances and improvement in the productive potential of the labour force, as well as the increase in resources available to enjoy

leisure. In line with the Atkinson Review recommendation, ONS has produced an experimental output measure for the NHS using an adjustment based on the post-war historical UK annual growth trend of 1.5 per cent in real earnings/income.

There is reason to believe that this is a conservative number and a 2 per cent adjustment is more in line with the recent trend in real earnings/income growth. However, it should be noted that the complementarity principle has attracted wide debate since the review and Atkinson himself called for prudence in applying the principle. Following recent consultations, a decision has now been made against the use of this principle to adjust NHS output in the National Accounts (see **Box 13.1**).

Total adjustments to NHS output – data for the NHS quality adjusted output series as described above are only available from 1999 onwards. When all the experimental quality adjustments proposed are incorporated in the measurement of health

service output, the average annual growth in output increases from 3.9 per cent (without quality adjustment) to 5 per cent during the period 1999 to 2004. **Table 9A** and **Figure 9A** provide detail on the impact of the individual quality adjustments. When NHS output is measured including an adjustment for private/public sector complementarity (termed the 'value of health' impact), the annual average growth increases to 6.5 per cent per year.

The quality indicators used to adjust NHS output growth are based on available research and data, which can cause problems of bias if all the relevant quality domains are not represented in these selected quality indicators. Further work is also needed concerning the relative weights to be used. The questions of whether or not value weights should replace the existing use of cost weights and the conditions and the practicality of implementing value weights need to be further explored.

Source: UKCeMGA (February 2006)

9.2 Measuring public service inputs

Public service inputs are the labour, goods and services and capital used to produce public service output. For example, doctors, nurses and support staff use medical equipment in a hospital to produce health care services. Teachers and assistants use educational equipment in schools to produce lessons.

Using existing ONS, Atkinson Review and OECD guidelines, there are essentially two ways to measure inputs. The traditional indirect method is based on on wages and prices to deflate current expenditure on labour and goods and services to estimate the volume of these inputs. For capital, depreciation methods have traditionally been used. Alternatively, a more direct method would be to use data that allow counting the volume of inputs, for example, hours worked by employees, the number of goods and services that are purchased, and the services that can be generated from capital. Currently, both of these methods to measure inputs have been deployed.

9.2.1 Public service inputs produce public service output

Measurement of inputs is the second element to deriving the productivity measure (using the formula output/inputs). Input is the collective term that defines all resources used to produce the output. The three broad categories of input are: labour, intermediate consumption and capital consumption.

Examples for public service inputs include:

- **labour** – all employees involved in producing output, for example, doctors, nurses, healthcare assistants for health service output; teachers, teaching assistants, administrative staff for education service output

- **goods and services** – prescription drugs, hospital beds, surgery equipment for health service output; textbooks, writing equipment, desks for education service output

- **capital** – hospitals and operating theatres for health service output; schools and computer equipment for education service output. Capital input reflects the services obtained from the use of fixed assets that depreciate and needs to be replaced at the end of their lives

The volume measurement of public service input is relatively more straightforward than is the case for public service output. This is because inputs are resources that are purchased within the market framework where prices exist; therefore it is similar to the measurement of private sector inputs. Total expenditure on inputs is available with relative ease and frequency from public sector spending units. However, getting detailed expenditure data is still a challenge.

An important consideration in measuring inputs in the public sector is that some of its services are jointly produced by the service provider and the individual. This is the case in education, where the effort put in by the individual pupil contributes significantly to the outcome of his or her own education attainment. In such cases the characteristics of the recipients of services, for example the ability of pupils, can be important 'inputs' in the actual production function.

Also, for some services such as education, the volume of education received from previous stages in the education system by default becomes an input of the next stage. For these reasons, care must be taken to ensure that where output is not properly adjusted to isolate that part of it attributable to the service provider's contribution, then the inputs must be appropriately adjusted to reflect the additional resources used.

Table 9.3: Quality criteria for deflators for government services

Label	Short description	Examples/explanation
1. Comprehensiveness	The set of deflators should cover all components of expenditure to be deflated	UK expenditure should be deflated using UK, not just English, deflators; Health deflators should cover the whole of NHS, not just hospitals.
2. Coverage	The individual deflator should relate to the expenditure on the individual item to be deflated.	Deflators for labour expenditure should cover National Insurance contributions and pensions as well as earnings.
3. Relevance	The deflator should correspond to the expenditure item to be deflated.	Expenditure on books should be deflated using an indicator of price change in books.
4. Sustainability	The deflator should be available for the foreseeable future, and for a reasonable number of periods in the past.	Micro studies on changes in price for only a single year have limited use: long time series are preferable.
5. Homogeneity	Deflation should be carried out at a level of disaggregation that maximises homogeneity of items within category.	Significant difference in the movement of pay between staff grades would suggest that separate deflators are needed.
6. Timeliness	The deflator should be available in good time after the end of the reference period.	Estimation for missing periods may introduce bias.
7. Periodicity	The deflator should be available on a quarterly basis.	Annual figures may be satisfactory but only where there is evidence of insignificant short-term change.
8. Quality change	Where changes in characteristics of a good/service occur, price indices should reflect pure price changes only.	Improvements in composition and consequently effectiveness of a drug should be should be distinguished from pure price change.
9. Availability of cost weights	Corresponding weights (of the same periodicity) for deflators should also be available.	

Source: The Atkinson Review 2005

9.2.2 Atkinson Review's principles for public service input measurement

Principles F and G from the Atkinson Review relate specifically to the measurement of inputs:

Principle F: the measurement of inputs should be as comprehensive as possible, and in particular should include capital services; labour inputs should be compiled using both direct and indirect methods, compared and reconciled.

Principle G: criteria should be established for the quality of pay and price deflators to be applied to the input spending series; they should be sufficiently disaggregated to take account of changes in the mix of inputs; and should reflect full and actual costs.

These principles highlight that comprehensive coverage and the appropriate level of differentiation are critical elements for measuring the accuracy of volume of input. When using an indirect method, it is important to ensure that the deflators used are suitable. **Table 9.3** provides further detail from the Atkinson Review on quality criteria for deriving new deflators for government services.

9.2.3 Indirect and direct methods are used to measure public service inputs

Following **Principle F** from the Atkinson Review (and Organisation for Economic Co-operation and Development (OECD) guidelines for labour inputs), there are two alternative approaches to measure the volume of inputs
or resources required for producing public services output: an indirect approach or a direct approach. The indirect approach involves deflating the expenditure on labour, intermediate consumption and capital consumption using suitable price and pay indices. The deflators capture the change in price over time and, when applied to expenditure figures, remove the price effect leaving behind only the change in volume. See **Chapter 4** for more detail of deflators.

The direct method to measure the volume of inputs is the preferred approach (*Measuring Productivity: OECD Manual, 2001*) and involves counting the quantity of labour in the case of labour inputs and using capital services as a measure of capital consumption. See **Chapter 5** for more details of quality-adjusted labour input and the measurement of capital services.

9.2.4 Quality adjustment of inputs also needs to be considered

Quality is defined for inputs similarly to the way it is for output. The key approach to adjusting for the change in quality of inputs is the use of differentiation. This technique is equivalent to what has already been explained for quality adjustment in output. By making input categories more homogeneous, the changes in quality are automatically adjusted for when there are changes in the composition of inputs used. See **Chapter 6** for more details on quality adjustment.

In the case of labour inputs, although it can seem to be a homogeneous input group, in fact it consists of diverse characteristics such as skill levels, experience, age and ability, which determine the productiveness of the labour input. There is more about adjusting labour input in **Chapter 5**.

Box 9.4: Example: Measurement of NHS inputs

The NHS provides a good example of how inputs are measured in the public sector. Out of total general government health expenditure on inputs (in current prices), labour is the biggest expenditure category, accounting for around £38.7 billion (50 per cent) of total expenditure in 2004. The next largest area of expenditure is on intermediate consumption, accounting for £36.6 billion (48 per cent) of total expenditure in 2004. Finally, capital is the smallest component, accounting for £1.8 billion (2 per cent) of total expenditure in 2004. The most recent work in measuring NHS inputs includes new and more detailed deflators and refined methodologies that include direct and indirect methods for measuring labour.

Labour

A Paasche Price Index deflator is the most recently developed technique for measuring the volume of labour input using the indirect method. The index measures the weighted average increases in unit staff costs for each staff group using quantity, rather than current price expenditure, as weights (previously a Laspeyres Index in the National Accounts used the latter measure). Using the Paasche Price Index for the period 1995 to 2004, cost inflation of NHS staff was rising more slowly than is the case when the previous Laspeyres Index was used (4.9 per cent annual growth compared to 5.7 per cent per annum). The Expenditure on labour is obtained from DH reported expenditure.

The new direct NHS labour input measure, similar to the quality-adjusted labour input measures detailed in **Chapter 5**, is therefore an index measure based on staff count by differentiated categories. These are then weighted together by earnings for each of the staff categories. Differentiated staff categories by skill in the NHS include for example, consultants, registrars, general practitioners, qualified ambulance staff, managers, nurses and practice staff. The

volume growth in labour input using the direct method for the period 1995–2004 is estimated to be 3 per cent per annum compared to 3.4 per cent per annum when using the indirect method.

There are, however, advantages and disadvantages in using the two methods identified for estimating NHS labour inputs, these are summarised in **Table 9B**:

Intermediate consumption

Prescription drugs form a major part of NHS intermediate consumption (see Chapter 4 for more details of intermediate consumption within the National Accounts). Expenditure on prescription drugs can change for a number of reasons including:

- population changes
- prescribing practice
- guidelines
- changes in drug formulation and innovation
- disappearance of old drugs and entry of new drugs
- changes in the price of drugs

With so many factors affecting prescription drug expenditure levels, it becomes very difficult to separate the price and volume effects. Part of the entry effect may be price change. For example, if a relatively new and expensive drug increases its market share because it constitutes a clinical breakthrough, then it would be

Table 9B: Estimating NHS labour inputs

Method	Advantages	Disadvantages
Indirect Method: Deflated NHS expenditure on labour	Method differentiates between different types of labour input in hospitals	Does not take account of possible salary differences between those employed directly by NHS and agency staff
		Method is based on assumptions about the split between labour and non-labour costs in primary care
		Uses wages, not total labour costs
		Based on England only
Direct Method: based on NHS sources	Based on official sources: censuses of NHS staff and extracts from payroll systems	Does not take account of salary differences between those employed directly by the NHS and agency staff
	Takes into account some aspects of the difference between headcount and hours worked (uses 'whole time equivalents')	The index does not take into account changes in the relative costs of different types of staff (cost weights are fixed at 2002 values)
		Hours worked is based on contracted hours and not hours actually worked
		Uses wages, not total labour costs
		Based on England only

a quality change. If, on the other hand, the drug is therapeutically similar to existing drugs but has been successfully marketed at a higher price, then most of the change in expenditure can be construed as a price change.

Similarly there is an argument to link the price of branded and generic drugs, so that when brands fall out of patent and generic drugs move in, the change in cost needs to be factored in as a price effect. Based on this analysis, when a Paasche Price Index for generic and branded drugs is applied, the price of prescription drugs fell by 0.5 per cent during the period 2002 to 2003 and by 3.4 per cent from 2003 to 2004.

Capital

At present two approaches are used to measure the volume of capital. The first method is the more traditional approach applying deflated capital consumption using inventory depreciation. The second approach is the new measure of capital services advocated in the Atkinson Review (see **Section 9.1.3**). Using the traditional capital consumption method, the estimated growth in the volume of capital input for the period 1995 to 2004 is 3.3 per cent growth per annum, and it is 4.3 per cent per annum when the direct method is employed for the same period.

Aggregating all the inputs

To aggregate all the three different input estimates into one volume index, a Laspeyres Index is adopted, similar to the methodology used for the output measure. The three components of labour,

Source: UKCeMGA (February 2006)

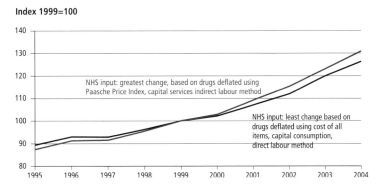

Figure 9B: NHS input measures giving the greatest and least change in volume inputs, 1995–2004

Index 1999=100

NHS input: greatest change, based on drugs deflated using Paasche Price Index, capital services indirect labour method

NHS input: least change based on drugs deflated using cost of all items, capital consumption, direct labour method

intermediate consumption and capital input are aggregated together using the current price expenditure of the items in the previous period. As expected, the different methods described above will give rise to different growth rates of NHS inputs. The growth in NHS volume input using the various methods is estimated to range between an average increase of 3.9 and 4.6 per cent per year during the period 1995 to 2004 (see **Figure 9B**). For the period 1999 to 2004, where output quality adjustment data are available, the input volume growth using the newly trialled methods is on average 4.8 per cent and 5.5 per cent per year depending on the method used.

In summary:

The methods that give the highest growth in the volume of input for the period 1995 to 2005 are the:

- indirect (deflation) approach for labour

- Paasche Price Index for prescription drugs, for intermediate consumption and

- capital services approach for capital

The methods that give the lowest growth in volume input for the period 1995 to 2005 are:

- the direct (counting) approach for labour

- average cost of index approach for prescription drugs, for intermediate consumption and

- capital consumption (depreciation) for capital

A major weakness persisting in estimating the volume of input for health services is that coverage of the key deflators is still based on England data. The deflators used need to be extended to cover the other UK countries as soon as detailed data become available.

9.3 Measuring Public Service Productivity

Significant progress has been made in developing methods for measuring public service output, and ONS has published the findings to date in productivity articles that act as a vehicle for experimental series. However, for changes to be made to the National Accounts, any new methodologies and data sources need to be subjected to a rigorous peer group appraisal, particularly as public service output makes a significant contribution to estimates of GDP.

Consensus is building towards a general agreement that the National Accounts might best be used to portray core economic estimates of productivity, that is, estimates that are based purely on the costs of producing output such as market sector productivity (see **Chapter 8**). It may be the case, however, that other publications best serve the wider welfare objectives.

The rationale is that unit costs cover a certain amount of economic welfare, in the sense that higher cost outputs would usually reflect higher levels of welfare. More welfare could be covered, though, if the weight of importance for outputs were based on values rather than costs, and if output were fully adjusted for its contribution to valuable outcomes. The ideal situation would, of course, be one that sees National Accounts estimates being adjusted as the evidence on values and quality adjustment gather consensus both domestically and internationally.

9.3.1 Public service productivity measurement

As mentioned earlier, because of the difficulties of measuring the growth of public service output in the absence of markets, the traditional approach in national accounting was to assume by convention that the output of the non-market government sector was equal to whatever was spent by government and public authorities. This is the so-called <output = inputs> convention.

The convention implies that productivity in the non-market sector by definition cannot change over time. This means that there is no possibility for the government to make any improvement in the services it provides using the existing resource levels, at least in measurement terms. It also precludes the possibility that the quality of government services could deteriorate for any given level of inputs over time.

Clearly this does not represent reality. Productivity in the public sector can and does change over time just as in the market sector. For example the quality of service in a particular NHS primary care unit can improve or deteriorate depending on the leadership and management of the unit even if all input resources are held at exactly the same level.

A justification that can be offered in the defence of the traditional convention is that governments behave as a perfectly rational agent, where the spending decisions on public services are based on optimisation criteria. In this case the government would be spending up to the point where the additional output from an extra unit of spending equalled the cost of that spending – no more, no less. Where the behaviour of the government is true to this, using the <output = input> definition can be plausible.

There are however, more compelling reasons to suggest that in reality governments cannot be the rational agent as described, on the basis that:

- governments do not possess the degree of knowledge required to operate in such a totally rational way
- even if governments were rational to the high extent

implied, they might not have the fiscal latitude to be able to afford to spend to the point where marginal costs of spending equal the marginal benefits

In view of all these compelling arguments, it became the prevailing opinion among national accountants that the convention was no longer tenable. As early as 1993, the SNA93 incorporated a movement away from the <output = inputs> convention in favour of direct measurement of the output of government/public services. The same change was reflected in the European System of Accounts (ESA95) promulgated in 1995 which applies to all European Union countries.

In addition, the *Eurostat Handbook* on Price and Volume measures also advocates a direct approach to measuring government output. It rejects the zero productivity assumption used in the old convention and argues that:

A harmonised assumption about productivity does nothing to make the resulting estimates of output more comparable. The more different the developments in productivity among member states, the less comparable are the results from using the same productivity change assumption (*Eurostat Handbook*, paragraph 3.1.2.1).

The work done by Sir Tony Atkinson highlights the soundness and importance of rejecting the assumption of constant productivity for the public sector. The report endorsed discarding the old convention and advocated a more principled and consistent approach to direct measurement of public sector services, as outlined in **Sections 9.1 to 9.1.6**. Atkinson's work is the most recent project lending weight and providing guidance that public service productivity should be defined by the standard ratio of the volume of output to the volume of input:

$$\text{Public services productivity} = \frac{\text{Public services output}}{\text{Public services input}}$$

Public service productivity measured by ONS for any of the government services is measured in terms of multi-factor productivity (MFP), where the volume input measure is the aggregate of all the inputs including labour, intermediate consumption and capital. This is a form of total output MFP similar to the approach used in the KLEMS project (see **Chapter 12**) and different from the labour-capital value added MFP produced by the ONS for the whole economy and some industries (see **Chapter 7**).

Box 9.5: Example: Measurement of productivity for the National Health Service

NHS productivity is calculated by dividing the volume of NHS outputs by the volume of NHS inputs and observing the changes on a yearly basis. Following the information provided in earlier sections, there are currently three sets of productivity estimates of interest:

- NHS productivity without quality adjustment

- NHS productivity with quality adjustment but no allowance for private/public sector complementarity

- NHS productivity with quality adjustment and an allowance for private/public sector complementarity

Using the different input measures and the output volume series for the period 1999 to 2004 without quality adjustment, NHS productivity is estimated to have **fallen** between 0.9 per cent and 1.5 per cent per annum, as shown in **Figure 9C**.

When quality adjustment is applied to NHS output, but excluding any allowance for private/public sector complementarity, NHS output growth during 1999 to 2004 increases by an average of 1.1 per cent per year. Applying these quality adjustment indicators therefore improves NHS productivity growth figures for the period to between an average **increase** of 0.2 per cent and a **fall** in productivity of 0.5 per cent per annum, as shown in **Figure 9D**. The adjustment for quality has the effect of changing a falling productivity trend into one that is relatively flat.

When an allowance for private/public sector complementarity is applied to quality adjusted NHS output, productivity is estimated to have increased by 0.9 per cent and 1.6 per cent annum for the period 1999 to 2004.

Figure 9C: New estimate of NHS productivity, excluding quality change for NHS output, 1995–2004

Index 1999=100

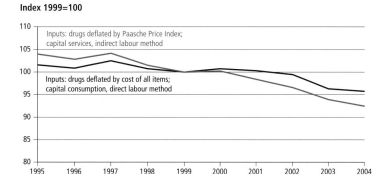

Figure 9D: NHS productivity based on output including quality change in NHS output but no allowance for private/public sector complementarity, 1999–2004

Index 1999=100

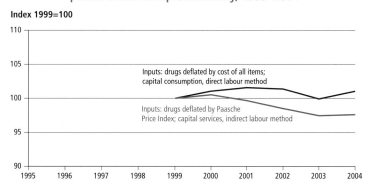

Figure 9E: NHS productivity including quality change in NHS output and allowance for private/public sector complementarity, 1999–2004

Index 1999=100

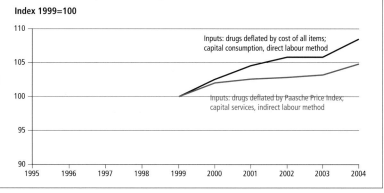

Source: UKCeMGA (February 2006)

135

9.4   Triangulation

Since the productivity measure is a residual or an implied measure determined by the vagaries of output and input measurement, there is validity in checking it against other sources of corroborative evidence. This sentiment is supported in the Atkinson Review in the statement that 'no single number, however carefully constructed, can fully capture the performance of complex public services with multiple objectives. Productivity change should be interpreted in the light of a range of other information'. The Atkinson Review named this the 'Triangulation principle' which is outlined in **Principle H:**

Principle H: Independent corroborative evidence should be sought on government productivity, as part of a process of 'triangulation', recognising the limitations in reducing productivity to a single number.

Triangulation is about checking the plausibility of productivity numbers by analysing information from independent sources. The Atkinson Review sets out three levels at which the triangulation can be carried out.

1. The first stage should be one of cross-checking. At the minimum, the growth trend of outputs, inputs and productivity should be checked for coherence and reconciled with reliable sources of information on each of the elements

2. The second stage of triangulation would be to systematically relate the derived productivity figures against departmental Public Service Agreement (PSA) targets and the corresponding trend of the performance indictors

3. The third level of triangulation is a very ambitious one and would involve undertaking a government-wide productivity measurement programme

The outcome of the triangulation process of cross checking is, in the first instance, the verification of the single measure of productivity using alternative sources. Secondly, the result of the first and second stages of triangulation will provide evidence to weight the inputs and output so as to adjust the implied productivity number to reflect reality. However, the evidence based used so far for triangulation purposes is still firmly pinned to the first level recommended by Atkinson.

9.4.1 Triangulation in practice and further recommendations for its use

Since a single measure of productivity is unlikely to be sufficient to capture the complexity of pubic services with its multiple objectives and multiple quality domains, triangulation is The Atkinson Review's systematic approach. It supplements the findings from the implied measure of productivity by seeking evidence on each of the three elements in the equation <productivity = output/input>. For example, corroborative evidence in terms of wider departmental performance indicators, inspection reports, or even patient or customer satisfaction surveys, can be used for the purpose of triangulation.

The key issue with triangulation, however, is that the wider evidence base does actually say something meaningful about the output and inputs used for productivity estimates. At the lower but perhaps more practical end, it may be sufficient to simply look at the wider evidence for support. At the higher end, but less practical, would be a more analytical and technical approach to align key indicators and productivity estimates.

It is clear that the single productivity number generated will be only as good as the two elements of output and input that are measured in the first place. Measured changes in output and inputs involve some uncertainty because of the limitations on data availability, multiplicity of outcomes, quality dimensions of public services, and the complexity of measuring quality changes of services operating outside the market system.

For example, in the absence of prices and good information on choice by recipients of public services, it is difficult to value the marginal benefit or unit benefit of public services by which to weight all the different outputs. If value weights are used then, depending on whose valuation is adopted, the growth rates of output and thereby the productivity growth rate can be significantly different. Also, on the input side, specific deflators at a sufficiently disaggregated level may not be available to accurately filter out price movements which could make input growth figures less than accurate.

Box 9.6 Example: Wider evidence on the performance of the National Health Service

To corroborate the productivity story obtained from the measured volume of output and input series, a triangulation exercise can also be carried out for the health sector. The evidence presented below provides a richer understanding of the productivity picture than what the trend of a single productivity number can tell. At the 'first level' of triangulation, the independent information considered so far includes the following:

Average length of stay in hospital – the average length of stay in hospitals has fallen from just over 8 days in the beginning of the 1990s to just below 7 days in 2003/04. The length of stay in hospital is a major part of NHS costs and a decline in average stay would be consistent with a rise in productivity. This effect will be augmented if the freeing up of beds had allowed more patients to be treated.

Elective day case rates – the elective day case rate increased from 39 per cent in the 1990s to 67 per cent in 2003/04. Day case surgeries are surgical procedures where the patients are discharged on the same day of the admission. Increased day case rate helps to reduce costs to the NHS, contributes towards timely treatment, reduces the risk of cross infection and

reduces the number of procedures cancelled. Increase in day case surgery also reflects an improvement in quality of NHS services provided for patients. This is because the procedure is likely to have a shorter waiting time, it enables patients to return home the same day and back to normal activities sooner than otherwise would be possible. It also allows patients to receive care better suited to their needs. The evidence of an increase in elective day care rates is therefore consistent with the view of rising NHS productivity.

Emergency readmissions – the rate of people readmitted into hospitals within 28 days after being discharged – increased across different age groups for the period between 1998/99 and 2003/04. Readmission rates is a measure of the quality of treatment received by patients, however the indicator is a developing one. There are many factors that can contribute to readmission: level of after care, whether treatment took place in a hospital, the length of overnight stay, and others issues. While the readmission rate is an informative statistic, a firm judgement on the implication to productivity is difficult to make at this stage.

Public attitudes to health care – results from the British Social Attitudes Survey

(BSAS) can be used to determine public attitudes towards health care. The BSAS is not a patient survey but a public survey and therefore is not directly linked to patient experience or the performance of the NHS (although clearly some respondents may have encountered at least some health care in the past or present). Results obtained from the public satisfaction questions indicate that public satisfaction with NHS has fluctuated over time. Nevertheless, over the period 1990 to 2003, 'the quite satisfied with NHS' has remained the highest public response. Again, although this statistic is informative, it does not yet lend any real weight as to whether productivity is rising.

The evidence above adds to the story of how NHS productivity has been changing over the recent years. Although the information is not comprehensive, the triangulation exercise does provide evidence that is in keeping with the rising trend in productivity. In the limit, it would of course look odd if estimates show that NHS productivity is rising (or falling) but all the key performance indicators suggest otherwise. But getting the right balance between wider evidence and productivity estimates is still developing, and there needs to be more rigour when interpreting the exact trends.

Source: UKCeMGA (February 2006)

9.5   Conclusions

9.5.1 Atkinson Review has advanced measurement of public service productivity

Since 1998, ONS made good progress in taking forward an internationally driven agenda for measuring public service output by direct methods. However, the true turning point for making significant advances in this technically challenging area was the publication of the Atkinson Review in January 2005.

ONS set up the UK Centre for the Measurement of Government Activity specifically to take forward the principles and recommendations made by the Atkinson

Review. So far, significant progress has been made in the measurement of output and productivity for following public services: health, education, adult social care and the administration of social security. These services form a major share of total government expenditure on public services. Progress has also been made in the areas of public order and safety, but to a lesser extent.

9.5.2 Measurement of public service output is now firmly based on direct methods

Following major changes in the methods used to measure public service output since 1998, the process has become more transparent. The first step is to identify as many outputs, covering as much expenditure dedicated to them, as possible and practical. The second and most challenging step is to identify the quality of these outputs, in particular the contribution they make to outcomes.

In terms of moving forward on these steps, please refer to the UKCeMGA strategy paper that was published in July 2007.

9.5.3 Measurement of public service inputs are now based on improved methods and expenditure data

Compared to public sector output, the measurement of public service inputs is relatively more straightforward given the presence of wages and prices. There are still major challenges ahead, particularly in getting better and more detailed expenditure data that allow a more accurate assessment of the volume of inputs used to produce output in the specific public sector services. But given the data that are currently available, the use of both indirect (deflation) and direct (counting) methods has progressed to a higher level of sophistication.

9.5.4 Consideration of economic and wider welfare measures of public service productivity are required

It is likely that, at least in the short term, more than one measure of productivity will be required to fit different major objectives. For the National Accounts, initial output measures of public service productivity are likely to be based more on economic cost weights and, at best, partial measures of quality. This is because it takes time for new methods and data to be accepted in the National Accounts – a framework that requires serious and technical scrutiny. In the meantime, when new and more appropriate measures of output evolve, in particular those that include new measures of quality and therefore welfare, it is important to publish these new findings. The current series of ONS productivity articles serve this purpose very well.

Finally, it should be acknowledged that this chapter draws heavily from a number of key publications. In particular these are the Atkinson Review Final Report and key productivity articles on taking up the challenges set by the review already published by UKCeMGA. We have also relied on key research findings published by the National Institute of Economic Research and the University of York, the Department for Health, and the Department for Education and Skills.

9.6   References

Atkinson A B (2005) *Atkinson Review: Final Report. Measurement of Government Output and Productivity for the National Accounts*, Palgrave Macmillan: Basingstoke, available at: www.statistics.gov.uk/about/data/methodology/specific/publicSector/atkinson/final_report.asp

Pritchard A (2001) *Understanding government output and productivity*, Office for National Statistics: London.

UKCeMGA (October 2005) *Public Service Productivity: Education*, Office for National Statistics: London.

UKCeMGA (February 2006) *Public Service Productivity: Health*, Office for National Statistics: London.

UKCeMGA (October 2006) Establishing the Principles Consultation, *Measuring performance in our public services*, Office for National Statistics: London.

UKCeMGA (November 2006) Education Consultation, *Measuring performance in our public services*, Office for National Statistics: London.

UKCeMGA (January 2007) Health Consultation, *Measuring performance in our public services*, Office for National Statistics: London.

UK Centre for the Measurement of Government Activity (2007) 'Measuring Quality as Part of Public Service Output', Office for National Statistics: London, available at: http://www.statistics.gov.uk/about/data/methodology/specific/PublicSector/output/consultations.asp

York, NIESR Study (December 2005) *Developing new approaches to measuring NHS outputs and productivity: Non-technical Summary of the Final Report*, University of York and National Institute for Economic and Social Research: York.

Chapter 10

Micro, or Firm Level, Productivity

All ONS productivity outputs, whole economy, sector or industry level series, are constructed from data for individual firms collected through ONS surveys. Since 1995 information technology has made it possible to look behind the overall figures to understand better how they are driven by the performance of individual firms. This is valuable in developing statistical evidence for the design and assessment of policy.

Most ONS business surveys are carried out under the Statistics of Trade Act 1947, which makes completion of the survey compulsory but limits the use to statistical purposes. A programme to develop microdata access began in 1997, and to link microdata from different surveys in 2001.

Since 2004, ONS has provided secure access to confidential microdata for statistical research through a 'virtual microdata laboratory' (VML) facility. This VML provides useful research access to these data, for statistical analysis by accredited experts. Analysis of individual survey returns, rather than macro level statistics, has enabled these researchers to look at individual drivers of productivity.

This chapter describes the VML, and the use and policy impact of micro productivity work. It gives an overview of the datasets and information currently available to researchers while maintaining security.

The History of the Business Data Linking Project

Productivity can be measured at the firm level, allowing businesses or policy makers to understand firm performance, dispersion of performance, and productivity drivers at firm level (HM Treasury, March 2006).

Creation of linked data sets for business demography and productivity work in manufacturing has been under way in ONS – in different forms – since 1997. Work began in the late 1990s to create a longitudinally linked data set from the 1970s onwards. The aim of this is to bring together, in one database, all the data about sales, value added, employment and various inputs relating to one firm from as many different surveys as possible. This work formed the foundation of the Business Data Linking (BDL) project and used survey data from the Annual Business Inquiry (ABI) and its predecessors to form the Annual Respondents Database (ARD). The first work using this resource looked at the distribution of productivity across manufacturing firms, and how it was affected by the creation of new firms and the death of old ones.

From these beginnings, the BDL project set out in 2001 to link the ARD to other surveys to assess inputs to productivity beyond labour and capital. The project was run as a partnership between ONS and Queen Mary College London, and sponsored by HM Treasury (HMT) and the Department of Trade & Industry (DTI). It combined returns from a number of ONS surveys with ARD productivity information to assess the performance impact of inputs such as skills, research and develpment (R&D), innovation and ICT use, and of organisational characteristics such as multinational reach.

Early work focused largely on manufacturing firms but, once the principles were well established, the project undertook the first major microdata analysis of the distribution and dynamics of productivity in the services sector. As this work was published, access and popularity of data linking by academics and policy researchers increased, resulting in a rise in the number of projects assessing a range of issues and industries.

This project has now linked, using the Inter-Departmental Business Register (IDBR) as its key reference point, data from successive surveys from several sectors. In doing so it has tackled a number of difficult problems caused

by changes in register structure, sampling strategy and survey design. (For more information about the IDBR, see **Section 5.1.**) The virtual microdata laboratory (VML) was set up in 2004 to bring together all data for research in a consistent format and secure environment. It now houses numerous data sets that are available for productivity research in many areas and is a technically secure solution providing common access to ONS business data across all ONS sites. The VML can be accessed under supervision by selected researchers (Ritchie, 2005).

To ensure that the trust placed in the researchers using the data is justified, access is subject to a range of procedural restrictions and access agreements. These are modelled on arrangements that have been successfully developed in other National Statistics Institutes in North America and Europe, but adapted to the UK legal framework. The access to UK data and the sharing of methodologies and techniques internationally has now generated a huge amount of work on micro level productivity. Given the skills and reputation of UK economic researchers, this has quickly brought ONS to a position among the world leaders in providing data and facilities for this type of productivity research.

10.1 Areas of Productivity Research

In its original form, the main purpose of the ARD was to investigate how output and productivity developed at the level of the individual firm. This permitted researchers to test how far overall growth in market sector productivity was caused by:

- improvement in performance by firms continuing in operation
- faster growth by firms with better productivity performance
- the death of low productivity firms and their replacement by newer firms with better performance

These data can also be used to research the behaviour, as well as the performance, of firms with different types of characteristics. For example, LSE researchers have used the ARD, linked to other surveys, to investigate what types of firms invest most heavily in computer hardware, before going on to test what the effects of such investment might be.

A large proportion of microdata work is used to answer productivity questions. The combination of enterprise level data on employment, turnover, value added, purchases of intermediate materials and services and investment data, which can be used to derive firm level capital stocks, enables users to construct productivity estimates for each enterprise. Unique firm identifiers then allow linking both across time and over different surveys. Consequently information from numerous business surveys can be linked to ABI data to create cross sections or panels.

Micro level productivity analysis has already played an important role in informing policy, particularly in providing evidence on how and where key drivers of productivity improvement can be seen at work (see **Chapter 3** for further information on these). Indeed, microdata work has proved particularly powerful in assessing how HMT's strategic 'five drivers' of productivity work in practice, and perhaps more important, suggesting areas of market failure where potential productivity gains are not being achieved.

The productivity supplement to the 2006 Budget (HMT, 2006) provides a good summary of microdata work, which has been used to guide and assess policy. Below are examples of some studies undertaken by academic researchers on the 'five drivers' of productivity using ONS data.

10.1.1 Competition
The effects of competition on productivity, in enabling more productive firms to grow at the expense of others, and in giving firms a clear incentive to improve performance, can be seen in firm level data. One study shows that these processes, and the entry and exit of businesses associated with them, account for 20 per cent to 50 per cent of the increases in UK manufacturing productivity (Disney, Haskel and Heden, 2003). Similar effects have also been shown in the retail sector (Haskel and Khawaja 2003). There is also considerable evidence that businesses that are able to compete internationally, as multinationals in global markets, are able to reap productivity benefits (Criscuolo and Martin, 2003).

10.1.2 Innovation
Studies have shown that competition is positively associated with innovation by firms (Aghion, Bloom, Blundell, Griffiths and Howitt, 2001). Innovation can boost productivity in two ways, by firms investing in R&D themselves and reaping the benefits from new or improved products and processes, or by 'spillovers' from

creators of knowledge to other firms to compete. Studies have shown that both these processes – R&D investment and the use of external knowledge – influence the ability of firms to innovate (Criscuolo, Haskel and Slaughter, 2004). International sales and innovation have been shown to be associated with superior productivity (Harris and Li, 2005). Innovation includes not only technical development but also design and this too has been shown to generate positive returns (Haskel, Cereda, Crespi and Criscuolo, 2005).

10.1.3 Investment
Investment improves labour productivity by increasing the stock of capital available to workers. A number of studies have estimated the effects, and recent work has shown the specific productivity impacts associated with investment in IT hardware (Bloom, Van Reenen and Sadun, 2005). Investment in software and the use of ICT by employees have also been shown to be associated with higher levels of firm productivity (Farooqui, 2005). These effects are particularly large when supported by modern, broadband, communications networks (Farooqui and Sadun, 2006).

10.1.4 Skills
The quantity and quality of skills in an economy – or a firm – affect its productive capability. Linking of skills variables to ABI information has produced a series of analyses showing that both qualifications and occupations are associated with productivity effects (Haskel, Hawkes and Perriera, 2004). UK scope for this type of analysis is limited by available data, usually from the Annual Survey on Hours and Earnings (ASHE) – for occupations and the Employee Skills Survey – for qualifications. In Scandinavian countries, where individual worker characteristics can be linked to their employers, much more detailed studies are possible.

10.1.5 Enterprise
Enterprise – the creation of new firms to exploit new ideas – is essential to the competitive process. Studies into the demography of enterprises and the effect of entry of new firms on productivity have been carried out in a number of countries (Scarpetta, Hemmings, Tressel and Woo, 2002). ONS and Dutch work on the effects of ICT investment has shown that newer firms are better able to secure larger productivity gains.

The impact of VML work is increasingly important for policy makers. For example, the majority of microeconomic studies on productivity referenced in the 2006 *Budget Productivity Report* are based on VML analyses. This stands in sharp contrast to 2001, when productivity analysis relied almost entirely on aggregate data and research from other countries. The range of productivity analyses at a national level has stimulated the use of these data for regional analyses, with devolved assemblies being particularly keen to carry out more local analysis.

10.2   Advantages of microdata analysis

One of the key advantages of microdata is that they permit the examination of a great deal of variability that occurs at lower levels, and that macro statistics often mask. Microdata make it possible to analyse relationships between economic variables more closely. The presence of linked demographic information in many data sets allows more complex tabulations and regression results to be extracted than by simply using aggregates. In terms of productivity, it is possible to isolate the effects of factors such as region, firm size and foreign ownership on the productivity of individual businesses.

The wealth of information available through the VML has been reflected in the many productivity analyses that have been conducted since its advent. The increase in use of these data has also lead to increased scrutiny of the datasets. This has allowed problems and techniques to be shared among researchers, and has given ONS valuable feedback on the quality of data.

The applications of firm level analysis are still being developed, with new researchers coming to the field in an increasing number of countries. As future work progresses, productivity, analysis using microdata will become more sophisticated, more widely recognised and practiced.

10.3   The available data sets and their use in productivity research

There are several data sets that are now used for micro productivity analysis. The following is a summary of some of the key sources and their use in research.

10.3.1 Annual Respondents Database (ARD2)

The Annual Respondents Database (known as ARD since 2000 and ARD2 since 2006) combines a number of ONS business surveys and reference numbers taken from the IDBR, a register of legal units and the most comprehensive list of UK businesses available. Together they form a

longitudinal database of firm information with the data, in recent years, taken solely from the ABI.

Since 1997 this survey has collected over 50,000 records per year from most industries with information on employment, turnover, purchases, investment and stocks for all industries, as well as more specific variables for individual sectors. The combination of these variables allows the calculation of gross value added, which can be combined with employment and capital stock measures to form estimates of productivity. Most VML productivity analysis uses the ARD2 to some degree.

The ARD2 also contains 'non-selected' records for those businesses that either did not return or did not receive a survey form. These records are taken from the IDBR and by using them ONS can correctly weight each firm by turnover, employment or industry. The IDBR reference number also allows businesses to be linked across surveys to combine the variables collected. Consequently, multiple surveys can be used to conduct productivity analysis using the variables collected from the ABI. For further information see Robjohns (2006).

10.3.2 Business Structure Database (BSD)

The IDBR is the key sampling frame for UK business statistics and is maintained and developed by the Business Registers Unit (BRU) within ONS. The Business Structure Database (BSD), also held by the BRU, creates a longitudinal version of the IDBR for research use, taking full account of changes in ownership and restructuring of businesses.

An advantage of the BSD over previous sources is that it enables researchers to distinguish between a business merely exiting a survey and that business exiting an industry altogether. This allows the effect of firm entry and exit on productivity to be analysed more accurately. As every local unit, reporting unit, enterprise and enterprise group is given its own unique reference number when it enters onto the IDBR, it is possible to link firms longitudinally. This reference remains unique to that business while it remains in the same form on the register. It is therefore possible to make inferences about business entry and exit from the register.

An example of how this works is presented by Foster, Haltiwanger and Krizan (1998), who proposed a method of decomposing productivity growth into entry and exit components. This method requires information on whether a firm has entered or exited an industry in any given period and also an estimate of each firm's productivity. The combination of business survey data and the BSD allow such analyses to be carried out. For example, this analysis for computer services between 1997 and 2003 demonstrated that during that period the industry's labour productivity grew 5 per cent because of low productivity firms exiting.

10.3.3 Annual Foreign Direct Investment (AFDI)

The Annual Inquiry into Foreign Direct Investment (AFDI) is conducted in two parts: an inward inquiry and an outward inquiry. The inward inquiry concerns the subsidiaries/associates of foreign firms operating in the UK, while the outward inquiry covers the investment made by UK firms in their overseas operations.

An example of the use of this is that linking the ARD2 and AFDI permitted researchers to identify enterprise productivity effects associated with multinational operations, and to separate them from the issue of foreign ownership. The results show (as similar work in the US and Sweden has done) large productivity advantages associated with multinational operations, irrespective of country of origin, after taking account of sector, scale, capital input and other relevant factors. It suggests that multinationals are able to exploit shared intellectual capital not captured by current surveys. These results have had a major impact on the productivity agenda in the UK.

10.3.4 E-Commerce Survey

The e-commerce survey asks for information on firms' use of ICT and e-commerce in their business. The survey has been run since 2001, so has a relatively short span of data, but has provided a useful source for analysis of the productivity impacts of ICT use.

Recent projects have used responses from both the e-commerce and ABI surveys to create a matched data set of firms that have answered both of them, plus the quarterly Capital Expenditure survey. Internal ONS projects have identified a number of productivity effects including the positive impact of investment in computer hardware and software, and employee use of the Internet in firms on labour and multi-factor productivity.

10.3.5 Community Innovation Survey (CIS)

An EU wide survey on innovative activity in both manufacturing and service firms, the Community Innovation Survey (CIS), has been carried out every four years since the mid 1990s and is about to become a biennial survey. As a voluntary survey, it has not been carried out under the Statistics of Trade Act, and is more widely used for firm level analysis of the innovation process than any other dataset. For productivity analysis it is linked to the ABI and to surveys on R&D expenditure.

10.3.6 Other Surveys

The VML also houses a number of other datasets that have been used in productivity work. Combined together, these allow a wide range of research to be carried out, including:

- examining the link between changes in productivity and wages in the UK over the last two decades

- investigating the importance of knowledge transfer as a driver of productivity within UK retailing

- an explanation of the existence of non-linearities and interaction effects for capital and labour scale economies in productivity

- matching ARD with skills data to examine the importance of human capital in determining plant level productivity in various manufacturing and non-manufacturing sectors of the UK economy

- studies introducing travel time and geographical information to look into the regional impacts, such as closeness to major conurbations and proximity to relevant transport hubs

There are currently over 200 academic and government researchers accredited to use the VML facilities.

10.4   Issues with microdata analysis

One challenge for microdata researchers is that surveys are almost always designed and sampled with a view to producing macro statistics. Consequently, the questions asked on survey forms are not always ideal for microdata analysis. For example, recent employment questionnaires have asked respondents for number of employees at a point in time as opposed to an average over a period, which is generally more useful for productivity research purposes. Another issue for microdata research is the updating and changing of classifications and variable definitions. The Standard Industrial Classification (SIC) has changed several times, most recently in 2003. This requires complicated mappings to be made at each period where a change is introduced. Similarly, when variable definitions are changed over time it creates complications for longitudinal analysis.

Other problems with business microdata stem from issues with sampling and consistency across surveys. ONS rules on sampling ensure that small firms are sampled on an irregular basis and the smallest are not selected at all so as not to over-burden respondents. This has the effect that business surveys include only a minor percentage of small firms, which may be particularly problematic when trying to analyse areas such as new start-ups. Survey design weights are available to help correct for this problem. In terms of consistency, it has become evident that similar variables on different surveys do not necessarily match. Coding to denote foreign ownership has often been noted to differ for the same firms across surveys.

A further caveat to note when conducting analysis on linked datasets is the low frequencies that can be expected. There may only be a couple of hundred firms who are present in both the datasets that are being used in a piece of analysis. This limits the numbers of degrees of freedom for complicated regressions, which will be exacerbated if further subsections need to be drawn from the dataset.

In addition to this, it is likely to be only the largest firms that are present across several surveys and hence it may be difficult to make inferences about the population from matched datasets. The problem of testing whether conclusions from the limited number of observations available from linked datasets can be extended to the wider population is a complex one. The solution depends on good understanding of the sample design in the surveys that are being linked. Recommendations on how to deal with these issues have been developed to aid researchers (Cheshire and Nisheim, 2004).

10.5   Producing macro statistics from microdata

An issue that attracts a lot of comment is the use of microdata to produce macro level statistics. The process of 'grossing-up' individual survey returns to form population estimates is, in theory, quite a simple one. In reality, though, replicating published figures often proves difficult. A major reason for the lack of consistency between published and independently derived figures is the balances and adjustments that are made on comparison with other data sources. Differences in weighting techniques may also contribute to differing results. The ongoing development of these techniques has given increased understanding of the issues relating to grossing up individual returns and will hopefully lead to a more standardised approach. These issues should be noted,

however, when trying to use ONS business microdata in producing aggregate productivity figures.

10.6   Accessing data

Access to restricted microdata through the VML requires an application to Business Data Linking (BDL) branch at ONS. Projects must demonstrate some level of statistical or research benefit to ONS in order to be accepted. Only named researchers are allowed to access the data and all outputs are subject to Statistical Disclosure Control (SDC) methods that are in line with ONS standards and administered by BDL staff. For people outside the civil service to use these data, an institutional agreement is required with the research organisation or university.

The VML facility provides an exceptionally high level of security while still offering researchers the flexibility of full access to the data. As part of the security, VML staff vet all statistical results generated by researchers to ensure the confidentiality of respondent data. A training course in the legal requirements and the basic disclosure control is required for all VML users, and recommended for those commissioning work. More information can be obtained from bdl@ons.gov.uk.

10.7   Conclusion

The VML provides researchers with a technical solution to accessing confidential ONS business surveys. The increase in use of this resource has led to a better understanding of its use in productivity analysis. The linking of ABI variables to other datasets has allowed researchers to isolate the productivity impact of a number of factors. The wealth of firm-specific information that is available gives microdata a key advantage over macro statistics in this area. As further work is produced and more data are added to the VML, the scope for productivity research will broaden.

10.8 References

Aghion P, Bloom N, Blundell R, Griffiths R and Howitt P (2001) 'Empirical Estimates of the Relationship between Product Market Competition and Innovation', *Quarterly Journal of Economics* 120, pp 701–728.

Bloom N, Van Reenen J and Sadun R, (2005) *It Ain't What You Do, it's the Way that You do IT*, Centre for Economic Performance, London School of Economics: London.

Cheshire A and Nisheim L (2004) 'Statistical Properties of Linked Datasets', DTI research paper, Department of Trade & Industry: London.

Criscuolo C, Haskel J and Slaughter M (2004) *Why are some Firms more Innovative? Knowledge Inputs, Knowledge Stocks and the Role of Global Engagement*, NBER: Cambridge.

Criscuolo C and Martin R (2003) *Multinationals and US Productivity Leadership, Evidence from Britain*, draft note, Ceriba, Centre for Research into Business Activity, ONS: London.

Disney R, Haskel J and Heden Y (2003) 'Restructuring and Productivity Growth in UK Manufacturing', *Economic Journal* 113, pp 666–694.

Farooqui S (2005) 'IT use by Firms and Employees, Productivity Evidence across Industries', *Economic Trends* 625, pp 65–74, available at: www.statistics.gov.uk/ CCI/article.asp?ID=1233

Farooqui S and Sadun R (2006) *Broadband Availability, Use and Impact on Returns to ICT in UK Firms*, ONS and Centre for Economic Performance, Organisation for Economic Co-operation and Development: Paris.

Foster L, Haltiwanger J and Krizan C J (1998) *Aggregate Productivity Growth: Lessons From Microeconomic Evidence Working Papers 98–12*, Center for Economic Studies, U.S. Census Bureau: Washington.

Harris R and Li Q (2005) *Establishment Level Empirical Study of Links between Exporting, Innovation and Productivity*, Report to UKTI.

Haskel J, Cereda M, Crespi G and Criscuolo C (2005) *Creativity and Design Study*, Economics Paper No.15, Department of Trade & Industry: London, available at: www.dti.gov.uk/files/file13654.pdf

Haskel J, Hawkes D and Perriera S (2004) *How much do Skills Raise Productivity? UK Evidence from Matched Plant, Worker and Workforce Data*, Ceriba, Centre for Research into Business Activity, ONS: London.

Haskel J and Khawaja N (2003) *Productivity in UK Retailing, Evidence from UK Microdata*, Discussion Paper, Ceriba, Centre for Research into Business Activity, Queen Mary College: London, available at: www.qmul.ac.uk/~/CERIBA/publications/services.pdf

HM Treasury (2006) *Productivity in the UK; Progress and new evidence*, HMT: London.

Ritchie F J (July 2005) 'Business data linking: recent UK experience', *Austrian Journal of Statistics* 33, Number 1&2, pp 89–100.

Robjohns J (2006) 'ARD2: the new Annual Respondents Database', *Economic Trends* 630, pp 43–51, available at: www.statistics.gov.uk/CCI/article.asp?ID=1556

Scarpetta S, Hemmings P, Tressel T and Woo J (2002) *The Role of Policy and Institutions for Productivity and Firm Dynamics, Evidence from Micro and Industry Evidence*, Organisation for Economic Co-operation and Development: Paris.

Chapter 11

Regional Productivity

Regional differences in productivity performance across the UK are seen by government as important policy targets. For a number of years, government objectives have been set not only in terms of improving UK productivity performance against other countries but also in creating conditions to allow less productive regions to reduce the 'gap' between themselves and the most productive.

This chapter discusses the issues surrounding the measurement of productivity at a regional level. It introduces the uses and importance of regional statistics before describing regional productivity in terms of the historical and current measures available. Clarification is provided about what the different measures show – whether they describe economic performance, welfare or productivity – and the effect that using different measures can have.

Some of the factors that explain differences in the productivity of regions are identified, with discussion of the issues surrounding data capability and availability at the regional level. The chapter finishes with discussion of future development plans, with particular reference to the recommendations made to better satisfy the pressing needs for improved regional data that were highlighted in the 'Review of Statistics for Economic Policymaking' (Allsopp, 2004).

The Link between Regional Productivity and Policy

Regional and local statistics have become increasingly important in recent years, reflecting the greater emphasis on regional and area-based policies. The European Union's (EU) Structural Funds have used regional gross domestic product (GDP) per head as the indicator that determines which regions of the EU are eligible for the highest levels of support under the Convergence Objective, a policy that aims to help areas 'lagging behind'.

Within the UK, devolution to Scotland, Wales and Northern Ireland, and the creation of the Regional Development Agencies in England, have added to the demand for more regional data. In particular, the Government has also set a joint public service agreement (PSA) target for the Department for Communities and Local Government (DCLG), HM Treasury (HMT) and the Department of Trade and Industry (DTI) within the Spending Review Period 2005 to 2008:

> Make sustainable improvements in the economic performance of all English regions by 2008 and over the long term reduce the persistent gap in growth rates between the regions, demonstrating progress by 2006 (DCLG, 2006).

Regional data are important to support this target.

11.1   Producing regional statistics

Estimates of regional GDP became available in the 1970s and since then GDP per head has been used as the main indicator of regional performance. Since the introduction of the European System of Accounts 1995 (ESA95), gross value added (GVA) and GVA per head have been used as the main indicators of regions' performance. GVA is preferable to GDP at regional level because it excludes taxes or subsidies on products that are difficult to attribute to local units (see **Chapter 4** for further details). Until recently, these have been the only indicators of regional performance that were available on a consistent basis across Europe. For an in-depth discussion of regional GVA please see **Section 11.2**.

Similar to measures for the UK (detailed in **Chapter 1**), regional GVA per head does not provide a good measure of the economic productivity of a region or the wellbeing of those living in the region. GVA, the numerator, is generally a workplace-based concept, allocating the incomes of workers to where they work, whereas the denominator is the residence-based population of the area. GVA per head is therefore inflated upwards in those areas where there is a significant amount of in-commuting. Consequently, GVA per hour worked is the preferred productivity measure. Recent improvements in levels of detail and quality of information on hours worked has enabled past data limitations to be overcome and the preferred measure of productivity to be developed.

It is also recognised that there is a need for a wider range of indicators to support regional policy. In particular, methods have been developed to produce gross disposable household income (GDHI) and GDHI per head as indicators of the welfare of people living in a region. For measuring the economic performance of individual regions, it is recognised that there is a need for regional measures of economic activity and productivity, based on GVA and labour market indicators. This chapter looks particularly at the issue of regional productivity and its measurement within the context of the UK and its constituent countries, regions and sub-regions.

Box 11.1: Defining regional geographies

For the purposes of European regional statistics, geographical distinctions are made according to the European Union's Nomenclature of Units for Territorial Statistics (NUTS), allowing comparison of regions across the European Union. There are three NUTS levels in the UK, as follows:

- NUTS level 1: 12 areas – Scotland, Wales, Northern Ireland and the nine Government Office Regions in England

- NUTS level 2: 37 areas within the UK, generally groups of unitary authorities and counties.

- NUTS level 3: 133 areas, generally individual counties and groups of unitary authorities or districts, also known as local areas.

The compilation of regional statistics raises specific problems less relevant to the national level. First, the quality and accuracy of data collated based on sample surveys depends on sample size. The finer the detail, for example at NUTS3 level compared to NUTS1 level, the smaller the sample size and therefore the greater the uncertainty about precision of estimates.

Next, multi-region activity poses a particular problem for regional statistics. The statistics collected generally relate to reporting units. National productivity measures are calculated by aggregating data for reporting units; see the description of the jobs series created for productivity measurement in **Chapter 5**. A reporting unit corresponds to either the entire enterprise or the major activity within a business, with the head office of the organisation sending a statistical return for the whole organisation. Each reporting unit can consist of one or more local units or individual sites such as factories or retail outlets. These local units may be based in different regions or may each have its own industry associated with it.

Statistical methods are used to apportion the activity of a reporting unit to the areas where its constituent local units are based. There is the potential problem of 'head-office effects' – that a business reports at its enterprise level (at which the business has some control or independence) because it cannot provide full data for each local unit (individual site). Making the necessary apportionments to local units then becomes more difficult. Developments to the business register will incorporate surveying of local units to improve this aspect of regional statistics. **Section 11.5** provides further details.

11.2   Measuring regional productivity

A common definition of productivity is 'a ratio of a volume measure of output to a volume measure of input use' (Organisation for Economic Co-operation and Development (OECD), 2001). To measure productivity at the regional level, it is preferable to use GVA per hour worked where GVA is a measure of regional economic activity or output, and the hours worked are a measure of the labour input used to produce the output.

The historically-used GVA per head does measure the economic performance of a region against an input measure (the population). However, population does not take into account potential regional demographic differences, including different dependency ratios. Neither does it represent cross-regional commuting that causes disparities between the number of people who live in a region and the number who work there. Using a residence-based denominator against a workplace-based GVA numerator is not comparable and therefore using GVA per head as a measure of productivity gives a distorted picture.

For example, where there are large commuting inflows, such as in London, fewer people live than work there. In these regions, more people contribute to the workplace-based GVA than would be accounted for by a residence-

based population denominator, which would, on this basis, be too small. GVA per head for that region would therefore overstate the relative 'productivity' and therefore present an inaccurate picture of productivity for that region and the surrounding regions.

Labour productivity, therefore, provides a more comparable indicator of productivity as it measures both the numerator and denominator on a workplace basis. GVA per worker apportions GVA to the number employed in the region.

GVA per worker = GVA/Total number of people employed

This method is not, however, the most appropriate because it does not take into consideration regional labour market structures or different working patterns, such as the possible mix of part- and full-time workers, home workers and job share availability. Therefore while GVA per worker is the headline UK measure, it is not the preferred regional measure.

The preferred measure is GVA per hour worked, which apportions GVA to the total hours worked by the workforce and therefore is a more appropriate measure of productivity.

GVA per hour worked = GVA/total workforce hours worked

The recent overcoming of the data limitations on hours worked data has been important in developing this as the preferred measure. The differences between these indicators are discussed in more detail later in the chapter.

11.2.1 Productivity indicators – what is currently published

ONS publishes regional productivity indicators annually. The three productivity measures are:

1. output per filled job (as a proxy for output per worker)

2. output per hour worked

3. output per head

The figures published are indexed to a UK average to enable description of the variations within the UK. Published productivity estimates currently only relate to NUTS1 level. It is anticipated that experimental sub-regional productivity estimates will be able to be published (at NUTS 2 and 3 levels) for GVA per filled job and GVA per hour worked in 2007.

Other ONS publications that incorporate information on regional productivity include the quarterly article 'Regional Economic Indicators' published in *Economic & Labour Market Review*. This article extends analysis beyond the primary productivity indicators already identified by investigating some of the drivers of productivity identified by HMT and the DTI (HMT, 2001). The productivity drivers identified are investment, innovation, enterprise, competition and skills. For more information on the five productivity drivers, see **Chapter 3**.

The DTI also publishes productivity indicators for the 12 NUTS1 regions and countries of the UK in its annual publication *Regional Competitiveness and State of the Regions* (DTI, 2006). GVA (workplace basis) per head is tabulated on both a UK Index and pound sterling per head basis. For fairer comparisons across differently sized regions and to remove the effects of using a residence-based denominator against a workplace-based numerator, labour productivity indicators are also included. GVA per workforce job provides absolute regional indicators for broad industry sectors. In addition, and like those produced in the ONS *Productivity First Release*, GVA per job filled (as a proxy for GVA per worker) and GVA per hour worked are included, both on an index basis.

11.2.2 The significance of different productivity measures

Figure 11.1 shows how using different indicators can alter the perceptions of relative regional performance. Three indicators for comparison of the productivity measures are presented: GVA per head (although **Section 11.2** identified this historic measure as a measure of economic performance rather than productivity, it is useful for comparison), GVA per filled job (a proxy for GVA per worker) and GVA per hour worked. It provides the percentage divergence from the UK average of each region in terms of each indicator in 2001.

Figure 11.1 shows that when GVA per hour worked is used to measure productivity, the regional differences (from the UK average and between each other) decrease compared to when GVA per head of population and GVA per filled job are used. Conversely, it is evident that regional performance differentials are considerably greater when using GVA per head, with London far out-performing all the other regions. When GVA per hour worked is used, it can even change the ranking of regions and this further supports the thesis in the beginning of this section that GVA per head can be a misleading productivity indicator.

To help understand the distinctions between the different indicators, an OECD methodology was applied to UK data (New and Virdee, 2006). This showed that the differences

Figure 11.1: Comparison of regional economic performance indicators, 2001 NUTS 1 Regions

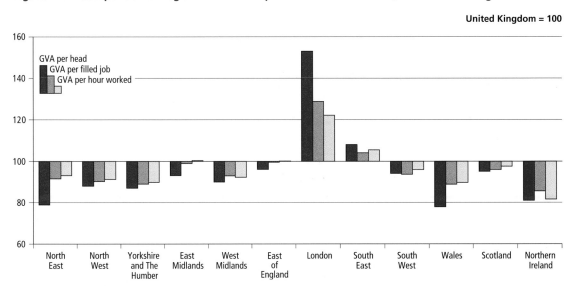

United Kingdom = 100

GVA per filled job and GVA per hour worked are consistent with the regional productivity publication of March 2007.
GVA per hour worked are consistent with the December 2006 Regional Accounts release, based on headline workplace based GVA.

in GVA per head of individual regions from the UK average were only partially explained by differences in labour productivity. The OECD methodology decomposes GVA per head into four components:

1. average labour productivity

2. employment rate

3. activity rate

4. commuting rate

All of these can contribute to a regional divergence from the UK average and identifying the reasons for these regional differences can be useful to inform effective policy formation. If the significance of these components can be identified in each region as being linked to natural features that cannot be changed except in the long run, or to untapped resources, then appropriate policies can be formulated. Examples of natural features might include geographical location and natural resources, while untapped resources might be skills or transport infrastructure.

Productivity and commuting effects are the primary factors that explain regional differences from the UK average. **Formula 1** below combines these factors with employment rate and activity rate to show how GVA per head can be decomposed:

As differences in labour productivity provide a large contribution to the explanation in divergences from the UK average, a new indicator of GVA per hour worked can

Formula 1:

$$\frac{GVA}{P} = \frac{GVA}{EW} \times \frac{EW}{LFW} \times \frac{LFW}{LFR} \times \frac{LFR}{P}$$

GVA per head = Productivity x employment rate x commuting effect x activity rate

Where:

P = population.

EW = employment at the workplace .

LFW = labour force at the workplace.

LFR = labour force at place of residence.

be incorporated into **Formula 1**. GVA per worker divides into two separate components of GVA per hour worked and hours per job, as **Formula 2** shows below.

Formula 2:

$$\frac{GVA}{P} = \frac{GVA}{HW} \times \frac{HW}{EW} \times \frac{EW}{LFW} \times \frac{LFW}{LFR} \times \frac{LFR}{P}$$

Where HW = hours worked.

Figure 11.2 shows the 2001 results for the NUTS1 regions and how these components explain the differences of GVA per head from the UK average. The 0 per cent vertical line represents the UK average of GVA per head for the

Figure 11.2: Factors contributing to differences in regional GVA per head from the UK average in 2001 NUTS1 Regions

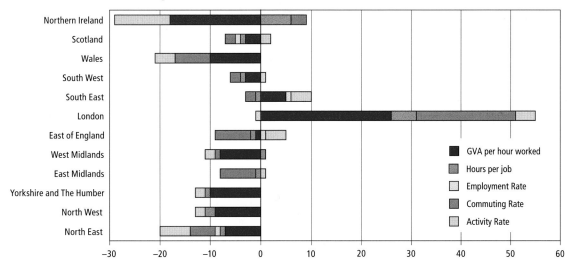

relevant year. The factors that contribute negatively to the economic performance of each region are shown on the left side, whereas the factors that increase performance are shown on the right. **Figure 11.2** shows how each component has a varying influence on economic performance in different regions and therefore what is of specific importance within each region.

Labour productivity is shown to contribute significantly to the divergence of regions' economic performances from the UK average. Activity and commuting rates are also important. Because of the UK's relatively low level of unemployment, the employment rate plays a less significant role for the period covered by this analysis. Taking the example of activity rates, this shows that the regions appearing to lag behind the UK average in terms of GVA per head have relatively low activity rates. These low labour market participation rates can reflect demographic structures of the population, a natural characteristic that cannot be changed except in the long run. The large divergence of GVA per head above the UK average in London is attributable primarily to productivity (GVA per hour worked) and the commuting rate.

This analysis has been extended to a time series basis during 2007 in an article in *Economic & Labour Market Review* (Swadkin, 2007).

11.3 Measure of output: gross value added

As defined in **Section 11.2** and in **Chapter 1**, productivity is the ratio of a volume measure of output (the numerator) to a volume measure of input use (the denominator). Therefore, a volume measure of regional GVA is the preferred measure for output. Because of the absence of regional deflators in the UK however, this measure of regional GVA does not yet exist for the UK regions (see **Chapter 4** for details on deflators). Current estimates of regional productivity use a nominal measure of regional GVA, based on current prices using the income approach, as the numerator.

Relative regional consumer price levels were published for 2004 (the results compared average regional prices against a UK average price benchmark of 100). Other investigative work has also been carried out within ONS to estimate the viability of regional deflators based on current data availabilities. Regional deflators can be estimated from national deflators. Improvements to the industry deflators available at the national level will enable weighting by industry structures in regions. The first estimates for

a constant price regional GVA (chain-linked volume measure) are planned to be available in December 2009.

Nominal GVA does not, by definition, take account of inflation or any regional price differences. It could cause comparison of trends (either between regions or based on movements relative to the UK average) to be misleading if regional price change differentials are significant. Current productivity analysis using nominal GVA therefore does not currently account for these effects.

Regional GVA is published annually every December by ONS Regional Accounts. The headline indicator is a five-period moving average designed to smooth the volatility effects of sampling and non-sampling errors of raw data. The raw, unadjusted data are also published. Under the EU Regulation covering the ESA95, GVA is required to be produced at NUTS levels 2 and 3. For the UK, GVA data are also produced at NUTS 1 level because of the importance of these areas as the devolved countries and the Government Office Regions of England. At NUTS1 the figures are published one year in arrears with a 31 industry breakdown. At NUTS2 and 3 the data are published two years in arrears with 17-way and 3-way industrial breakdown respectively.

At NUTS1 level only, regional GVA is calculated both on a workplace and a residence basis. Residence-based GVA allocates the income of commuters to where they live, not to where they work and where the added value is produced. Residence-based estimates only differ from those published on a workplace basis for London, the South East and the East of England (*Regional Trends* 39, p. 267), as these are assumed to be the only NUTS1 areas with significant net commuting effects.

Current published productivity figures use a numerator based on the workplace basis for GVA per filled job and GVA per hour worked, but a residence place based numerator for GVA per head. However, a measure of GVA per head on a workplace basis is available in the annual Regional Accounts release, as used in **Figure 11.1**.

11.3.1 How is GVA calculated?

At the national level there are three approaches to measuring economic activity – production, expenditure and income approaches – which are then balanced to deliver one final measure of GDP; more detail is provided in **Chapter 4**. Owing to insufficient data availability, regional output (GVA) is measured using the income approach only; the sum of incomes earned from the production of goods and services in the region.

Regional GVA is subject to National Accounts *Blue Book* controls and is calculated using a top-down approach based on the national results. To derive estimates of regional GVA, regional shares are apportioned to the national totals, using various data sources. Each regional level is constrained to the level above, for example, NUTS 1 results must aggregate to the UK results. In the same way, NUTS 2 are constrained to the corresponding NUTS 1 headline results (these being the smoothed, not raw, data). Constraining to the headline smoothed results is important for the purpose of comparability at the lower levels of geographical detail.

Regional estimates are calculated for the individual income components of GVA which include compensation of employees (CoE), gross trading profit (GTP), gross trading surplus (GTS), mixed income, taxes and subsidies on production, rental income and financial intermediation services indirectly measured (FISIM). Within these categories, several different sources are used as indicators that provide the basis on which to apportion national totals to regional and sub-regional splits.

At NUTS1 level, for example, CoE is split into manufacturing and non-manufacturing. The Annual Business Inquiry Part 2 (ABI/2) provides regional indicators for manufacturing industries. Non-manufacturing sources are made up of a calculation using earnings data from the Annual Survey of Hours and Earnings (ASHE) multiplied by employment data from the Short Term Employment Survey (STES). The exceptions to this are data on the agriculture industry and on armed forces, which are supplied by the Department for Environment, Food and Rural Affairs (DEFRA) and the Defence Analytical Services Agency (DASA) respectively.

CoE at NUTS1 level involves a complex iteration process between these regional indicators to control results using a two-way pro-rata method. The first control is by industry according to the overall national accounts input-output results. The second control is based on pay as you earn (PAYE) income data collected by HM Revenue & Customs (HMRC), an administrative data set considered the best source of total earnings data by place of residence. This source provides the total share of CoE for each region. At NUTS2 and 3, GVA is only published on a workplace based series so although similar sources are utilised, the

PAYE data are not applicable. Constraints to the higher geographic detail level are maintained, as previously mentioned.

The sources used for the regional indicators in compiling GVA provide examples of the issues with collating regional statistics previously mentioned, such as the head-office effects. The ABI/2, for example, collects data at the reporting unit (or enterprise) level and so results have to be estimated for local units (the level of detail necessary for regional data). Information on industry classification, number of employees and region is obtained from the Inter-Department Business Register (IDBR) for each local unit and used to accordingly apportion the ABI/2 results.

11.4 The input measure: labour

As previously outlined, a measure of labour provides the input part of the productivity calculation. There are two main sources of this information in the UK: employer-based surveys from which a workforce job (WFJ) series is compiled, and the household-based Labour Force Survey (LFS).

Employer-based surveys are known to be more informative about productivity effects in general, which is why current productivity calculations utilise the WFJ series and a workforce hours series. However, jobs that are omitted by employer surveys would, if households report accurately, be picked up in the LFS. The LFS also prevails as potentially more informative about commuting effects since it utilises the same source for compiling both workplace and residence-based data. Workplace based data from the LFS does rely on the respondent accurately knowing their place of work. For more information about the LFS, see **Chapter 5**.

The choice of source can have important impacts on productivity calculations because different sources can produce different estimates for measuring people in employment by their place of work. From a regional perspective, the differences are not evenly distributed and so can be more significant in some regions than others. The OECD (2001) recommends combining the best aspects of each survey to minimise the data limitations affecting productivity calculations.

The Review of Employment and Jobs Statistics, The National Statistics Quality Review Series; Report No. 44 (ONS, 2006) – also called the Employment and Jobs Review – reviewed employment and job statistics and made recommendations for increasing the coherence of the estimates from the different sources. Work is being carried out within the Office for National Statistics towards the implementation of these recommendations. Supplementary updates to the report have been published (Walling, 2006) that further explain the regional differences in the data sources.

The LFS estimates for most regions are lower than the equivalent WFJ figures, but this is not the case for all. The differences may be attributable to head office effects when companies report WFJ in the region of their headquarters but the actual jobs are outside that region. Regional variations in industrial composition may also cause differences. If a particular source over or underestimates a certain industry, these impacts will be more evident in the regions where those industries are most concentrated.

Other differences may be caused by the IDBR, from which the samples for employer-based 'surveys' or 'enterprise surveys' are drawn. It may contain out-of-date local unit information or omit some jobs because of the nature of the register, being that it only includes businesses with a VAT and PAYE record. It excludes non-UK organisations that are registered abroad but hold a UK VAT reference, for example embassies. Jobs in these organisations, private households or in the hidden economy would therefore be omitted.

11.4.1 The denominator in published regional productivity

Workforce jobs (WFJ) provide the denominator for the output per filled job indicator of both full and part-time jobs published at NUTS1 level. This is equal to the sum of:

- employee jobs
- self-employment
- jobs in the HM Forces
- numbers enrolled in government supported trainee (GST) schemes

WFJ are used rather than the jobs series created for productivity measurement because the latter is not available at a regional level. The difference between these is the basis on which they are reported. The jobs series for productivity measurement is based on reporting units and workforce jobs on local units (see **Chapter 5** for a definition of this jobs series). Therefore, for regional purposes WFJ are more useful. Regional WFJ are not seasonally adjusted, nor constrained to the LFS, as the jobs

series used for productivity is for national productivity calculations.

To calculate hours worked, average annual hours for each region are taken from the LFS and multiplied by the region's WFJ total. The regional hours data are not seasonally adjusted. The annual average hours figure consists of:

- the average of the four quarters' LFS data for employees and self-employed
- annual LFS data for GST
- HM Forces data provided by the Ministry of Defence

These data are then constrained to the total UK hours worked series (as calculated on a local unit basis) to derive the total workforce hours worked series at the NUTS 1 level. This compares to the national productivity calculations, which use UK hours on a reporting unit basis and constrained to the LFS.

11.4.2 Sub-regional Productivity

Compiling experimental sub-regional productivity estimates would involve, for the denominator part of the equation, constraining NUTS 2 and 3 data to any published NUTS 1 results. A WFJ series is calculated at local authority level (and grossed up to NUTS2 and 3 levels) by ONS each year, but there is no comparable workforce hours series at these geographical levels.

To calculate GVA per hour worked sub-regionally would involve using the LFS series on total actual hours worked. To maintain consistency with the method identified above and between the geographical levels, the NUTS 2 and 3 results for this series would be pro-rated and constrained to the relevant NUTS 1 workforce hours worked total. This was first utilised in regional analysis (New and Virdee, 2006) to calculate, at NUTS 2 and 3 levels, the contribution of the GVA per hour worked and hours per job components to the regional divergences in GVA per head from the UK average.

11.5   Future plans

The *Review of Statistics for Economic Policymaking* (Allsopp, 2004) examined the statistical requirements for regional economic policy and provided a strategic direction for the development of economic statistics through various recommendations. One of the primary recommendations was to satisfy the pressing need for better regional data, including the development of a production-based measure of regional gross value added in real terms. It is the role of the Regional Economic Analysis and Allsopp Division at the ONS to leverage the recommendations. The primary benefit for regional productivity analysis (identified in **Section 11.3**) will be the development of the production-based measure of regional gross value added in real terms.

The enhancements planned under the Allsopp programme include development and quality improvement of the business register to enable the surveying of businesses at each individual establishment. This will reduce head-office effects. Parallel to this, the development of the Business Register Employment Survey (BRES) will provide improved integrated employment data by replacing that currently produced through the Business Register Survey (BRS) and the employment part of the Annual Business Inquiry (ABI). The annual employment estimates then produced will enable better apportionment of business survey data, in particular the turnover part of the ABI/2. These schemes will improve the local unit data available for regional analysis.

Improvements to the current Regional Accounts approach and enhanced development of the technical framework will reduce the reliance on large expansions of business surveys. Combined with the above projects, they will help deliver the first estimate of a production-based chain-linked volume measure of regional real GVA in 2009.

A consideration for future regional productivity analysis is the publication timing of relevant data. GVA and labour market measures are not published simultaneously. For example, the two year time lag of GVA publication at NUTS 2 and 3 levels leads to a corresponding delay in producing productivity analysis. Additionally, the different sources employed may be surveyed on different time frames. The LFS, for example, is surveyed continuously throughout the year whereas the ABI is a snapshot at a point in time and this may limit their comparability. However, the survey improvements within the Allsopp remit outlined above will ensure data on productive resources and employment can be acquired from the same sample surveys and so be more reliable to use together in productivity calculations.

11.6　References

Allsopp C (2004) *Review of Statistics for Economic Policymaking: Final Report*, HM Treasury and HMSO: London.

Department for Communities and Local Government (2006) 'PSA Target 2 Regional Economic Performance', available at: www.communities.gov.uk/index.asp?id=1122989

Department for Trade and Industry (2006) *Regional Competitiveness and State of the Regions*, available at www.dtistats.net/sd/rci/

HM Treasury (2001) *Productivity in the UK: 3 – the Regional Dimension,* available at: www.hm-treasury.gov.uk.media/97F/regional_policy.pdf

HM Treasury (2004) *Productivity in the UK 5: Benchmarking UK Productivity performance: A consultation on productivity indicators*, available at: www.hm-treasury.gov.uk.media/D8A/3B/productivitychs.pdf

Marais J (2006) 'Regional Gross Value Added', *Economic Trends* 627, pp 27–57, available at; www.statistics.gov.uk/CCI/article.asp?ID=1400

Office for National Statistics (2006) *Review of Employment and Jobs Statistics*, Office for National Statistics: London, available at: www.statistics.gov.uk/about/data/methodology/quality/reviews/labour.asp

New D and Virdee D (2006) 'Analysing Differences in Regional Economic Performance', *Regional Trends* 39, pp 1–10, Palgrave, Macmillian: Basingstoke.

Organisation for Economic Co-operation and Development OECD (2001): 'Measuring Productivity, Measurement of Aggregate and Industry-Level Productivity Growth', OECD: Paris.

Office for National Statistics (2006) *Regional Trends* 39, Palgrave Macmillan: Basingstoke.

Swadkin C (2007) 'Regional Economic Indicators with a focus on the differences in regional economic performance', *Economic & Labour Market Review* 1(2), pp 52–64, available at: www.statistics.gov.uk/CCI/article.asp?asp=1729

Walling A (2006) 'Comparison of statistics on jobs', *Labour Market Trends* 114 (11), pp 373–388, available at;www.statistics.gov.uk/CCI/article.asp?asp=1648

Chapter 12

International Comparisons of Productivity

Designed to be consistent across countries, international comparisons of productivity are measures that allow the UK economy's performance to be assessed against both that of other nations and domestic objectives. This is particularly of interest to the Department of Trade & Industry (DTI) and HM Treasury (HMT), which assess these series when determining the UK's progress against their Public Service Agreement productivity target. Understanding how international comparisons of productivity are estimated is important when considering what progress is being made.

This is an area in which the Organisation for Economic Co-operation and Development (OECD) also carries out a great deal of work. OECD compiles productivity statistics for member countries to monitor economic performance, analyse labour and product market rigidities, and generally use productivity as an input to econometric models and forecasting.

This chapter discusses the various international comparisons of productivity, their purpose and limitations. It includes a section provided by the OECD which gives their perspective on productivity comparisons. There is also a section on the *International Comparisons of Productivity First Release* produced by ONS, with detail on data, methodology and some recent results. The chapter ends with a description of the ongoing EU KLEMS (Capital, Labour, Energy, Materials and Services) project, which aims to produce an international growth accounts database for EU countries. This section provides background to the project, some interim results and discusses future work.

How and Why Organisations Create International Comparisons of Productivity

As a National Statistics Institute (NSI), the main role of ONS is to produce statistics and analysis to inform and improve policy and decision-making in government, as well as to assess outcomes to judge the effectiveness of policy. Therefore international comparisons serve a useful purpose in allowing assessments to be made between the performance of the UK and other nations. This provides the evidence to judge whether policy is achieving its desired objective. The comparisons can lead to explanations of why one country is outperforming another and policy is sometimes reshaped according to findings.

In addition to NSIs, there are other organisations that make international comparisons, particularly between economic variables such as the Structural Indicators collated by Eurostat. These include the Organisation for Economic Co-operation and Development (OECD), other Government departments (OGDs) and Eurostat, the statistical office of the European Community. Comparisons are widely used by other government departments, especially the Department for Trade & Industry (DTI) and HM Treasury (HMT), academics, firms, students, research organisations, the media, the public and others.

The most common international economic comparison is that of gross domestic product (GDP) per capita. GDP is frequently compared across countries in some form or other because it is a performance indicator and a measure of a country's economic health or wellbeing. Another example of a productivity comparison is the International Comparisons of Productivity (ICP) produced by ONS, versions of which are also produced by OECD and the US Bureau of Labour Statistics. The ONS ICP compares the productivity performance of the UK relative to the G7 group of countries, both individually and as an aggregate.

However, although international comparisons are informative and widely used, there are a number of issues with regard to measurement and comparability as well as interpretation. The main problem lies in the difference in concepts and measurement practice across countries. For instance although most countries follow the UN System of National Accouts 1993 (SNA93) – see **Chapter 4** for more details – different countries treat some components of National Accounts differently. Some of

the most obvious examples are Financial Intermediation Services Indirectly Measured (FISIM), (see **Box 8.5**), software expenditure and military expenditure. Issues of comparability mainly stem from the method of measurement used and are discussed later in the chapter.

Additionally, it needs to be recognised in international comparisons that some countries (as mentioned in **Chapters 2** and **9**) still adopt an input cost approach to government sector output. This is particularly important in interpreting whole economy productivity growth rates because the way they are calculated varies from country to country.

Although the most obvious examples are components of GDP, measurement issues also exist with virtually every other variable. For instance, although the preferred measure of labour productivity is 'per hour worked', making hours worked data internationally comparable is notoriously difficult – specific issues with components of productivity are discussed later in the chapter.

12.1 Regional and international productivity comparisons – the OECD perspective

OECD compiles productivity statistics for its member countries to monitor economic performance, to analyse labour and product market rigidities, and as an input to its econometric model and forecasting. Periodic productivity measures published by OECD comprise labour productivity growth at the level of the total economy and by industry, as well as multi-factor productivity measures for 19 OECD countries. All OECD productivity measures are constructed with a view to maximising international comparability. This is their strength – for the analysis of individual countries, national productivity data will often be the preferred source.

12.1.1 OECD interest in productivity measures

There are several analytical reasons why the OECD is interested in the measurement of productivity:

- productivity growth is considered a key source of economic growth and competitiveness and, as such, forms a basic statistic for many international comparisons and country assessments

- productivity data are also used in the analysis of labour and product markets of OECD countries. For example, Conway *et al* (2006) investigate the link between productivity and product market regulation across OECD countries

- productivity change constitutes an important element in modelling the productive capacity of OECD economies. This permits computation of capacity utilisation measures, themselves important to gauge the position of economies in the business cycle and to forecast economic growth. In addition, the degree to which an economy's capacity is used informs analysts about the pressures from economic demand and thereby the risk of inflationary developments

Productivity measures can be found in many OECD publications. However, since 2004, a core set of productivity measures has been made available on an ongoing basis through the OECD Productivity Database, with periodic updates and expansions and free availability via the internet (www.oecd.org/statistics/productivity). Since 2005, there is also an *OECD Compendium of Productivity Indicators* that draws on the Productivity Database and other sources to bring together a broad set of productivity-related statistics available at the OECD.

The international perspective typically embraced by OECD gives rise to some additional possibilities for analysis but also poses added difficulties for measurement. Some of these analytical possibilities, as well as the associated measurement issues, are discussed below, along with indications of how they are addressed by the OECD.

12.1.2 Labour productivity comparisons

Labour productivity is typically measured as the ratio between output and the hours worked to produce this output. At the level of the total economy, the most frequently used measure of output is GDP. Therefore, GDP per hour is the central measure of labour productivity at the macroeconomic level. See **Chapters 7** and **8** for more details on the different UK productivity measures.

12.1.2.1 GDP levels

In the OECD estimates of productivity levels, data on GDP are derived from *OECD's Annual National Accounts* (ANA). The data from ANA are based on the replies to OECD's annual national accounts questionnaire for OECD member countries. For GDP to be comparable, a common conceptual framework is required. This is provided by the SNA, which almost all OECD countries follow in the compilation of their accounts. Generally, the data resulting from this questionnaire are considered comparable across countries although some differences remain, for example, in the treatment of expenditure on military equipment,

FISIM or the treatment of the non-observed economy. At the same time, practices are converging in some of these fields so that comparability of GDP levels will further improve – see Ahmad *et al* (2004). Below is some detail of the issues that exist in some of these areas.

Military expenditures – US GDP data are affected by a wider treatment of military assets than is recommended by the SNA. Other OECD countries strictly adhere to the SNA in this area, meaning GDP levels are not strictly comparable. However US GDP data in the ANA database adjusts for this difference. Also the impact of this difference in classification on US GDP growth is relatively small, 0.03 per cent (Ahmad *et al*, 2003), meaning that the impact on US productivity growth will also be relatively small, although this could change. International convergence in this area is expected in the next SNA, due to take place in 2008.

FISIM – since charges for most banking services are implicit (for example there is no explicit charge for chequing services or debit cards), the output of this financial sector is estimated using the difference between interest received and interest paid, or FISIM to use the SNA terminology. This component of GDP is estimated by all OECD member countries. However according to SNA, this should also be broken down into final consumers (households) and intermediate consumers (businesses), with only the former having a direct impact on GDP. Such a breakdown has long existed in the United States, Canada, Australia and, more recently, Europe and Japan, but has yet to be implemented in other countries including the UK. ONS intends to introduce this breakdown at some point in the near future, although a definite date has not been set. Again the impact on levels of GDP (estimates suggest up to 3 per cent for some countries) is greater than the impact on growth rates. Convergence on this issue is expected soon (Ahmad *et al,* 2003).

Software investment – SNA93 recommended software expenditure should be treated as investment if it satisfies conventional asset requirements. However the effect of the implemented change varies wildly across countries. The issue of comparability can be seen when comparing the share of total software expenditures that are recorded as investments. This would be expected to be similar across OECD countries but actually ranges from 4 per cent in the UK (although this will change in 2007) to 70 per cent in Spain, mainly as a result of different estimation procedures, for instance supply-side versus demand-side. An OECD/Eurostat Task Force has produced a set of recommendations to harmonise estimation, most of which will be implemented by countries. But until they are, differences in software investment and GDP will remain. The impact of these differences on GDP growth can be substantial, although may not be as large from 2000 onwards, since software expenditure before this date was exceptionally high because of attempts to avert the threat of the 'millennium bug'.

12.1.2.2 Real GDP

Comparability of real GDP throws up more measurement issues since this area takes price and quality changes into account. The group of products that has seen the largest changes in price and quality are in ICT, and different countries apply very different methodologies in compiling price indices for these products. Quality adjustments also vary considerably.

For example the US price index for 'office accounting and photocopy equipment' (which includes computers) fell by 20 per cent per annum between 1995 and 1999, compared with 13 per cent in the UK and 7 per cent in Germany (Ahmad *et al* 2003). Since computers are internationally traded, price movements should be similar. The same issue exists in deflators for software investment. More details of quality adjustment in the UK are given in **Chapter 6**.

However the direct impact on the growth rate of GDP is limited by three factors:

1. only final products impact on GDP so differences in the price indices of different intermediate goods will distort an industry's contribution to GDP growth but not GDP growth itself

2. GDP will only be affected if the product in question is manufactured in that country and

3. if imports are used as intermediates, then the absence of accurate quality adjustments will mean that real GDP growth will be overstated as imports will be lower and imports have a negative impact on GDP. As a result, simulations to estimate the impact of ICT price adjustments on GDP growth suggest modest effects of around 0.1 per cent (Ahmad *et al* 2003)

Real output in services – the share of services as a proportion of total output – is high and growing among OECD economies. However measuring output in this sector is much more difficult than in production; there is some discussion of why in **Chapter 8**. Measuring output

in non-market services is even more difficult as there is no associated market price. The majority of OECD countries employ an input-based approach, while other countries attempt to construct output measures, resulting in very different productivity estimates. ONS work in this area is set out in **Chapter 9**.

Choice of index numbers – the choice of index numbers used to express GDP can also affect comparability. Although the trend is moving toward the use of chained indices, as recommended by Eurostat, fixed-base Laspeyres indices are still used in some OECD countries. OECD work has shown that with significant changes in relative prices, use of different indices can affect GDP growth. The use of chained Fisher indices in the United States, which decrease GDP growth compared to other methods, is an example of this (Ahmad *et al*, 2003). There are more details of UK deflators in **Chapter 4**.

12.1.2.3 Purchasing power parities

The comparison of income and productivity across countries also requires purchasing power parities (PPP) for GDP to convert measures of output into a common currency. A PPP is a ratio of prices created by taking the prices of goods that make up GDP in one country and expressing them relative to another country's currency (usually the US dollar). Exchange rates are not suitable for this purpose since they reflect a wide range of things including:

- interest rate differentials
- capital flows
- speculation on currency
- international prices of good that are traded internationally

The PPP estimates used by the OECD are derived from its joint programme with Eurostat.

There are many conceptual and practical measurement issues associated with PPPs, and these are described in OECD (2005). For example, just as with inter-temporal comparisons, it is notoriously difficult to compare the prices and volumes of non-market services across countries. Akin to the national accounts, PPP comparisons are typically based on the comparison of input prices such as compensation of medical personnel to carry out cross-country comparisons of health services. Other difficult areas include the pricing of investment goods and of services such as air travel. The pace at which methods can be improved is sometimes hampered by the available resources for PPP work in national statistical offices but also by very basic conceptual and empirical questions.

One simple mechanism to improve the consistency between price concepts used in PPP work and in national accounts is to improve communication between national accountants and price specialists. At the European level, joint meetings have taken place but establishing close links between price statisticians and national accountants is even more important at the national level so countries are encouraged to promote such cooperation. There is more about PPPs later in the chapter.

Also if PPPs are used to make sub-national international comparisons, another comparability issue needs to be borne in mind. This is that price data collected for PPPs tend to be from major cities, usually capitals, and so is not necessarily representative of a particular region.

12.1.2.4 Employment and hours worked

Equally important for international comparisons of productivity levels are comparable measures of labour input. In most comparisons of labour productivity levels, labour input is measured along two dimensions: the number of persons employed and the total number of hours worked by all persons employed. A possible third dimension concerns labour composition (quality). This dimension is currently not considered in the OECD approach.

Basic data for employment can be derived from several sources, including administrative records, labour force surveys and establishment or enterprise-based surveys. Labour force surveys are typically conducted to provide reliable information about personal characteristics of the labour force, such as educational attainment, age, or the occurrence of multiple job holding, as well as information about the jobs. This might include, for example, hours at work, industry, occupation and type of contract.

Compared with most other statistical sources on employment, labour force surveys are quite well standardised across OECD countries. Because most countries collect their numbers on the basis of agreed guidelines, they therefore pose few problems for international comparisons. In addition, labour force surveys have fairly comprehensive coverage of the economy. For more details about the UK Labour Force Survey (LFS), see **Chapter 5**.

The main difficulty with employment estimates from labour force surveys is that the data are not necessarily consistent in coverage with other data needed, notably GDP and hours worked. Labour force surveys are mostly defined within geographic boundaries, whereas national accounts, for example, are defined within economic boundaries. This implies that a country's military bases and diplomatic premises on foreign soil are part of its economic territory, and that the residence of an enterprise is determined according to its 'centre of economic interest'. Moreover, labour force surveys may have lower and upper age thresholds and may exclude institutional households. Despite these shortcomings, labour force surveys are often an important source of information for comparisons of productivity levels for the aggregate economy.

A second major source of employment data is therefore countries' national accounts. Many countries now provide data on employment in the framework of their national accounts. In principle, national accounts information on employment is preferable over labour force surveys, because of the conceptual issues discussed above and since the national accounts are likely to integrate a wider range of basic source data on employment. However, in the UK, the LFS is regarded as the more accurate measure (see **Chapter 5** for more details).

On these grounds, the OECD Productivity Database uses the national accounts as the default source for employment data. Despite this principle, it is important to be cognisant of the statistical problems that are still associated with national accounts information on employment. The first important limitation is that only 14 OECD countries currently include data on total hours worked in the framework of national accounts. For these countries, the OECD has moved to estimates of total hours worked from the national accounts. For the other 17 countries, OECD uses data on hours worked collected for the annual publication *OECD Employment Outlook* from a variety of sources, including labour force surveys, and combines these with employment figures from national accounts to derive an estimate of total hours worked. Since such data are often not consistent with national accounts there are issues of comparability, although there is less uncertainty for the growth rate of hours worked.

As more countries publish hours worked data in their national accounts, these will be progressively introduced into the OECD productivity measures (see **Chapters 5** and **13** for details of UK work in this area). However, much

Figure 12.1: Income, productivity levels and labour utilisation, 2004

Percentage points difference with respect to the United States

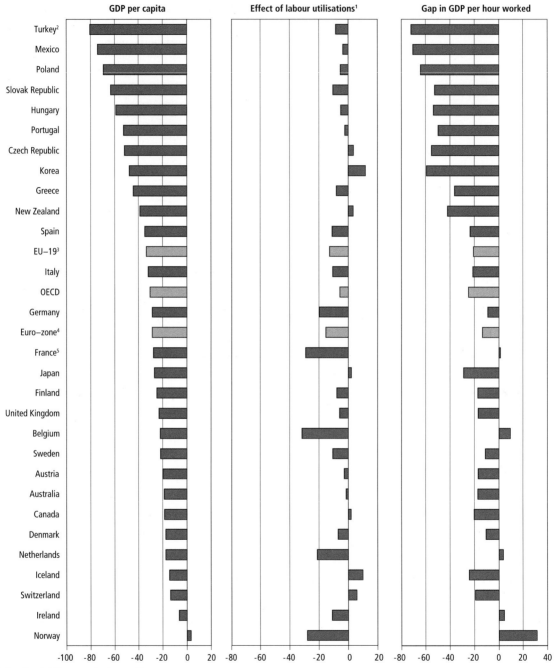

1. Based on total hours worked per capita.
2. GDP for Turkey is based on the 1968 System of National Accounts.
3. EU member countries that are also member countries of the OECD.
4. Austria, Belgium, Finland, France, Germany, Greece, Ireland, Italy, Luxembourg, Netherlands, Portugal, Spain.
5. includes overseas departments.

Source: OECD Productivity Database.

needs to be done to improve international comparability, in particular of hours worked measures hampered by national differences. These include employment concepts, survey concepts and design as well as exclusions or inclusions of certain parts of the population. The comparability of measures of hours worked across OECD countries therefore remains an issue, and work is currently underway – notably through the 'Paris Group', an international statistics forum on labour and compensation – to further improve the available measures of hours worked.

12.1.2.5 Labour productivity and GDP per capita

A useful analytical device is the comparison between labour productivity and GDP per capita. GDP per capita is a measure more directly related to economic wellbeing than GDP per hour worked or labour productivity, the difference being the number of hours worked per inhabitant, or labour utilisation in the economy.

Figure 12.1 opposite presents the differences of these two measures relative to the USA. It is apparent how differences in GDP per capita deviate from differences in labour productivity for many countries. The gap is particularly marked for certain European countries, such as France, Italy, Belgium and the Netherlands. They all have levels of GDP per hour worked that are higher or comparable to the USA but much lower levels of GDP per capita.

Lower labour utilisation, for instance lower employment rates and shorter working hours, explains the bulk of this gap. Therefore, although high labour productivity is often associated with strong economic performance, it should be interpreted jointly with estimates of GDP per capita to understand whether high productivity is accompanied, and perhaps caused, by rigidities in labour markets.

12.1.2.6 NDP and GDP per hour worked

Despite the widespread focus on GDP, it is well known that a gross measure such as GDP does not account for capital used up in production and for obsolescence of capital goods. The associated loss in value, depreciation, reduces the net value of production that is available as net income in any given year. The observation has often been made that an increasing number of capital goods are short-lived (for example computers), and that this structural shift in the composition of assets results in higher overall depreciation. For purposes of measuring and comparing economic wellbeing, it is therefore useful to examine net as well as gross measures.

Consequently, net domestic product (NDP, which equals GDP minus depreciation on a country's capital goods) and NDP per hour worked are complementary measures of productivity. Countries with a structure of fixed assets that is biased towards short-lived assets would exhibit a relatively lower NDP per hour worked than GDP per hour worked, reflecting relatively higher depreciation.

Net measures require reliable estimates of depreciation and the empirical basis for estimating depreciation is not generally well established. In many countries, asset service lives are based on rough-and-ready assumptions often held unchanged over time. To put depreciation measures on a more solid empirical basis, additional studies and research will be required, for example through one-off surveys on assets and through analysis of second-hand market prices. ONS does not currently produce productivity measures using NDP.

12.1.2.7 Industry-level labour productivity

There is much interest in international comparisons of productivity at the industry level. OECD has long produced labour productivity measures broken down by the international standard industry classification within its STAN Database for Industrial Analysis and available online. Generally, hours worked data are not available by industry and therefore the industry-level productivity measures are based on value-added per employed person. As of 2006, an additional information source has been used for labour productivity: business survey data. The *OECD Structural and Demographic Business Statistics* are based on this source which is complementary to STAN because it permits a more detailed break-down, it provides an additional dimension of analysis – the employment size class of enterprises – and it ensures good concordance between employment and output data. At the same time, the data do not add up to national accounts totals and the coverage of enterprises may vary across countries, thereby reducing international comparability.

12.1.3 Multi-factor productivity comparisons

In addition to labour productivity measures, OECD estimates indices of multi-factor productivity (MFP) change over time. MFP growth shows how much of labour productivity growth is left once account has been taken of capital used in production (see **Chapter 3** for more details). A prerequisite for the computation of MFP measures is therefore the availability of measures of capital input. In line with the conceptual basis, OECD capital input is measured as a flow of capital services. See Schreyer (2003) for a description of capital services measures and Schreyer and Webb (2006) for capital stock data at OECD (see **Chapter 5** for details of UK measurement). Major statistical issues from an international perspective include:

- availability of investment data by major type of asset – investment data constitutes the 'raw material' for the computation of capital measures which can be thought of as cumulative investment, adjusted for wear and tear, obsolescence and retirement. Detailed investment data are not generally available in statistical offices. In a number of cases, the OECD has to come up with its own estimates to extend or complete national series. This introduces uncertainty into the estimates

- comparability of price indices for investment – price indices are required to account for asset-specific inflation and for certain capital goods such as ICT products. Methods for price indices are not always comparable across countries so OECD therefore uses a set of 'harmonised' deflators for this type of investment

- comparability of asset lives calculations used by statistical offices is limited and the OECD applies the same set of asset lives across all countries

Figure 12.2 below shows how estimates of MFP are presented in the context of growth accounting. The total height of each bar indicates the average annual growth

rates of GDP for each country. The differently shaded parts of the bars indicate the estimated contribution of the various factors of production to output growth. These are labour, capital (broken down into ICT capital and other capital) and MFP, which is the remaining output growth that could not be allocated to changes in labour or capital. For the period under consideration, it is apparent that MFP growth along with ICT capital investment has accounted for an important part of output growth with the most impressive example being Ireland.

The resulting indices of MFP growth are widely used in analysis and modelling although care has to be taken to avoid over-interpretation. In particular, MFP growth is often interpreted as an indicator of technological progress. This is not entirely correct for three reasons:

1. technological change does not necessarily translate into MFP growth because embodied technological change, such as advances in the quality of new vintages of capital, is reflected instead in the measured contributions of capital and labour to output growth

2. MFP growth is not necessarily caused by technological change. Other factors include adjustment costs, economies of scale, the influence of the business cycle, measurement errors, effectiveness of management and organisational structure and omitted inputs (for example, energy, materials and services)

Figure 12.2: Contributions to average annual rates of GDP growth, 1995–2005

Percentage points

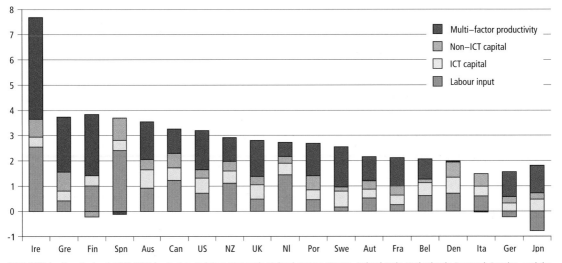

1995–2002 for New Zealand; 1995–2003 for Austria, Belgium, Denmark, Finland, France, Greece, Ireland, Italy, Netherlands, Portugal, Sweden, and the United Kingdom; 1995–2004 for Australia, Japan and Spain; 1995–2005 for the United States, Canada and Germany

3. measures of MFP are therefore better interpreted as measures of improvements in overall efficiency than as pure expressions of technical change. For a comparison with ONS measurement please see **Chapter 7**

12.1.4 Conclusion

This section of the chapter has summarised OECD interest in, and work on, international productivity comparisons and also some of the measurement issues faced in making such comparisons. These problems are significant, although international practice in many areas is converging. There are also other measurement issues which have not been explored in this chapter such as imputed rents and other smaller methodological differences. Indeed some differences may not yet even have been discovered. Therefore, while difficult, the process of making international comparisons is being made easier through work done by OECD in its aim of maximising methodological convergence and providing a better statistical base for analysis.

12.2   ONS's International Comparisons of Productivity

International Comparisons of Productivity (ICP) are produced biannually by ONS with the release dates usually being in September and February. ICP has been published by ONS since October 2001 and all data are sourced from the OECD. The release incorporates two different types of labour productivity measures: output per worker and output per hour worked. The latter was previously released as an experimental statistic. However, since February 2006 it has been reclassified and now both measures have National Statistic status. The main reason for this is that work done by OECD improved the comparability of data on hours worked across countries.

Comparisons of productivity levels are made between the rest of the G7 group (Canada, France, Germany, Italy, Japan and the USA) and the UK. These countries have been chosen because they are key competitors of the UK. France, Germany and the USA are listed in the DTI's Public Service Agreement (PSA) productivity target. In the future, as emerging economies grow, ONS may choose to include additional countries in the ICP release, particularly if extra countries are added to the DTI's PSA target.

12.2.1 Data sources

As mentioned above, ICP is released on a biannual basis reflecting the publication and revision cycles of the OECD component data series, those being current price GDP, PPPs, employment and hours worked:

- GDP is taken from the Main Economic Indicators published on a monthly basis
- PPPs are published on the OECD PPP website (at www.oecd.org/std/ppp) and are updated annually at the beginning of January
- employment data are published in Annual Labour Force Statistics in August
- hours worked are published annually in Employment Outlook in June/July

Therefore the February release incorporates revisions to the PPPs and GDP data. In September new employment and hours data are available and the series is extended by one year. Revisions to the back series, caused by revisions to employment, hours and GDP data, are also included in the September release.

12.2.2 Methodology

The two alternative productivity measures, GDP per worker and GDP per hour worked, are calculated using the four component data series published by OECD. First, comparable levels of productivity are calculated, then they are divided by the UK estimate and multiplied by 100 to express the level as an index relative to the UK (UK=100). Therefore a country with a value greater than 100 has a higher level of productivity than the UK and vice versa. The respective calculations are set out below in equations (1) and (2):

$$\text{GDP per worker} = \frac{GDP/PPP}{Employment} \qquad (1)$$

$$\text{GDP per hour worked} = \frac{GDP/PPP}{Employment \times Hours} \qquad (2)$$

where:

GDP = current GDP in market prices (calculated using the expenditure method) expressed in the country's own currency,

PPP = current purchasing power parities relative to the US (US=1),

Employment = number of people in employment, and

Hours = actual average hours worked per person per year.

PPPs are used to convert GDP so that point in time cross-country comparisons can be made. The PPP itself is a measure of how much a representative basket of goods, in this case worth $1 in the USA, costs in a particular country and so is a measure of relative prices.

12.2.3 Purchasing Power Parities

PPPs are used to convert variables such as GDP from a nominal currency into comparable measures of the same unit. The PPP itself is a type of exchange rate that equalises the purchasing power of currencies for a representative basket of goods. So if a basket of goods costs £0.50 in the UK and $1 in the USA, then the PPP is equal to:

$$PPP = \frac{P_{UK}}{P_{US}} = \frac{0.5}{1} = 0.5$$

Therefore dividing UK GDP by 0.5 will mean UK and USA GDP can now be viewed on a comparable basis.

As mentioned previously, the use of PPPs is preferable to the use of exchange rates, which are highly volatile and influenced by factors other than relative prices. These include interest rate movements, which result in capital flows, and currency speculation. Also market exchange rates will only reflect the relative prices of those goods and services that are traded internationally; in contrast PPPs reflect the prices of all goods and services that make up GDP. Further detail on the PPP programme is provided in **Box 12.1**.

12.2.4 GDP versus GVA

GDP is defined as the total value of goods and services produced within a country and gross value added (GVA) is the residual of total output minus intermediate consumption. More detail is given on these measures in **Chapter 4**.

For productivity analysis it is preferable to use GVA as the numerator because it is a measure of the value actually created during the production process. However because of the limitations of international data sources, GDP is used instead. Since countries conform to the United Nations SNA93, this measure is internationally comparable. Also it would not be appropriate to use PPPs to convert GVA into internationally comparable volume measures because PPPs are specifically designed to be used on GDP. The reason for this lies in their construction – the weights used to

aggregate PPPs up to a whole economy basis are the shares of products that make up final expenditure GDP.

Following the methodological change in the compilation of the official UK productivity estimates in September 2004, the definition of the headline productivity measure (GVA per worker) is now closer to that used in ICP. Prior to this date the ONS headline measure was GVA per job, a fundamentally different measure (see **Chapter 5** for more detail).

12.2.5 Interpretation of ICP results

ONS ICP numbers are calculated using current PPPs. This means that they should be interpreted as point-in-time comparisons based on current international prices and should **not** be treated as a time series to infer volume productivity growth. This is an important point because movements in the ICP reflect changes in relative prices, relative volume changes and possibly changes in methodologies or definitions. However they can be seen as broadly indicative of trends over a long period of time. Because of the volatility of the PPPs and issues regarding whether all component series are strictly internationally comparable, ICP users are advised that differences of a few index points between countries should not be regarded as significant.

To allow comparisons over time, ICP would need to be calculated using the constant PPP approach, where the PPP is extrapolated from the base year using the countries' implied GDP deflator. This is the approach adopted by OECD and the Bureau of Labour Statistics (BLS) when they produce their own versions of ICP. Under this approach, movement in the results can be interpreted as volume growth over time.

However, the results obviously depend highly on the choice of the base year and there is the implicit assumption that price structures are fixed across time. In reality this assumption clearly does not hold and so the further one moves from the base year, the more questionable is the result. The other main difference between figures published by ONS and OECD is the choice of employment data. OECD uses data from National Accounts while ONS uses data from countries' Labour Force surveys.

The ICP series begins in 1990 but data produced after 1995 are considered to be of higher quality because of improvements made to the PPP programme by OECD and Eurostat since then.

Box 12.1: The PPP programme

The calculation of PPPs is undertaken by OECD and Eurostat in a shared programme that began in the early 1980s. The PPPs are compiled using data collected in price surveys, GDP weights to reflect expenditure shares and other input data such as government salaries and rents. First, relative prices are calculated for individual goods and services. Then relative prices for products in each product group are averaged to produce unweighted PPPs for that particular product group. Finally PPPs for products and product groups are weighted together to form an aggregate using expenditure shares of GDP.

An overview of the PPP programme is provided below in **Figure 12A** Since 1995 PPPs for the European countries have been calculated using the results of annual benchmark surveys where one-third of consumer goods are surveyed every year.

The remaining two-thirds are calculated by interpolation using suitable consumer price indices. Surveys for capital goods and construction are completed every two years while rents and government salaries are collected annually. GDP weights are obviously subject to regular revisions as part of the National Accounts process. Therefore provisional PPPs are released toward the end of each year, 12 months after the reference period, and final PPPs are released two years after the reference period.

PPPs for non-European countries are calculated using triennial benchmark surveys (the last two being in 2002 and 2005. Results of the 2005 benchmark will be released during 2007 and are extrapolated backward and forward for years outside the benchmark period. To take advantage of all the information

available, the OECD has integrated Eurostat's annual benchmark results into the programme for all OECD countries. This involves fixing the relative price ratio of the European and non-European groups and only allowing the relatives to be changed internally within the same group (European or non-European).

For non-European countries, PPPs prior to 1999 are extrapolated backward from the benchmark using countries' implied GDP deflators. This is also true of European countries prior to 1995 when Eurostat's annual benchmarking process began.

It should be noted that ICP can only be calculated at whole economy level and not for individual or even broad sectors as the OECD/Eurostat programme does not construct PPPs at sector level.

Figure 12A: Overview of the OECD-Eurostat Programme

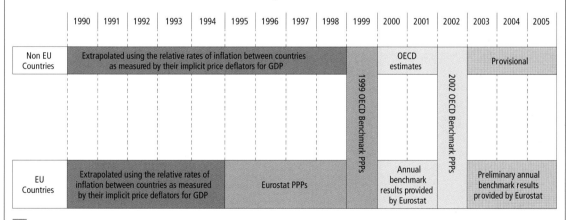

Revisions expected due to revisions in implicit price deflators for GDP.

Revisions not expected here. However note that revisions in OECD published PPPs may occur for EU countries from 1995 to 1998 as the relative position of the EU group may change relative to the non EU countries as a result of revisions to non EU PPPs (PPPs are reported as USA = 1). The relative PPPs within the EU will not however change.

Revisions expected due to 2002 and 2005 benchmark exercise.

Revisions expected. Provisional estimates. For non EU countries these are OECD estimates. For EU countries these are preliminary annual benchmark results provided by Eurostat.

Box 12.2: Revisions

As mentioned previously, the February release of ICP incorporates revisions to countries' PPPs and GDP data. The September release incorporates revisions to employment, hours and GDP data and extends the series by an additional year. In general the major source of revision to ICP is the PPP data with the largest revisions usually occurring in benchmark years. There are, however, occasionally significant revisions to countries' employment and hours data, such as when data are benchmarked to new census results.

That said, PPP revisions are prevalent because of the high degree of estimation and their provisional nature until they are finalised. Revisions to current price GDP are frequent but usually smaller in magnitude except when there has been a major methodological change such as the introduction of a new SNA, such as SNA93. Countries tend to respond to such changes at different times and this should be borne in mind when interpreting ONS's ICP results. Therefore the volatility of ICP is caused by regular and irregular revisions to the four component data series, all of which impact at different times.

12.2.6 ICP: February 2007

The following analysis refers to results contained in the *ICP First Release* published in February 2007 which contained revised data up to and including 2005. Results for GDP per worker are presented in **Figure 12.3** below.

As can be seen, when using the GDP per worker measure, the productivity of UK workers is higher than those in Japan, similar to those in Canada, Germany and Italy, lower than those in the G7 group excluding the UK, and lower than those in France and the USA. The USA is the leader with productivity 25 per cent above that of the UK. This pattern is the same as was reported in the earlier releases in 2005 and 2006. A fuller description of current and previous ICP results, using both measures, can be found at:

www.statistics.gov.uk/StatBase/Product.asp?vlnk=9671

As an aside, when using the per hour worked measure, the best performers are France, the USA and Germany, followed by the G7 group, then the UK, Italy, Canada and finally Japan. The reason for the different ranking is comparative labour utilisation and working hours. The main point is that GDP per hour worked takes into account how long workers in individual countries work on average. Because working patterns differ this affects the ranking of countries.

For instance, since workers in the USA work longer hours than those in the UK, then UK performance relative to the USA is better on a per hour basis than it is on a per worker basis. In contrast, workers in continental Europe work shorter hours on average, and therefore the relative performance of the UK compared to France and Germany is lower on a per hour basis than it is on a per worker basis. The positions of France and Japan are fundamentally a reflection of working patterns in those countries – the long hours worked in Japan compared to the relatively short hours worked in France.

Figure 12.3: International Comparisons of Productivity: GDP per worker

Index UK=100

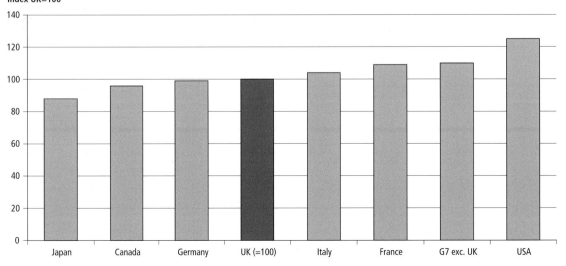

12.3   The EU KLEMS project

The EU KLEMS project is a three-year project, running from September 2004 to September 2007, led by the University of Groningen and the National Institute of Economic and Social Research (NIESR) on behalf of the European Commission. Its purpose is to create a database of internationally harmonised growth accounts by industry for EU member states with a breakdown into contributions from capital (K), labour (L), energy (E), materials (M) and business services (S). KLEMS productivity estimates are multi-factor total output productivity and when the project is completed will allow for detailed comparisons to be made across countries. (See **Chapter 1** for more information on KLEMS and **Chapter 3** for more details about multi-factor productivity.)

12.3.1 Background

When input-output tables are integrated with the system of national accounts, they provide a powerful tool for obtaining measures of value added and productivity. In the context of KLEMS productivity measures they are an indispensable source for the identification, measurement and weighting of intermediate inputs, *Measuring Productivity* (OECD Manual, 2001).

The KLEMS project aims to create a database to facilitate international comparisons of economic growth, productivity, employment creation, capital formation and technological change at the industry level for all European Union member states from 1970 onwards. Comparisons will also be made with several EU candidate member countries, and additionally with the United States, Japan and Canada, by linking to 'sister' KLEMS databases. This work will provide important input to economic policy making and evaluation, including the assessment of competitiveness and economic growth potential.

The EU KLEMS growth accounts are based on principles established in the latest System of National Accounts (1993) and the European System of Accounts (1995). In particular the recommendations to move towards the use of an input-output system for the construction of National Accounts, the use of chain indices for the measurement of prices and quantities, and the capitalisation of software are key ingredients for improved productivity measurement using a KLEMS input structure. Most recently, the various

methods to measure output, productivity and (capital) inputs have been described in two OECD documents (OECD, 2001a and 2001b) and in two Eurostat manuals (Eurostat, 2001 and 2002).

During the first two years of the project (September 2004 to September 2006), data have been assembled using the methodologies of national accounts and input-output analysis. The input measures include capital, labour, energy, material inputs and service inputs, and are adjusted for quality differences over time and across countries. Productivity measures are being developed, in particular with growth accounting techniques that are strongly rooted in statistical conventions and economic theory (see **Chapter 3** for more information on the growth accounting framework). Substantial methodological research is being carried out on measures of output, inputs, prices and productivity to improve international comparability. The development of a flexible database structure and implementation of the database in official statistics will occur when the project is finalised.

During the third year (September 2006 to September 2007), the database will be used for analytical purposes, by relating productivity to international transactions, human capital creation, price formation of capital, market structure and innovation. To facilitate this type of analysis the database will be expanded by trade and technology measures and a link will be sought with existing micro (firm level) databases. The balance in academic, statistical and policy input in this project will be realised by the participation of 15 organisations from across the EU, representing a mix of academic institutions, national economic policy research institutes and the OECD. Support from various statistical offices will also contribute.

12.3.2 Role of ONS

Beyond its oversight responsibilities regarding the quality of the data produced, ONS has been closely involved with producing the various components of the EU KLEMS project, specifically in supplying data on employment, hours worked and capital services. Constant price Supply and Use tables are central to the project and consequently the ONS National Accounts team has sought close cooperation with the project. However, NIESR are responsible for producing the UK part of the KLEMS database.

12.3.3 Role of National Institute of Economic and Social Research (NIESR)

NIESR are jointly leading the KLEMS project with the University of Groningen on behalf of the European Commission. NIESR have been taking forward the UK KLEMS work in co-operation with ONS's National Accounts modernisation team and productivity economics team. NIESR has funded ONS's involvement.

The main advantages for ONS are:

- linking the KLEMS project with the NA modernisation work to ensure that there is consistency with other countries

- a time series of comparable productivity data within Europe

- avenue for quality assurance of new methods

- expertise in linking in new data onto published data

12.3.4 Releases in 2007

The public release of the KLEMS database is taking place during 2007; the analytical model has already been released. This will consist of deflators and Supply and Use Tables based on a 72-industry breakdown for the EU's member states, provided in current and constant prices, and backdated to 1970. The database will also include output and productivity measures in terms of growth rates and (relative) levels, as well as newly developed measures on knowledge creation (research and development, patents, embodied technological change, other innovation activity and co-operation). There will be two interdependent modules, the analytical module and the statistical module.

The *Analytical Module*, released in March 2007, is the core of the EU KLEMS accounts. It provides a research database at the highest possible quality standards for use in the academic world and by policy makers. Using 'best practice' techniques in areas of growth accounting, it focuses on international comparability, and aims at full coverage (country by industry by variable).

- It is a research database and falls outside the statistical responsibilities of the National Statistics Institutes (NSIs)

- A disclaimer will appear next to any NSI data used

- It uses the available data and applies the most state-of-the-art methods that are judged best by the consortium

- In addition to filling gaps in the data through transparent estimation procedures, this database will contain alternative approaches regarding certain statistical conventions, which go beyond ESA95 and SNA93

The Statistical Module of the database will be developed parallel to the analytical module and will be released in December 2007. It includes data as consistent as possible with those published by NSIs. Its methods will usually correspond to the rules and conventions on national accounts, supply and use tables, commodity flow methods and other measures (SNA93, ESA95), and any deviations from these standard rules should at least be supported by the NSIs.

- It aims to contain data which are either fully consistent with the rules and conventions of SNA93 and ESA95 or verified by NSIs

- A disclaimer is not required

- This is the ideal status the consortium would like to reach for the majority of its input and output data

The release of the databases will spur the beginning of the analytical phase of the project, which will consist of four research areas:

1. analysis of Productivity, Prices, Structures and Technology and Innovation Indicators

2. research on labour market and skill creation

3. research on technological progress and innovation and

4. research on linkages to firm level databases

Concerning the fourth research area, important analytical gains will come from integrating micro database measures of 'within-industry' firm level distributions with the EU KLEMS 'between-industry' macro results. The integration of microdata is seen as potentially increasing the quality of a future extension of the EU KLEMS database (van Ark, 2005). More information can be found at: www.euklems.net/

12.4 References

Ahmad N, Lequiller F, Pilat D, Wölfl, A and Schreyer P (2003) 'Comparing labour productivity growth in the OECD Area: the role of measurement', *OECD Statistics Working Papers 2003/05*, available at: www.olis.oecd.org/olis/2003doc.nsf/LinkTo/std-doc(2003)5.

Ahmad N, Lequiller F, Marianna P, Pilat D, Schreyer P and Wölfl A (2003) 'Comparing growth in GDP and labour productivity: measurement issues', *OECD Statistics Brief* 7, Organisation for Economic Co-operation and Development: Paris, available at: www.oecd.org/searchResult/0,2665,en_2649_34257_1_1_1_1_1,00.html

Brereton M (2006) 'Methodology Notes: Links between Gross Domestic Product (GDP) and Gross Value Added (GVA)', *Economic Trends* 627, pp 25–26, available at: www.statistics.gov.uk/cci/article.asp?ID=1416

Camus D (2006) *ICP First Release*, 4 October, available at: www.statistics.gov.uk/cci/nugget.asp?id=160

Conway P, de Rosa D, Nicoletti G and Steiner F (2006) 'Regulation, Competition and Productivity Convergence', OECD *Economics Department Working Paper No 509*, Organisation for Economic Co-operation and Development: Paris.

Dey-Chowdhury S (2006), 'Methodological Notes: International Comparisons of Economic Activity', *Economic Trends* 633, pp 23–28, available at: www.statistics.gov.uk/cci/article.asp?id=1614

Eurostat (2001) *Handbook on Price and Volume Measures* in National Accounts, Eurostat: Luxembourg.

Eurostat (2002) *The ESA 95 Imput-Output Manual: Compilation and Analysis*, Eurostat: Luxembourg.

Lau E and Wallis G (2005) 'International Comparisons of Productivity: a technical note on revisions and interpretation', *Economic Trends* 617, pp 42–56, available at: www.statistics.gov.uk/cci/article.asp?ID=1069

OECD (2001a) *Measuring Productivity: OECD Manual*, Organisation for Economic Co-operation and Development: Paris.

OECD (2001b) *Measuring Capital: OECD Manual*, Organisation for Economic Co-operation and Development: Paris.

OECD (2004), *Purchasing Power Parities and Real Expenditure*, Organisation for Economic Co-operation and Development: Paris.

OECD (2005) *OECD PPP Methodological Manual*, Organisation for Economic Co-operation and Develpment: Paris.

OECD (2006) *Structural and Demographic Business Statistics 1996–2003*, Organisation for Economic Co-operation and Development: Paris, available at: www.oecd.org/statistics/industry-services

OECD (2006) *OECD Compendium of Productivity Indicators 2006*, Organisation for Economic Co-operation and Development: Paris, available at: www.oecd.org/statistics/productivity.

Schreyer P (2003) 'Capital Stocks, Capital Services and Multi-Factor Productivity Measures', OECD *Economic Studies* 37, 2003/2, pp 164–183, Organisation for Economic Co-operation and Development: Paris.

Schreyer P and Webb C (2006) *Capital Stock Data at the OECD – Status and Outlook*, Organisation for Economic Co-operation and Development: Paris, available at: www.oecd.org/statistics/productivity.

van Ark B (2005) The EU KLEMS Project: Towards an Integrated System of Growth, Productivity and National Accounts for the European Union. Paper presented at OECD Workshop on Productivity Measurement organised jointly with Fundacion BBVA and IVIE, Madrid, Spain 17–19 October 2005, available at: www.euklems.net/workpackages/paper_madrid_ark.pdf

Chapter 13

Productivity: The Way Forward

UK productivity statistics, and the measures provided by ONS to support productivity assessments by users, have made significant strides over recent years. Some of the newer developments have been outlined in earlier chapters, but users – and the changing economy – continue to place new demands.

A significant challenge for productivity measurement is responding to structural changes in the economy. Research into new forms of investment shows that this can quite fundamentally affect interpretation of productivity analysis. In addition, the development programme for measurement of public sector output and productivity has been taking shape through a UK-wide consultation exercise. ONS also helps to influence international standards in this area.

This chapter outlines ONS's ongoing work to improve the consistency of input and output measures in a number of areas. Within the market sector this includes covering how better measures of labour input by industry are being created and also details of ONS work to improve definition of new types of capital.

This chapter also describes how ONS will continue to promote the development of international measurement standards to reflect change, but remains committed to producing its productivity outputs to agreed international definitions. In particular, this chapter includes details of future plans within ONS to improve measures of services within the public sector.

Plans for Continuing Improvement in Statistics and Analysis

ONS aims to provide users with the productivity estimates and analyses they require. To do this, ONS continues to tackle the main outstanding issues identified in previous chapters:

- consistency between output and input measures
- consistency of methodology across ONS systems and data series
- locating new, detailed sources of data
- producing new series tailored to users' needs
- meeting changing regional, national and international standards

Continuing improvements in these areas cover a wide range of economic measurement, starting with labour market statistics.

13.1   Labour market statistics

Various improvements to labour market statistics are being pursued in ONS, following the National Statistics Quality Review of Employment and Jobs Statistics (2006). A key project is to develop routine linkage of the Inter-Departmental Business Register (IDBR) with Labour Force Survey (LFS) records, using the address and postcode of respondents' workplaces. If successful, and subject to ONS resources required, this would increase the accuracy, consistency and coherence of estimates of employment and jobs statistics from household and business surveys. For more information on the IDBR and LFS, please see **Chapter 5**.

Statistics on employment by industry and location of workplace from the LFS and other household surveys are subject to error because of the difficulties in getting accurate responses from individual workers. It is necessary to use business survey sources for more reliable information, based on industry, sector and locations of businesses as recorded on the IDBR.

The Allsopp Review (2004) suggested there should be considerable potential benefits for National Statistics from linking the household survey data with the IDBR as a means of providing improved information on respondents' workplaces (as discussed in **Chapter 11**). This would make it possible to make much better use of the LFS and other survey data – including in due course the Annual

Population Survey (APS) and the Integrated Household Survey (IHS) – for productivity statistics as well as for a wide range of other purposes. Coherence will be much improved between corresponding output and employment/hours estimates used to derive productivity series.

These improvements will result in better productivity measures as detailed below.

Productivity by industry – ONS's published productivity measures are now based on LFS-based denominators for whole economy level. If the LFS-industry link could be improved, this whole economy methodology could be applied coherently to the estimation of industry specific productivity measures, potentially allowing a more reliable and more detailed industry breakdown to be published.

Productivity by public/private sector – Private sector employment is currently estimated as the difference between the LFS whole economy employment estimate and an estimate for the public sector. If IDBR information about employer status in the public/private sector could be linked to LFS records, more coherent private sector employment estimates could be generated. These would be very valuable for a number of purposes including improving ONS estimates of market sector productivity.

Productivity and skills – If LFS-based data could be fully integrated into the productivity analysis framework as described above, the potential would be released to use the information about occupations, education and skills in the LFS to generate improved 'quality adjusted' labour input (QALI) measures. It would also strengthen current analytical research on combining information for the LFS and the Annual Survey of Hours and Earnings (ASHE).

13.2   Whole economy and market sector productivity

Taking advantage of these projects, each of the issues identified earlier can be tackled to produce better ONS productivity estimates. For more detail on planned productivity work see Camus and Lau (2006).

13.2.1 Consistency between output and input

While work is under way to improve labour input measures, there are also plans to strengthen the role of labour market data in the National Accounts. Consequently, ONS is currently working on a project to achieve greater consistency between data used in the National Accounts and in labour market statistics (LMS).

This will result in recommendations of data to use in the new modernised National Accounts system:

- recommendations for compensation of employees data
- recommendations for employment data
- the self-employed and unpaid elements being included in a consistent manner
- recommendations for earnings data

13.2.2 Consistency of methodology across ONS systems and data series

In order to take full advantage of the current redevelopment within the National Accounts systems, a structure for long-term productivity analysis will be included in the modernised National Accounts (see Beadle, 2007). This structure will be composed of National Accounts data sources along with checks and calculations to automatically produce detailed productivity estimates consistent with National Accounts.

This structure will incorporate:

- consistent national accounts/labour market data – recommendations from the LMS/NA Consistency Project (detailed in **Section 13.2.1**)
- constant Price Input-Output (KPIO) tables – these are required for the construction of multi-factor productivity estimates because of the need for information on the flow of intermediate inputs
- double deflation – this is needed, along with KPIO, to ensure that the intermediate input and outputs are correctly deflated; this ensures that there is consistency between GDP and industry output when calculating productivity (see **Chapter 4** for more details on double deflations)

Additionally, this structure should ensure that productivity estimates can also be used as a check for the National Accounts themselves. This will be strongly linked to the development of a growth accounting framework. This structure will also include improved public services outputs developed by UK Centre for the Measurement of Government Activity (UKCeMGA).

13.2.3 Locating new, detailed sources of data

ONS will continue to support and develop the microdata business lab which was established in early 2003. Productivity analysis projects using microdata will be taken on in-house or in partnership when ONS is sponsored to do so and/or where the work contributes to measurement improvements.

ONS will also look into the possibility of using administrative data, particularly HM Revenue & Customs (HMRC) PAYE records where appropriate either as quality assurance or as data in their own right.

13.2.4 Producing new data series tailored to users' needs

This covers a number of different productivity series for a range of users and requirements.

13.2.4.1 Developing market sector productivity measures

From March 2007, ONS has published market sector productivity measures on both a per worker and a per hour worked basis. In future, increasing emphasis will be given to measures of market sector productivity and of productivity for the public services (see **Chapters 8** and **9** for more details).

13.2.4.2 Service sector productivity estimates

ONS currently produces some service sector productivity estimates on an experimental basis for Distribution, Hotels and Catering and also Agriculture, Forestry and Fishery as well as total services estimates. In future ONS will be looking to expand this range further and to review the 'experimental' status of existing series.

13.2.4.3 International Comparisons of Productivity (ICP)

Comparisons of GDP per worker and per hour worked are currently produced comparing the UK with key competitors from the G7 countries. Given the changing nature of the world economy, other countries may be added to this comparison in future.

13.2.4.4 Capitalisation of Research and Development (R&D)

Research and Development is currently treated as intermediate consumption instead of as a form of investment. The SNA 2007 discussion group has recommended that the SNA93 should be changed to recognise the outputs of R&D as assets. A project is under way, funded by Eurostat, to assess the practical and methodological issues involved in capitalising R&D.

13.2.4.5 Inclusion of the Information and Communication Technologies (ICT) investment revision

Revisions to software investment, which indicate that this is a greater proportion of GDP than previously thought, were published in *Economic Trends* (Chesson and Chamberlin, 2006). These results will be included in the revisions procedure for National Accounts.

13.2.4.6 Intangibles

A research project, jointly owned by HM Treasury (HMT), is in progress to produce and analyse productivity measures for this area of work. While software is recognised as an asset and R&D is planned for recognition by 2008, other areas, such as advertising, are not. These areas suffer from measurement problems but are generally recognised as important. Analysis in this area has previously been carried out in the United States (Corrado, Hulten and Sichel, 2004).

13.2.5 Meeting changing regional, national and international standards

The way forward for regional productivity was tackled as part of the *Review of Statistics for Economic Policymaking* (Allsopp, 2004). A primary aim of the review is to obtain better regional data, including regional gross value added. Further details are given in **Section 11.5**.

The UK also developed national standards through the Atkinson Review and ONS is the first national statistics agency to follow UN and Eurostat guidance in how to treat public services output and productivity differently. All of this helps improve ONS's productivity work compared to past performance.

The details of this are tackled in detail in the next section.

13.3   Public service productivity work programme

The way forward when improving public service productivity can be divided into three distinct categories:

1. improvements in measuring outputs

2. improvements in measuring inputs

3. improvements in using triangulation information to support productivity estimates

More detail is provided below, including some examples in the context of health service output.

13.3.1 Improvements in measuring outputs

Market sector outputs for productivity tend to come directly from the National Accounts as total output or value added. Outputs for public services are much more difficult to define as there is not automatically an expenditure or volume associated with such things as improved hospital care or policing. Therefore defining and measuring public service output can be difficult. Future work can be categorised into the individual areas given below.

13.3.1.1 Coverage

Improving the coverage of output indicators will make them more representative of the departmental expenditure used to produce them. Principle D of the *Atkinson Review* outlines the conditions required for accepting new output indicators. For example it covers adequately the full range of services for a particular functional area and the effects of its introduction have been tested service by service.

13.3.1.2 Quality adjustment

UKCeMGA have just carried out a series of public consultations on measuring the quality of public services output. The detailed response to these consultations has been published in a strategy paper (ONS, 2007). But more generally, further developments in the quality adjustment of public service outputs are required. In particular, to have consistency with market sector output, the aim is to ensure the quality indicators are comprehensive and fit together in a robust framework. See **Box 13.1** for a summary of the main points from the strategy paper that addresses these issues.

13.3.1.3 Value weights

There are clear economic arguments to support the use of value weights rather than cost weights, however there is also general recognition that it is very difficult to derive value weights. It is likely, therefore, that cost weights will continue to be used in the short to medium term, but that should not preclude further research into the possibility of using value weights. When considering which type of weight to review, priority should be given to areas where cost and value weights are likely to be significantly different, as outlined in the *Atkinson Review*.

13.3.1.4 Collective services

There will be further investigation and consequent developments to assess how best to measure the output and productivity of collective services. As it currently

---

Box 13.1: How measurement of public service output will develop

The key methodological direction that will be used to measure the output, and subsequently productivity, of public services is the development of an overall quality measurement framework. This will allow UKCeMGA to develop authoritative, credible, and transparent estimates using the best data sources and research methodologies available, but also to make transparent, informed estimates when data do not allow definitive conclusions. A key objective is to reduce the measurement errors that would be associated with not measuring the quality of output at all.

The recently published UKCeMGA strategy paper starts with the key concepts required for quality measurement of public service output covering:

- dimensions – what outcomes do the outputs deliver

- techniques – such as measuring the contribution outputs make to outcomes and

- the capacity for benefit – consideration of the variables that affect the way individual users can actually benefit from the output delivered

The paper then considers three particular methodological issues:

- the relative importance of quality dimensions – for example how much weight should be given to education attainment compared with other objectives of the education system such as keeping children active and healthy

- using value weights instead of costs weights – recognising that cost weights traditionally used to measure output may not reflect the value of public services as perceived by users of the service and

- time lags – recognising the effects outputs have on outcomes may be delayed or spread over a number of years

The quality measurement framework will operate on the basis of professional statistical judgement and should be transparent to all who are interested. The strategy paper sets out the ways in which ONS intends to ensure the relevance and robustness of particular concepts, techniques and data sources used in this work.

Using the quality measurement framework and taking on board the contributions made by those who attended the ONS consultations, the key direction for measuring the quality of education output will include, for example:

- a more refined use of GCSE results

- developments to take account of the 14–19 initiative so diplomas and A levels are taken into account

- developments to measure quality of under-fives' childcare and education

All will be set in the context of the outcomes covered by the 'Every Child Matters' framework.

The key direction for measuring the quality of health output will include, for example:

- a refined set of quality dimensions putting more weight on those based on health gain

- more work on the activities that prevent illness and

- extending further beyond the current set of quality indicators, in particular for health gains from treatment

UKCeMGA will also be developing the quality measurement framework further through research funded by the Invest to Save Budget, with particular focus on adult social care and under-fives' education, and on tools for local use to measure the quality of services, whether provided by public, independent or third sector providers. The project will also be used to strengthen methodologies for quality measurement, which can be extended into other areas of public service.

Finally, after further consultation with a panel of economic experts in the UK, UKCeMGA will not be adjusting GDP output in the National Accounts to reflect complementarity, other than if such an adjustment already fits with existing conventions. However, UKCeMGA will be developing a wider welfare measure of GDP output for publication in productivity articles, but the methodology will need to be robust and clearly explained. Adjustments made will be tailored towards specific public services and not based on the uniform 1.5 per cent used so far.

---

stands, the <output =inputs> method is used to measure the output of collective services. Further development work will investigate the extent to which collective services can be divided into separate activities and associated costs and quality.

13.3.2 Improvements in measuring inputs

As for outputs, inputs for the public sector can also be difficult to define, but mostly at lower levels of

disaggregation. Again, planned future work can be divided into categories as shown below.

13.3.2.1 Expenditure data

This work will involve driving forward the agenda for getting better and more detailed expenditure data for both central and local government. There has already been a substantial improvement in the way central government expenditure data are collected using the new Combined

Online Information System (COINS) developed by HMT. But more progress is required for developing better systems for local government expenditure. ONS will be working with the Department for Communities and Local Government (DCLG) to achieve this.

13.3.2.2 Deflators

In association with the National Accounts and improved expenditure data, ONS will derive improved deflator measures for individual public services (see **Chapter 4** for more details on deflators and how they are used in productivity measurement), in particular better deflators for goods and services used for producing outputs.

13.3.2.3 Quality adjustment

There will be further work to improve the quality adjustment of inputs (see **Chapter 6** for details of the work already carried out).

13.3.3 Improvements in using triangulation information to support productivity estimates

It is unlikely that a single measure of productivity will ever fully capture the performance of complex public services, so it is essential that the wider evidence base is used in a more rigorous way to support productivity estimates. Further research and development of the evidence base and the direct links with measures of output and input will be carried out. This will improve all round confidence in published productivity estimates.

13.4   References

Allsopp C (2004) *'Review of Statistics for Economic Policymaking: Final Report'*, HM Treasury and HMSO: London.

Atkinson A B (2005) *Atkinson Review: Final Report. Measurement of Government Output and Productivity for the National Accounts*, Palgrave Macmillan: Basingstoke, available at: www.statistics.gov.uk/about/data/methodology/specific/publicSector/atkinson/final_report.asp

Beadle J (2007) 'Modernising the UK's National Accounts', *Economic & Labour Market Review* 1, pp 27–32, available at: www.statistics.gov.uk/cci/article.asp?id=1737

Camus D and Lau E (2006) 'Productivity measures and analysis: ONS strategy and work programme', *Economic Trends* 632, pp 14–21, available at: www.statistics.gov.uk/cci/article.asp?ID=1603

Chesson A and Chamberlin G (2006) 'Survey based measures of software investment in the UK', *Economic Trends* 627, pp 61–72, available at: www.statistics.gov.uk/cci/article.asp?ID=1401

Corrado C, Hulten C and Sichel D (2004) *Measuring Capital and Technology: An Expanded Framework*, Federal Reserve: Washington, available at: www.federalreserve.gov/pubs/feds/2004/200465/200465pap.pdf

Office for National Statistics (2006) *Review of Employment and Jobs Statistics*, National Statistics Quality Review Series Report No. 44, ONS: London, available at: www.statistics.gov.uk/about/data/methodology/quality/reviews/labour.asp

Tily G (2006) 'Improvements to timely measures of service sector output', *Economic Trends* 630, pp 29–42, available at: www.statistics.gov.uk/cci/article.asp?ID=1555

UK Centre for the Measurement of Government Activity (2006) 'Public Service Productivity: Education', *Economic Trends* 626, pp 13–47, available at: www.statistics.gov.uk/cci/article.asp?ID=1345

UK Centre for the Measurement of Government Activity (2007) 'Measuring Quality as Part of Public Service Output', Office for National Statistics: London, available at: http://www.statistics.gov.uk/about/data/methodology/specific/PublicSector/output/consultations.asp

Glossary

A

ABI (Annual Business Enquiry) – which since 1997 has collected over 50,000 records per year from most industries with information on employment, turnover and stocks for all industries, as well as more specific variables for individual sectors.

AFDI (Annual Foreign Direct Investment) – conducted in two parts: an inward inquiry and an outward inquiry. The inward inquiry concerns the subsidiaries/ associates of foreign firms operating in the UK, while the outward inquiry covers the investment made by UK firms in their overseas operations.

Allsopp Review – refers to the 'Review of Statistics for Economic Policymaking' led by Christopher Allsopp in 2004, which examined the statistical requirements for regional economic policy. Its recommendations provided a strategic direction for the development of economic statistics.

ANA (Annual National Accounts) – a set of accounts produced by the Organisation for Economic Co-operation and Development (OECD) based on the replies to OECD's annual national accounts questionnaire for OECD member countries.

ARD (Annual Respondents Database – known as ARD since 2000 and ARD2 since 2006) – a micro database that combines a number of ONS business surveys and reference numbers taken from the Inter-Departmental Business Register. ((IDBR), see below) Together they form a longitudinal database of firm information.

ASHE (Annual Survey of Hours and Earnings)

ASHE (Annual Survey of Hours and Earnings) – a business survey conducted by ONS that is sent to a representative sample of employers to measure earnings and hours worked by employees.

Atkinson Review – an investigation, led by Sir Tony Atkinson in 2005, into the measurement of output and productivity in the public sector. It produced a final report *Measurement of Government Output and Productivity for the National Accounts.*

B

Blue Book (National Accounts Blue Book) – comprises the annual UK National Accounts in published form. (See National Accounts, below).

BoE (Bank of England) – the central bank of the UK. Since 1997 it has been independent and has had the statutory power to set UK interest rates.

BSD (Business Structure Database) – a longitudinal version of the IDBR for research use, which takes full account of changes in ownership and restructuring of businesses.

C

Capital deepening – an increase in capital stock.

Capital input – in terms of input to productivity measures, this is the flow of productive capital services.

Capital services – the measure of capital input that is suitable for analysing and modelling productivity. Being a direct measure of the flow of productive services from capital assets rather than a measure of the stock of those assets, capital services essentially measures the actual contribution of the capital stock of assets to the production process in a given year. For example, capital services from computers refer to the service they provide rather than the value of the computers themselves.

Capital stock – a measure of the value of the capital stock of assets. Known either as wealth capital stock or net capital stock, on a national scale it is the current market valuation of a country or industry's productive capital.

Capital productivity – a measure of the amount produced per unit of capital input. It is a volume, or physical, partial productivity measure that is produced by comparing output with capital input. While ONS does not publish figures on capital productivity, it can be seen as an input to multi-factor productivity.

CEPS (Communal Establishments Pilot Survey) – a one-off survey, similar to the Labour Force Survey (LFS) and specifically for people living in communal establishments, that was done in conjunction with the LFS for the autumn quarter of 2000.

Chain Index – an index constructed by linking two or more index series of different base periods or different weights.

Chained value measures (CVM) – index numbers from a chain index of quantity. The index number for the reference period of the index may be set equal to 100 or to the estimated monetary value of the item in the reference period.

CoE (Compensation of Employees) – refers to wages, salary and other monies or benefits paid to employees.

Complementarity – a principle described in *The Atkinson Review* which proposes that there are links between the private and public sector that need to be accounted for in the measurement of the public sector output. *The Atkinson Review* identifies that for different public services the channel of influence of the complementarity principle may differ.

CPI (Consumer Prices Index) – the headline measure of UK inflation for macroeconomic purposes and the rate on which the government's inflation target is based. It is an internationally comparable measure of inflation – CPI inflation measures (as opposed to RPI measures) are analysed by the European Central Bank when setting interest rates in the Euro zone.

CSPI (Corporate Services Price Index) – the former name of the Services Producer Price Index (SPPI).

Current Value – the actual or estimated value of a monetary amount for the period and location of interest.

D

DASA (Defence Analytical Services Agency) – a UK government department which provides professional analytical, economic and statistical services and advice to the Ministry of Defence (MoD), and defence-related statistics to Parliament, other Government Departments and the public.

Defra (Department of Environment, Food and Rural Affairs) – a UK government department which brings together the interests of farmers and the countryside, the environment and the rural economy, food, air and water to champion sustainable development.

Depreciation – loss in value of an asset because of ageing.

DfES (The Department for Education and Skills) – a UK government department responsible for education and training for people from school age through retirement.

Direct inputs – also called primary inputs (or primary factor inputs), are resources that go into producing something but are treated as outside (or sometimes described as exogenous to) the production process. This includes labour and capital.

Disembodied technical change – advances in technology not embodied in capital. Examples of such a change are increased knowledge through research and development (R&D) or improvements in organisational structure or management.

Domar aggregation – a good measure of underlying productivity growth at the aggregate level because it traces aggregate MFP growth rates to their industries of origin. It also allows changes in aggregate MFP to be assigned either to changes in the underlying industry rates or to structural change (changes in the Domar weights).

Domar weights – weights to combine industry-level, gross-output based MFP (KLEMS) to higher-level aggregates. Domar weights are special in that they do not normally add up to one. This reflects the combined effects of integration and aggregation.

Deflation – the technique used to change figures from nominal terms (current prices) into real terms (constant prices or volume terms), expressing the production (or consumption) of goods and services in the prices of a common year.

Double deflation – a method for deriving GVA for each industry by deducting the volume of inputs from the volume of outputs. This means that an industry's output is deflated by the price of its output, while each input is deflated by its own price index.

DTI (Department of Trade and Industry) – a UK government department responsible for trade, business, employees, consumers, science and energy. This includes creating conditions and policy for business success both within the UK and internationally.

DWP (Department for Work and Pensions) – a UK government department responsible for helping people find and continue in employment. It also provides benefits and other support for those out of work, children and disabled people as well as helping retired people access their pensions and other entitlements.

E

Embodied technical change – advances in the quality of capital or other inputs that is captured when calculating the contribution of the inputs. An example of this is the rapid improvement in the quality of Information and Communication Technology (ICT) over the last 20 years.

Employee jobs – the total number of jobs in an economy or industry. They are measured using surveys of employers that are then summed and weighted across all firms. Because of the possibility that employees can work more than one job, they may be picked up more than once in these surveys. This is why it is a measure of jobs rather than employees.

Energy productivity – output per unit of energy used. Although a measure rarely used in macroeconomics, it is used at firm level and can be seen as an intermediate input to multi-factor productivity.

European System of Accounts 1995 (ESA95) – the integrated system of national and regional accounts used by members of the European Union. It was most recently updated in 1995 and is broadly consistent with the United Nations System of National Accounts (SNA93) in definitions, accounting rules and classifications. However, it incorporates certain differences, particularly in its presentation, that are more in line with use within the European Union. The United Kingdom National Accountes have been based on ESA95 since September 1998, while the previous 1979 ESA is still used for compiling gross national product.

EPI (Exported Price Indices) – a series of economic indicators that measure change in the prices of goods manufactured in the UK but destined for export markets.

Eurostat – the statistical office of the European Community. As an institution of the Commission of the European Union, member states are required under various EU laws to provide it with statistics.

F

FISIM (Financial Intermediation Services Indirectly Measured) – the output of many financial intermediation services is paid for not by charges but by an interest rate differential. FISIM imputes charges for these services and corresponding offsets in property income. FISIM, an innovation of the 1993 System of National Accounts, is soon to be incorporated into the UK National Accounts.

Five Driver Framework – a government productivity model that identifies five drivers that interact to underlie long-term productivity performance: investment, innovation, skills, enterprise and competition.

G

GDHI (Gross Disposable Household Income) – the total income available to a household. GDHI can also be measured per capita.

GDP (gross domestic product) per capita – the total output of an economy relative to its population. It is sometimes considered an indicator of prosperity.

GDP(P) (Production gross domestic product) – a measure of GDP as the sum of all the value added by all producers in the economy.

GDP(I) (Income gross domestic product) – a measure of GDP as the total of the income generated through this productive activity.

GDP(E) (Expenditure gross domestic product) – a measure of GDP as the expenditure on goods and services produced.

Growth Accounting – a specific, useful way of observing the changing structure of the economy, and assessing the contribution of each sector or industry to the whole. It also provides a very useful framework for the collection of economic statistics. This approach might be called 'joined up statistics' because it links various economic growth and labour measures together to provide a more detailed picture of the economy.

GVA (gross value added) – the difference between total output and intermediate consumption for any given sector or industry. That is the difference between the value of goods and services produced and the cost of raw materials and other inputs which are used up in production.

H

Hedonic regression – A quality adjustment based on a multiple regression of prices against product characteristics.

HMRC (Her Majesty's Revenue & Customs) – a UK government department formed in 2005 following the merger of the Inland Revenue and HM Customs and Excise Departments. It works in three areas: collecting direct and indirect taxes, distributing benefits to those entitled to them and protecting borders and frontiers.

HMT (HM Treasury) – the UK's economics and finance ministry. It is responsible for formulating and implementing the Government's financial and economic policy. Its aim is to raise the rate of sustainable growth, and achieve rising prosperity and a better quality of life with economic and employment opportunities for all.

I

ICP (International Comparisons of Productivity) – an ONS measure that compares the productivity performance of the UK relative to the G7 group of countries, both individually and as an aggregate. Versions of the ICP are also produced by the OECD, the US Bureau of Labour Statistics and others.

ILO (International Labour Organization) – a UN specialised agency that promotes internationally recognised human and labour rights. The ILO formulates international labour standards in the form of Conventions and Recommendations across the spectrum of work related issues. It also provides technical assistance and promotes and supports and the development and strengthening of independent employers' and workers' organisations. Workers, employers and governments all participate in ILO governance through a unique tripartite system.

Impute – to ascribe, charge or attribute value to a transaction in which, although no money has changed hands, there has been a flow of goods or services. It is confined to a very small number of cases where a reasonably satisfactory basis for the assumed valuation is available. In a more general sense, it is a procedure for entering a value for a specific variable where the response is missing or unusable.

Index Number – a measure of the average level of prices, quantities or other quantifiable characteristics relative to their level for a defined *reference period* or location. It is usually expressed as relative to 100 (for example, 105 would be an increase of 5 per cent) where 100 is the value for the reference period or location.

Input-Output Supply and Use Tables framework – now used to establish the level of GDP at current prices. The framework is built on a robust process of balancing demand and supply for 123 separate products and inputs and outputs for 123 industries, to deliver a single measure of GDP derived simultaneously from the production, income and expenditure approaches to GDP.

Intangible asset – an asset that does not have a physical, material existence. Examples of intangible assets are software, brand equity, firm-specific human capital, organisational capital, organisational structure and non-scientific research and development.

Inter-Departmental Business Register (IDBR) – a register of legal units, which is the most comprehensive list of UK businesses available. There are approximately 2.1 million businesses on this register and it covers almost 99 per cent of economic activity within the UK. It holds a wide range of information on business units, including the industry classification of each of these firms.

Intermediate consumption in GVA – the cost of raw materials and other inputs that are consumed in the production process.

Intermediate inputs – resources that are used up by the production process such as materials, energy and business services.

IPI (Import Price Indices) – a series of economic indicators that measure change in the prices of goods and raw materials imported into the UK.

IoS (Index of Services) – a constant price (Laspeyres) index providing a monthly indicator of gross value added in the service sector of the economy.

K

KLEMS – an approach to calculating multi-factor productivity (MFP), where the growth of real total output is accounted for by the growth of capital (K), labour (L), energy (E), materials (M) and business services (S).

L

Labour input – in terms of input to productivity measures, this is the flow of productive labour.

Labour Market Statistics (LMS) – a measure of many different aspects of the labour market that provide an insight into the economy. They are also very much about people, including:

■ their participation in the labour force

■ the types of work they do

■ earnings and benefits they receive

■ their educational qualifications and

■ their working patterns

Labour productivity – output per unit of labour input. It effectively shows changes in productivity over time for the same value or amount of labour input. It does not distinguish between productivity changes owing to new equipment, new technology advances, organisational changes (for example, a new management structure) or increased efficiency.

Laspeyres Index – a fixed-base index in which index numbers are weighted arithmetic means of price (or other) relatives, using value (or equivalent) weights.

LFS (Labour Force Survey) – an ONS survey of households in Great Britain and Northern Ireland that provides information about people's employment status and conditions. It asks individuals about their current and previous jobs including which industries they work in, which jobs they hold within the industry and how many hours they work. It also enquires about related topics such as training, qualifications, income and disability.

Longitudinal study or database – associates all the data about one person or firm from as many different surveys as possible.

LU (Local Unit) – a local unit represents one site within a larger firm that has its headquarters somewhere else. The site might be a factory or shop, for example.

M

Market sector – a portion of the overall economy formed by the following institutional sectors: private non-financial corporations, private financial corporations, households and public corporations (financial and non-financial). The remaining institutional sectors form the non-market sector, including central government, local government and NPISHs. Market sector activity is undertaken at prices that are economically significant and its output is disposed of or intended for sale through the market.

Materials productivity – the relationship between output of saleable products and the volumes of raw materials and energy required to produce them.

MFP (Multi-factor productivity) – the residual contribution to output growth of an industry or economy after calculating the contribution from all of its factor inputs. It is also sometimes called Total Factor Productivity (TFP) but is referred to a multi-factor productivity in this guide. MFP can also be viewed as the unexplained difference between the growth in cost of inputs and the growth in cost of output.

MFP (Multi-factor productivity) – sometimes called total-factor productivity (TFP) or growth accounting, apportions growth in output to growth in the factor inputs, capital and labour, and growth in a residual that represents disembodied technical change. Examples of such change are increased knowledge through research and development (R&D) or improvements in organisational structure or management.

Microdata – the variables such as names, addresses, statuses, quantities and periods referring to a statistical unit and entered on a statistical record.

Mixed income – income that accrues to both capital and labour.

N

National Accounts (NA) – a set of current values, volume measures and volume indices which, together, summarise all the economic activity of a nation. In the UK the National Accounts is a central framework for the presentation and measurement of the stocks and flows within the economy.

NDP (Net Domestic Product) – the gross domestic product (GDP) minus depreciation on a country's capital goods. This is an estimate of how much the country has to spend to maintain the current GDP. If the country is not able to replace the capital stock lost through depreciation, then GDP will fall. In addition, a growing gap between GDP and NDP indicates increasing obsolescence of capital goods, while a narrowing gap would mean that the condition of capital stock in the country is improving.

NPISH (Non-Profit Institutions Serving Households) – charities that provide services to older people or children are an example of this.

NSI (National Statistical Institute) – the statistical office, agency or bureau that represents its country. ONS is the NSI for the UK.

NUTS (Nomenclature of Units for Territorial Statistics) – a code used to identify areas within and for the European Union. NUTS levels are coded with two alphanumeric digits per level, from level 1 to level 5. The full level 5 code consists of ten digits that can be truncated to give the code of every NUTS level within it. NUTS level 1 has 12 areas – Scotland, Wales, Northern Ireland and the nine Government Office Regions in England. NUTS level 2 covers 37 areas within the UK, generally groups of unitary authorities and counties. NUTS level 3 has 133 areas, generally individual counties and groups of unitary authorities or districts, also known as local areas.

O

OECD (Organisation for Economic Co-operation and Development) – made up of 30 member countries sharing a commitment to democratic government and the market economy. With active relationships with some 70 other countries and economies, non-governmental organisations and civil society, it has a global reach. Best known for its publications and statistics, its work covers economic and social issues from macroeconomics to trade, education, development and science and innovation. The OECD plays a prominent role in fostering good governance in public services and corporate activity.

P

Paasche index – an index whose index numbers are weighted harmonic means of price (or other) relatives, using current value (or equivalent) weights such as the current unit cost or price. *The Eurostat Handbook* recommends using the Paasche index for price measures.

PIM (Perpetual Inventory Method) – a method used to convert time-series data for the volume of purchases of assets (constant price investment) into a net capital stock measure.

Pink Book – the annual UK Financial Accounts published in one volume.

PPI (Producer Price Index) – there are four individual Producer Price Index enquiries dealing with UK made or sold manufactured goods, UK exports of manufactured goods, imports of commodities and manufactured goods and UK sold corporate services.

PPI (Producer Price Indicators) – a series of economic indicators that measure the price movements of goods bought and sold by manufacturers using a wide collection of representative products. The sets are fixed and the figures collected monthly.

Primary inputs (or primary factor inputs) – resources that go into producing something but are treated as outside (or sometimes described as exogenous to) the production process. This includes labour and capital. They are also referred to as direct inputs.

Productivity – the ratio between what is obtained (output) and what was put in to obtain it (input).

Productivity jobs – a measure of jobs created by apportioning employee jobs as defined in the ONS Labour Force Survey (LFS) to industries using employer sources. The number of people who are defined as self-employed in the LFS (using the LFS industry categorisation) is then added.

Productivity hours – a data series created by multiplying the productivity jobs series at industry level by the actual hours worked for the industry recorded in the LFS. The resulting data series consists of the number of hours worked at the industry level.

PPP (Purchasing power parities) – a type of exchange rate that equalises the purchasing power of currencies for a representative basket of goods. It takes the form of a ratio of prices created by taking the prices of goods that make up GDP in one country and expressing them relative to another country's currency (usually the US dollar). The weights used to aggregate PPPs up to a whole economy basis are the shares of products that make up final expenditure GDP.

Q

QALI (Quality-adjusted labour input) – measures not only headcount or hours as labour's input into production but also an approximate quantification of their marginal productivity, using the characteristics of workers to adjust hours worked.

R

RU (Reporting Unit) – a measure on which National Accounts data are based, the reporting unit level corresponds with either the entire enterprise or the major activity within a business. This can be thought of as the head office of the organisation. Each reporting unit consists of one or more local units, each of which has its own industry associated with it. The local unit corresponds to a site such as a factory or shop.

RPI (Retail Prices Index) – an important domestic indicator of inflation in the UK. It measures the average change from month to month in the prices of goods and services purchased in the UK.

S

SIC or UK SIC (Standard Industrial Classification) – the basis that is used in the National Accounts to produce any industry level estimates of data, including the estimates of GVA that are used for productivity. The UK SIC classifies business establishments and other statistical units by the type of economic activity in which the establishment is engaged.

Solow Residual – what remains after the growth accounting framework breaks down the sources of economic growth from increases in capital and labour. This remainder is usually attributed to technology and, in theory, if all the factors contributing towards productivity were identified and measured correctly in the decomposition then this residual would be zero. It was named after the person who identified it, Robert Solow, in 1957.

SPPI (Services Producer Price Index) – this was formerly called the Corporate Services Price Index (CSPI).

Superlative Index – an index that uses more information in its construction than a base index and is more flexible, for example the Tornqvist Index is a superlative index. The OECD definition is as follows: 'Superlative indices are price or quantity indices that are 'exact' for a flexible aggregator. A flexible aggregator is a second-order approximation to an arbitrary production, cost, utility or distance function. Exactness implies that a particular index number can be directly derived from a specific flexible aggregator.'

SNA93 (The System of National Accounts 1993) – is an internationally agreed method for creating national accounts. It was published under the auspices of the European Community (EC), International Monetary Fund (IMF), Organisation for Economic Co-operation and Development (OECD), United Nations (UN) and World Bank.

T

TFP (Total Factor Productivity) – see MFP.

Total output (sometimes called output) – the value of the goods and services together with the work-in-progress. It is equal to the value of the sales plus any increase (and less any decrease) in the value of the inventory of finished products and work in progress.

Tornqvist Index – a form of index where the weight is constructed using an average of the relevant variable in the current and base period. The Tornqvist is widely used in the construction of Quality Adjusted Labour Measures and is recommended in the OECD methodology (2001), making it the preferred measure.

U

UKCeMGA (United Kingdom Centre for the Measurement of Government Activity) – This is a division of ONS that co-ordinates and drives forward development programmes to produce better measures of government output and productivity.

V

VICS (Volume Index of Capital Services) – a measure that captures the flow of services that stem from physical capital stock and are used in the production process.

VML (Virtual microdata laboratory) – a facility within ONS that provides secure access to confidential microdata for statistical research. A technically secure solution, it allows common access to ONS business data across all ONS sites allied to a range of procedural restrictions and access agreements to ensure that the trust placed in the researchers using the data is justified. The VML now houses numerous data sets that are available for productivity research in many areas.

Volume measure – a quantity describing the number of units produced. A more technical definition is: an index number from an index of quantity. The index number for the reference period may be set equal to 100 or to the estimated monetary value of the item in the reference period.

W

Weight or weighting – a number used to indicate the relative importance of each item in a group. The term is used in many contexts, including sample/population weighting, index weighting, non-response weighting.

Workforce jobs – a data series that measures the total number of jobs at both economy and industry level. It is the sum of employee jobs, self-employment, HM Forces and Government Supported Trainee Schemes. Although workforce jobs is not used to produce estimates of GVA per jobs, it is still used as a leading measure of the total number of jobs.

Index

Page numbers for tables and charts are in italics